Palgrave Studies in Governance, Leadership and Responsibility

Series Editors

The fall-out from many high profile crises in governance and leadership in recent decades, from banking to healthcare, continues to be felt around the world. Major reports have questioned the values and behaviour, not just of individual organizations but of professionals, industries and political leadership. These reports raise questions about business corporations and also public service institutions. In response this new series aims to explore the broad principles of governance and leadership and how these are embodied in different contexts, opening up the possibility of developing new theories and approaches that are fuelled by interdisciplinary approaches. The purpose of the series is to highlight critical reflection and empirical research which can enable dialogue across sectors, focusing on theory, value and the practice of governance, leadership and responsibility.

Written from a global context, the series is unique in bringing leadership and governance together. The King III report connects these two fields by identifying leadership as one of the three principles of effective governance however most courses in business schools have traditionally treated these as separate subjects. Increasingly, and in particular with the case of executive education, business schools are recognizing the need to develop and produce responsible leaders. The series will therefore encourage critical exploration between these two areas and as such explore sociological and philosophical perspectives.

More information about this series at
https://link.springer.com/bookseries/15192

Cláudia Simões · Alin Stancu ·
Georgiana Grigore
Editors

Corporate Responsibility, Sustainability and Markets

How Ethical Organisations and Consumers Shape Markets

palgrave
macmillan

Editors
Cláudia Simões
School of Economics and Management
University of Minho
Braga, Portugal

Georgiana Grigore
Brookfield Campus
University of Leicester
Leicester, UK

Alin Stancu
Bucharest University of Economic Studies
Bucharest, Romania

ISSN 2662-1304 ISSN 2662-1312 (electronic)
Palgrave Studies in Governance, Leadership and Responsibility
ISBN 978-3-030-79659-4 ISBN 978-3-030-79660-0 (eBook)
https://doi.org/10.1007/978-3-030-79660-0

This Palgrave Macmillan imprint is published by the registered company Springer Nature Switzerland AG
The registered company address is: Gewerbestrasse 11, 6330 Cham, Switzerland

Contents

Notes on Contributors

Alessia Anzivino is Post Doc at Catholic University of the Sacred Heart, university where she received her Ph.D. in Management. She is researcher at Centrimark (Marketing Research Center) and Professor of Marketing.

José Andrés Domínguez-Gómez is Ph.D. Holder and Professor of Sociology at University of Huelva. He is the CEO of EIS methods of the University of Huelva's Spin-off and research and academic Director of 'Fair Play Social' - LaLiga Foundation.

Carolin Ermer is a research fellow at HTW Berlin and is currently working on the Trans-Sustain model project. Her main areas of research are competencies and learning approaches in Education for Sustainable Development (ESD) and Higher Education for Sustainable Development (HESD).

Roberto Fernández-Villarino is External Director of 'Fair Play Social' - LaLiga Foundation; he is Associate Professor of Labor Law at University of Huelva and Lawyer Director at Gaudia Consulting and Legal Services

S.L.P. He is also a Ph.D. researcher at the course Doctorate Department Education, University of Huelva.

Marta Galli is Ph.D. student in Management and Innovation at the Catholic University of the Sacred Heart. She researches and collaborates at Centrimark (Marketing Research Center). Her topics of research for the Ph.D. are the digital innovation and sustainability in the wine industry.

Georgiana Grigore is an Associate Professor in Marketing at University of Leicester, School of Business. She is also chair of an annual international conference in 'Social Responsibility, Ethics and Sustainable Business', which she co-founded in 2012. Her major area of research is in marketing and corporate responsibility concepts and practices, including changes that result from digital media. In the last years, she has published several books, including 'Corporate Responsibility and Digital Communities' and 'Corporate Social Responsibility in the Digital Age' that explore a contemporary intersection of two fields: corporate responsibility and digital technology. Her publications also include applications of post-psychoanalytic theories to consumer-brand relationships and shopping in Marketing Theory. Her research received external funding, including from Arthur W. Page Center (2014/2015 and 2015/2016) and British Academy/Leverhulme (2017/2019). She completed an EU-funded doctorate in Marketing at the Bucharest University of Economic Studies using relationship-marketing theory to examine the impact of corporate responsibility on stakeholders. Prior to her doctorate, she received a master's degree in Strategic Marketing and a bachelor's degree in Marketing from the same university. Before her Ph.D., Georgiana was a marketing specialist and consultant in the retail industry and a trainer for a series of practitioner workshops and marketing and corporate responsibility courses.

Zahra Khamseh (BA, MBA, Ph.D. Researcher) is a Ph.D. Candidate in Marketing and Strategy in the School of Economy and Management at the University of Minho, Portugal, and a member of the Research Center of Marketing and Strategy (NIPE). She has an MBA from Nottingham

University's School of Business. Her primary research interests are in Strategy and Internationalization of Social Enterprises.

Marta Kightley is an Associate Professor at Warsaw School of Economics in Poland. She teaches and publishes on history of economic thought, macroeconomics, institutional economics, developmental economics, and ethics in finance.

Robert Kudłak is an Assistant Professor at the Adam Mickiewicz University in Poznań, Poland. His main research interests focus on corporate social responsibility and its institutional antecedents, corporate environmentalism as well environmental and social impacts of corporate behavior. His research has appeared in various journals, such as the *Long Range Planning, Ecological Economics, Journal of Cleaner Production, Journal of Corporate Citizenship*, and *European Planning Studies*. He is currently a member of the editorial board of the Long Range Planning.

Kamala Vainy Pillai is currently a consultant on strategic engagement with a state research agency. Her Ph.D. focused on CSR and minority stakeholder empowerment, particularly on Indigenous Peoples (IP). She has over 30 years of experience in various sectors—corporate, civil society, hospitality, biotechnology, cybersecurity, institution of higher learning, and international media. She has been involved in sustainable development-focused community and research projects and initiates collaborative engagements between corporations, universities, civil society, and community groups.

Kai Reinhardt teaches General Business Administration, Human Resources and Organization at HTW Berlin. He has many years of practical experience in strategy management and international organizational development for international corporations in the Internet and high-tech industry. In his research, he focuses on exploring new forms of strategic competence management and the creation of digital organizations.

Lúcia Lima Rodrigues is Full Professor of Accounting and a member of the Economic and Business Policies Research Unit at the University of Minho. She is Vice-President of the Portuguese accounting standards setting body and the Representative of Portugal at several accounting

European Union bodies. She is also a member of the Stakeholders Reporting Committee of the European Accounting Association.

Inês Salgueiro holds a Master's degree in Philosophy from NOVA University of Lisbon. Currently, she is preparing her Ph.D. thesis on Kant's Ethical Thought. She is a collaborating researcher at IFILNOVA. She is a member of the MetaCare project funded by FCT. Her research interests focus on Kant, ethics, applied ethics, business ethics, and environmental ethics. Her publications include book chapters in publishers such as Springer and Walter de Gruyter. She has also published articles in Germany, Brazil, Spain, and Portugal.

Aldina Lopes Santos was a credit risk analyst, manager, and head of business centers of small and medium companies. Currently, she is manager of medium and large companies in a Portuguese Bank. She has been an invited lecture of Management Control at the University of Aveiro.

Julia Schwarzkopf teaches sustainability management at the HTW Berlin Business School. In her research, she focuses on sustainable business practices, especially along the value chain.

Roberta Sebastiani is Full Professor of Management at Catholic University of the Sacred Heart. Co-Director of Centrimark—Center for Marketing Research—and Director of the Master Program in Marketing Management at the same University. The research and teaching interests include marketing strategy, sustainable strategy and business ethics, and sustainable innovation. Her main topics of research concern value creation in the management of strategies, business dynamics, and sustainability.

Sadaf Shariat (LLB, LLM, MBA, Ph.D., FHEA) is a Lecturer in Law, based in the University of South Wales Business School. She has a Ph.D. in Law from Durham University and an MBA in CSR from Nottingham University's School of Business. Sadaf's research is interdisciplinary, in law, business, and moral philosophy. Her research in business studies mainly focuses on Corporate Social Responsibility and Social Enterprise.

Cláudia Simões is a Professor of Management (Marketing and Strategy area) at the University of Minho in Portugal. She holds a Ph.D. in Industrial and Business Studies from the University of Warwick, UK. Her research interests and publications are primarily in strategic marketing, corporate marketing (corporate identity, image, brand, and reputation), service management, and customer experience. She has published in the Journal of Marketing, Journal of the Academy of Marketing Science, Journal of Business Research, European Journal of Marketing, Industrial Marketing Management, Business Ethics Quarterly, Studies in Higher Education, and others. She is Associate Editor of the European Journal of Marketing.

Alin Stancu is Professor of Corporate Social Responsibility and Public Relations in the Department of Marketing from The Bucharest University of Economic Studies, Romania. His main areas of research include customer care, consumer experience, corporate responsibility, and public relations. He is the co-founder of The International Conference on Social Responsibility, Ethics and Sustainable Business (www.csrconferences.org) and co-editor of the book series: Palgrave Studies in Governance, Leadership and Responsibility.

Sophie Strobl received a Master's degree in Business from the University of Vienna. Already during her studies, she worked as a research assistant in a recruiting study and in the field of ad hoc marketing research at a media agency. Currently, she is employed as an Analytic Consultant at Nielsen and supports business customers in the food and drugstore industry.

Nicola J. R. Thomas is an Associate Professor in Marketing at De Montfort University, Leicester, UK. Nicola is a critical realist whose research focuses on sustainability and systems change. Specific research interests include transparency in marketing, marketing system reproduction/transformation processes, and sustainability marketing in general.

Udo Wagner is Full Professor and holds the Chair of Marketing, University of Vienna, Austria. His main areas of research are marketing research, consumer behavior, marketing models, retailing, and pricing. His papers appeared in academic journals, including Journal of Marketing Research, Marketing Science, and International Journal of Research in Marketing.

List of Figures

List of Tables

1

Perspectives on Corporate Responsibility, Sustainability and Markets

Cláudia Simões, Alin Stancu, and Georgiana Grigore

Markets and organisations increasingly act on a new sensitivity to social responsibility and sustainability ideas, principles, practices, arrangements and agendas. As such, companies develop offers that are more responsible towards individuals, society and environment. For example, Samsung used research and development to improve the quality of life of consumers by developing an application that optimizes the colours aimed at publics with Colour Vision Deficiency (CVD). This product became a standard for the industry (Samsung, 2017). Governments also act to promote sustainability and change in markets. For instance, the UK

C. Simões (✉)
University of Minho, Braga, Portugal
e-mail: csimoes@eeg.uminho.pt

A. Stancu
Bucharest University of Economic Studies, Bucharest, Romania

G. Grigore
University of Leicester, Leicester, UK

C. Simões et al. (eds.), *Corporate Responsibility, Sustainability and Markets*, Palgrave Studies in Governance, Leadership and Responsibility,
https://doi.org/10.1007/978-3-030-79660-0_1

Government determined that by 2030, the fossil fuel cars will no longer be in use in the country. This decision is part of a set of measures called the "Green Industrial Revolution", which seeks to reduce the environmental impact of car emissions (GOV.UK, 2020). Such reorientations have wider implications at the level of energy sources (e.g., electricity production and the development of nuclear or wind production). Yet, this change only solves part of the problem. Other challenges still remain, such as the lack of accessibility to public transport (Greenpeace UK, 2020; Grigore et al., 2017).

Sustainability and markets also call for new practices and states of mind in the ways institutions operate. Organisations and stakeholders intertwine in a continuous articulated search for quality of life and well-being for current and future generations. Stakeholders gradually take part in business activities co-creating mutual realities, often based on trust. Consumers are increasingly more aware and committed to sustainability issues, wanting to be part in community causes through their buying decisions. Consistently, consumers look for brands that reduce environmental impact and operate under sustainable guidelines (Forrester, 2020). Employees' interest in the companies they work for also develops beyond the financial compensation for their job. They are concerned about the companies' values, mission and policies towards environmental and social issues (Scheer, 2021).

The COVID-19 pandemic made us aware of our ecosystems' vulnerabilities (Sörensson et al., 2021). Extreme conditions occur and novel and innovative measures are needed to combat them. Future severe situations may emerge and nations ought to be prepared for such events (Forrester, 2020). Under these types of trends and conditions, the scope and grounds of sustainability expand into the creation of wider and interconnected realities reflected in new interplays among market actors and institutions. Integrated and systemic approaches, as the circular economy and the smart city, entail such rationalities and become particularly relevant.

This context shows that organisations' environments entail evolving market logics and marketing purposes connecting with the determination of corporate responsibility, sustainability practices, and related community and societal connections. Such market conditions and events catalyse new business models and instigate innovative market and business arrangements.

In this book, we discuss how evolving purposes in organisations and/or market logics, connect with the perseverance of corporate responsibility and sustainability practices, or related community and societal rationales. We inquire about the individual buying styles and identify supporting emerging and existing markets and offers. We further question which markets might have been weakened by such principles. From the organisations' perspectives, we look at the integration and transformation of corporate responsibility strategies and practices revealing the ways in which organisations operate in their environments. The book addresses these questions including current thinking and developments by both academics and practitioners. The chapters combine theoretical foundations on markets and/or marketing and corporate responsibility with practical insights that help managers in decision-making processes.

The book is structured in two parts. In the first part, chapters explore changing market systems, including how these can be made more responsible and sustainable. The section starts with an intercultural study on whether consumers' value systems impact on the sustainable consumption of groceries (Chapter 2). The study conducted in Austria and Sri Lanka, identifies the motives and barriers for purchasing environmentally friendly groceries by taking into account the cultural and economic factors. The first part also includes chapters on sustainability and omnichannel strategies in the Italian wine industry (Chapter 3), a CSR map in the case of the Spanish professional football league (Chapter 4), an exploration of non-financial reporting in the banking sector in Portugal (Chapter 5), and ends with an overview of the risks of unethical behaviour in the Polish financial sector (Chapter 6). The variety of contexts (i.e., wine industry, professional football, banking) from different countries reveals new insights into the intersection of corporate responsibilities and markets, expanding knowledge in this field of inquiry.

In Part II, we discuss stakeholders' role in co-creating and co-constructing sustainability initiatives and agendas in different ecosystems. Chapter 7 provides a detailed account of the vulnerabilities and interconnectedness of markets as a result of climate change pressure and activism. Part II then discusses the role of competency management in integrating sustainability in the vocational education of German butchers (Chapter 8). It further shows ways of transforming linear marketing systems to circular ones (Chapter 9). The last three chapters in this part provide deeper theoretical investigations into corporate responsibilities and markets, through: an extensive systematic literature review of corporate social responsibility and social enterprise (Chapter 10), an overview of traditional ethics and their limitations in addressing environmental justice that might be better dealt with through sustainable policy tests (Chapter 11), and a study that shows how differences in CSR involvement between countries result from the specific models of welfare capitalism (Chapter 12).

These papers were presented at the 8th International Conference on Social Responsibility, Ethics and Sustainable Business in Braga, Portugal (October 2019). We gratefully acknowledge the insightful contributions from all authors in the book, and we hope you enjoy reading the book. We also wish to thank all anonymous reviewers for their insightful, tremendously helpful and enriching commentary on all the chapters.

References

Forrester. (2020). *Rethinking Sustainability in the Middle of a Pandemic*. Forbes. https://www.forbes.com/sites/forrester/2020/08/05/rethinking-sustainability-in-the-middle-of-a-pandemic/.

Forrester. (2021). https://www.forbes.com/sites/forrester/2021/01/21/empowered-consumers-call-for-sustainability-transformation/. Accessed February 2021.

GOV.UK. (2020). *PM Outlines His Ten Point Plan for a Green Industrial Revolution for 250,000 Jobs*. GOV.UK. https://www.gov.uk/government/news/pm-outlines-his-ten-point-plan-for-a-green-industrial-revolution-for-250000-jobs.

Greenpeace UK. (2020). *The 2030 Ban on New Petrol and Diesel Cars, Explained*. Greenpeace UK. https://www.greenpeace.org.uk/news/petrol-diesel-cars-vans-2030-ban-phase-out/.

Grigore, G., Molesworth, M., & Watkins, R. (2017). New Corporate Responsibilities in the Digital Economy. In *Corporate Social Responsibility in the Post-Financial Crisis Era* (pp. 41–62). Cham: Palgrave Macmillan.

Samsung. (2017). *SeeColors: A Whole New World of Color for Those with Color Vision Deficiency*. https://news.samsung.com/global/seecolors-a-whole-new-world-of-color-for-those-with-color-deficiency

Scheel. (2021). https://www.forbes.com/sites/forbesbusinesscouncil/2021/02/04/sustainability-in-2021-everything-companies-should-know/. Accessed February 2021.

Sörensson, A., Grigore, G., Lundström, A., Stancu, A., & Tesfaye, B. (2021). What Happens to Corporate Responsibility in a Worldwide Health Emergency? In *Corporate Responsibility and Sustainability during the Coronavirus Crisis* (pp. 1–12). Cham: Palgrave Macmillan.

Part I

Markets and Society

2

Consumers' Value Systems in the Consumption of Sustainable Groceries: An Intercultural Study

Udo Wagner and Sophie Strobl

2.1 Introduction

2.1.1 Problem Description

Sustainability has become a major topic in political and economic debates. This can be seen, among other things, in the world-wide gathering of public policymakers in events like the UN Climate Change Conferences in 2018 (Katowice) or 2019 (Madrid). While sustainability is well researched in the Western world, it is comparatively rarely studied in developing countries. Such endeavors would prove especially important to sustainability research, as the majority of the world's population is located in underdeveloped countries (Dissanayake et al. 2016, 169). The ecological footprint of populations in developing countries remains much smaller than that of populations in developed countries. However,

U. Wagner (✉) · S. Strobl
University of Vienna, Vienna, Austria
e-mail: udo.wagner@univie.ac.at

C. Simões et al. (eds.), *Corporate Responsibility, Sustainability and Markets*, Palgrave Studies in Governance, Leadership and Responsibility, https://doi.org/10.1007/978-3-030-79660-0_2

as prosperity increases, both per capita consumption of natural resources and CO_2 emissions increase (Ewing et al. 2010, 21ff).

Household consumption is of great importance in this respect, as it is estimated to cause 30–50% of the environmental impact (Knaus and Renn 1998, 104). Studies on household energy consumption suggest that it directly or indirectly consumes the bulk of energy through the consumption of goods and services. The proportion of energy spent is particularly high in developed countries, with values reaching 60% in the literature. In less developed countries, households' share in energy consumption is lower; however, it is all the more likely in these countries that energy is used for the production of goods that are exported and, thereby, help foster private consumption in other countries (Hertwich 2005, 4676). On the consumer side, however, and in contrast to the production side, no clear trend toward sustainable behavior has been found to date.

Given these considerations, the relevant literature highlights the importance of integrating consumer behavior into sustainability research (Blok et al. 2015, 28). Food consumption is the second largest factor in household expenditure in Austria, accounting for 12% of household expenditures (Statistik Austria 2011). However, this is comparatively low given that it accounts for just under 20% in the EU and between 30–60% in less developed countries throughout Asia and Africa. These figures show that changing food consumption habits in favor of sustainable approaches have the potential to reduce human pollution (Tobler et al. 2011, 592). For this reason, the current work explores how the demand for sustainable groceries occurs and possible ways for stimulating this demand.

2.1.2 Research Agenda

Essentially, the problem arises regarding the aspects related to the consideration of sustainability in the choice of food, and whether these are similar across cultures. Such findings would be of particular importance to policy-makers in guiding strategic decisions or for companies marketing sustainable foods to appropriate target groups. Given the global implications of food sustainability efforts outlined above, transcultural factors that mediate food purchasing behavior must be identified.

The relevant literature identifies one's personal life philosophy as an influential factor on food purchases. One study uncovered that ideologies affect participants' dietary habits (Lindeman and Sirelius 2001, 182f). This implies that ideologies in research can be determined by values, which has received support in the literature (Gatersleben et al. 2014, 375f). Numerous scholars investigating the relations between sustainable behavior and values base their research on the model of Schwartz and Bilsky (Gatersleben et al. 2014, 375f; Lindeman and Sirelius 2001, 175f).

Schwartz and Bilsky (1987, 560) determine ten basic motivational values that can be assigned to two supra-value dimensions: self-enhancement ↔ self-transcendence vs. openness to change ↔ conservation. Since this standard model is commonly referenced in the literature, Fig. 2.1 briefly summarizes the essentials. The authors validate their theory using data from transcultural studies that prove its effectiveness across different cultures (Schwartz and Bilsky 1990, 888). Stern

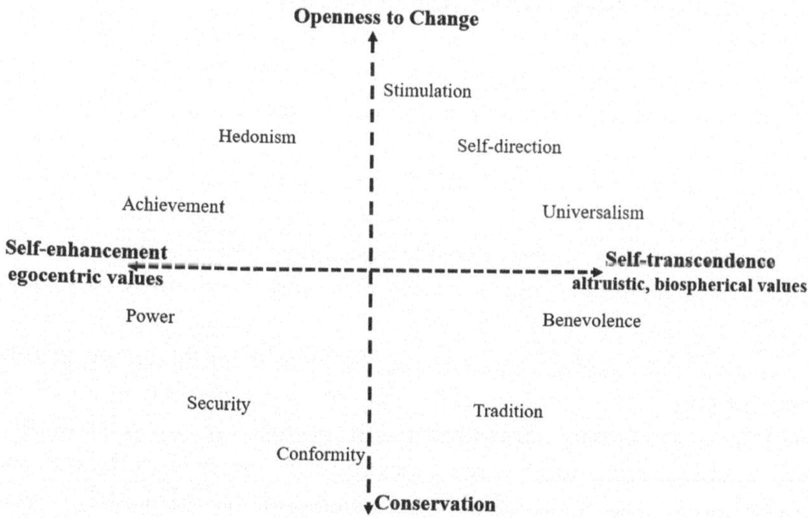

Fig. 2.1 Schwartz value system (*Source* Adapted from Schwartz 2012)

and Dietz (1994, 78) ultimately link the concept of values to sustainable behavior, identifying certain value ranges that promote or constrain sustainable conduct. Following this reasoning, the present study aims to link values with consumption of sustainable food in two culturally distinct countries, and to uncover principles that stimulate sustainability in the field of nutrition. In particular, we pose the following research question:

RQ : "How do transcultural values influence consideration of sustainability when purchasing groceries?"

2.2 Literature Review

The previous section outlined that sustainability and transcultural values are key concepts in this study. Therefore, this section elaborates somewhat deeper into these concepts and subsequently tries to link them.

2.2.1 Sustainable Consumer Behavior

This research follows the arguments provided by Ertz (2016, 4), and defines a sustainable consumer as someone who "…engages in a deliberate effort to acquire, use and dispose products in manners minimizing negative consequences and maximizing positive ones, on both environmental and social levels." The definition prioritizes the ecological and social dimensions of sustainable consumer behavior, whereas other authors also include economic, temporal, and developmental dimensions.

In terms of the *ecological dimension*, the focus is on the environmental compatibility of production and transport (i.e., whether and to what extent environmentally harmful emissions occur). This includes wastewater, exhaust gases, and all other types of waste materials. Obvious cues for consumers who are mindful of such emissions are official labels guaranteeing, for instance, organic production, packaging material—or lack thereof—and the seasonality and regionality of food.

Table 2.1 Properties of sustainable foods

Ecological dimension	Social dimension
Organic, seasonal, regional, no packaging	Regional, fair

The *social dimension* relates to the fairness of working conditions and wages of persons employed in manufacturing goods, and the influence of production on the environmental and living conditions in the product's country of origin. Again, labels (e.g., that certify fair-trade) may signal care for such considerations by the marketer to the customers; alternatively, buyers may possess actual knowledge about production conditions for locally or regionally produced food.

Based on these dimensions Table 2.1 presents the producers' view of properties of sustainable foods (Jungbluth et al. 2000; Flachowsky 2008; Ertz 2016). We note that properties might overlap and are not unique. Moreover, consumers might have different views in that they care of one of these properties without caring for sustainability (e.g., they purchase organic products for health reasons without concern for the environment; this will also become apparent from the empirical analysis later).

Evidently, one of the more effective ways to raise sustainability is to reduce consumption (Svensson 2012, 372); however, this approach is hardly viable for food products for several reasons. Firstly, nutrition is an unavoidable necessity of human survival. As long as only the amount of edibles required for sustenance is purchased—and no more—consumption does not represent an overaccumulation of possessions. Secondly, changing consumer behaviors towards abstinence remains remarkably difficult given the social facets at play. On the one hand, a reduction in the number of daily purchases may be due to financial constraints, which are associated with lower social status. On the other hand, a shift toward the purchase of sustainable products may indirectly signal wealth and high social status, as these goods are often more expensive than their conventional counterparts. Thus, rather than discuss reductions in food consumption, we focus on the motivations for purchasing groceries that display sustainable product characteristics.[1]

2.2.2 Transcultural Values

This research builds upon the Norm Activation Theory by Schwartz (1973, 352ff) developed to explain altruistic behavior. Thus, opinions and attitudes on a topic can affect the corresponding personal norms. These are to be understood as guidelines for action, which yield positive consequences when adhered to. By considering the consequences of one's own actions, and by personal responsibility for the outcome of a given action, personal norms (i.e., contextually dictated guidelines for action) are activated. An action is performed when the perceived costs in terms of time, effort, and available alternatives are deemed less detrimental than the negative consequences expected from behaviors that stray from such personal norms.

The social environment plays a role to the extent that the culture of the society inhabited by a person determines the internalized guidelines for action. Stern et al. (1995, 728) emphasize the importance of values in sustainable behavior. To this end, they extend the model of the Norm Activation Theory, beginning with the conceptualization of values as drivers of attitudes, opinions, and norms. According to their theory, personal values shape opinions on environmental issues, awareness of the consequences of environmental changes, and the belief in mutual responsibility. The further context of the effect is the same as that of Schwartz's model. In short, values affect opinions that, in turn, affect norms, which ultimately guide behavior. Therefore, the term Value-Belief-Norm model is used for their theory (Fig. 2.2).

Since the development of the Value-Belief-Norm model, it has often been used to investigate determinants of sustainable behavior. Because values are repeatedly employed to study discrepancies among

[1] For a more general context (not focusing on food) anticonsumption–on the micro level–describes actions against consumption or against specific products enabling consumers to express their values, ideas, beliefs, and overall identities (Seegebarth 2020, 34).

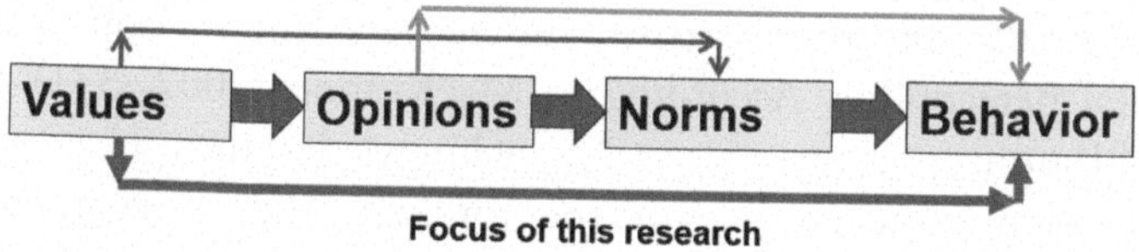

Fig. 2.2 Value-Belief-Norm model (*Source* Adapted from Stern et al. 1995)

cultures, this approach is also popular for scholars who conduct cross-cultural research on sustainable behavior. For example, Oreg and Katz-Gerro (2006, 464) analyzed environmentally conscious behaviors in 27 different countries, and Cordano et al. (2010, 229) compared results between South and North American subjects using the Value-Belief-Norm model.

This study also deals with cultural differences that manifest themselves in behaviors. Therefore, the Value-Belief-Norm model appears suitable for our research purpose and forms the basis for the established relationships (Fig. 2.2).

2.2.3 Linking Sustainable Consumer Behavior and Transcultural Values

The literature differentiates between three basic ethical concepts related to sustainable behavior: anthropocentrism, ecocentrism, and egocentrism. *Anthropocentrism* [also called (social) altruism] considers humans the most significant entity in the universe and, consequently, the maximization of the well-being of human societies as the utmost goal. *Ecocentrism* denotes a nature-centered, as opposed to human-centered, system of values. It identifies a philosophy that brings with it an intrinsic motivation to protect the ecosystem. Thus, ecocentric (or biospherical) values aim to protect the environment. *Egocentrism* is characterized by the inability to differentiate between oneself and others. Therefore, a person's own needs and those of the social environment are placed at the center of thinking and acting. This view differs from anthropocentrism in that only a small group of persons—rather than the whole of society—are included (Merchant 1992, 63f).

Conceptually, anthropocentrism and ecocentrism are opposing environmental perceptions. According to MacKinnon (2007, 331) people, who hold anthropocentric views "… acknowledge themselves as being the only significant entities in the universe and disregard animals and plants unless they provide life necessities." Consequently, human exploitation of the natural environment occurs. Contrariwise, ecocentrism recognizes value in all living species on earth regardless of their usefulness to humans. The anthropocentric perception is widespread and is considered responsible for current environmental crises. Unfortunately, the long-term perspective is missing, i.e., that a protected ecosystem serves humans in the long term; put differently, the conservation of the earth is relevant because it sustains human society. The egocentric mindset might be considered as an even more restricted anthropocentric view as it allows individuals to prosper without considering the cost to others. Surprisingly, however, Chandler (1981) found anthropocentrism to be unrelated to egocentrism in his studies.

Due to its complexity, Schwartz's (2012) ten-value system is frequently reduced to the two supra-value dimensions outlined in Fig. 2.1. In order to link sustainable behavior to this value system, we further concentrate on the supra-value dimension self-enhancement ↔ self-transcendence (dotted line in Fig. 2.1). Accordingly, it is quite obvious that altruistic and biospherical values are linked to self-transcendence, and that egocentric values are linked to self-enhancement. We note that a connection between egocentrism and sustainable behavioral intentions may operate bidirectionally. A positive influence is justified by the fact that people high in selfishness perform sustainable actions only when they prevent negative consequences. For example, a person buys organic food to improve his or her image toward others. Usually, however, the relationship is negative because selfish values prevent sustainable actions when the personal costs associated with them are perceived as high. Costs can comprise not only financial means, but any consequence perceived as undesirable. We complete a systematic investigation of the relationships between Schwartz's values and sustainable behavior and provide Table 2.2 which presents results of a literature review concerning this matter.

Table 2.2 Relations between Schwartz's supra-values and sustainable behavior

Literature	Schwartz's supra-value dimensions			
	Self-transcendence	Self-enhancement	Conservation	Openness to change
Stern and Dietz (1994)	pos.	neg.	no.	no.
Karp (1996)	pos.	neg.	neg.	pos.
Stern et al. (1995) study A	pos.	neg.	no.	no.
Stern et. al. (1995) study B	pos.	no.	no.	no.
Nordlund and Garvill (2002)	pos.	neg.	n. i.	n. i.
De Groot and Steg (2008)	pos.	n. i.	n. i.	n. i.
Vermeir and Verbeke (2008)	no.	neg.	pos.	no.
Cordano et al. (2010)	pos.	no.	no.	no.
Peyer et al. (2016)	pos.	n. i.	no.	no.
Sharma and Jha (2017)	pos.	neg.	neg.	neg.
Balderjahn et al. (2018)	pos.	neg.	no.	pos.

Notes pos./neg. statistically significant *positive/negative* relation between sustainable behavior and respective value dimension has been identified
no. *no* statistically significant relation has been identified
n. i. relation has not been investigated

As shown in Table 2.2, the supra-value dimension self-transcendence (mostly positive) to self-enhancement (mostly negative) is often associated with sustainable behavior. On the other hand, the research results on the supra-value dimension openness to change to conservation are often not significant and partly contradictory. This justifies our decision to focus our investigations on the former dimension. This evidence allows for the two following research objectives:

O1 : Analyze the type of role that values of self-transcendence, especially biospherical and altruistic values, have regarding the purchase of products with sustainable attributes.

O2 : Analyze the type of role that values of self-enhancement, especially egocentric values, have regarding the purchase of products with sustainable attributes.

Evidently, many other drivers may be at play (e.g., as moderators, limiting conditions). Whereas the universal character of Schwartz's value system should allow generalization across different cultures, availability of sustainable food, awareness of environmental issues, knowledge on sustainable food, and trust in information provided by marketers (e.g., accuracy of product labels), and sociodemographic variables may be relevant; therefore, they are included in the empirical part of this study.

2.3 Empirical Study

2.3.1 Method

The research question challenges the role of transcultural values in sustainable consumption; thus, cultural issues must be taken into consideration when undertaking an empirical investigation. Rather than analyzing a variety of cultures, we selected two markedly distinct cultures. For pragmatic reasons, Austria was selected to represent an industrialized economy in central Europe. Sri Lanka was chosen for comparison, as it is an Asian country in which the living conditions differ significantly from those in Austria. Sri Lanka is considered a developing country, but food safety and prosperity are ensured in urban areas to the extent that consumers are given a choice between traditional and sustainable food alternatives. In part, the population from Sri Lanka might be influenced by Indian, in particular Advaita, a philosophy which holds that the same soul is present inside everyone, including nature (Ranganathananda 1995, 83). Therefore, people's responsibility toward nature might be well established. Compared to Austria, however, clear differences in Sri Lanka can be seen in purchasing power, education, and other sociodemographic variables (Davis et al. 2016, 308).

Authors on the suitability of various survey methods in the field of sustainable consumption generally advise against the use of quantitative methods. Traditional quantitative surveys regularly lead to increased intent to act sustainably (Augner and Devinney 2007, 377f) due to its socially desirable response. The assessment of one's own values, attitudes, and behaviors are particularly susceptible to such bias (Cameron et al. 1998, 692). This effect is rare in qualitative studies; when it occurs, it only does so to a much smaller extent. Thus, an exploratory design was used in our study.

Two perspectives are deemed important in the present case. On the one hand, a direct investigation of common consumer practices when purchasing groceries is presumably relevant; therefore, focus group interviews were held. On the other hand, a more objective assessment of consumption habits and the underlying motives from a professional's point of view is also of value; thus, interviews of experts were held. This triangulation, the combination of multiple investigative methods, compensates for potential methodological biases. The subject of the study is considered from different perspectives, which complement each other, and allow a more objective view on the topic.

Focus group interviews. Two focus groups per country were carried out. Between groups, participants differed by their awareness of the sustainability of the foods they purchase. This approach was intended to create more homogeneous group compositions in terms of attitude toward sustainable groceries which, in turn, should stimulate honest and open communication among respondents.

In Austria, potential participants were approached at a farmers' market, supermarkets, or organic food shops. Although they were not financially compensated for participation, they received a small package of locally produced products (bottle of fruit juice, mixed fruits, and two fruit yogurts). Group interviews took place in rural areas and lasted approximately 90 min each. One of the authors moderated the discussion based on predetermined interviewer guidelines. In sum, fourteen females and two males (aged between 28–74 years) participated.

In Sri Lanka, recruiting subjects proved more challenging; however, a local organization helped by means of snowball sampling. The language barrier was a complicating factor because interviews were conducted in English and only a small proportion of inhabitants possess sufficient English fluency. Another obstacle was the economic disparities of participants. Many Sri Lankans earn low incomes and, therefore, rely on cheap food. However, our research requires participants whose grocery purchase decisions are not exclusively dictated by financial constraints (in order to reveal their value system).[2] Rather than financial compensation for participation, respondents received a bar of organic Austrian chocolate. Group interviews took place near a local food market in the capital, Colombo; these interviews had a slightly longer average duration than those in Austria.[3] The same moderator used the same interviewer guidelines as with the Austrian interviews. In sum, five females and five males (aged between 24–81 years) participated. In all cases, focus group interviews were audio-recorded.

Expert interviews. Experts were selected exclusively according to substantive criteria following the topic under question. The expertise required to participate was contextual knowledge in the field of sustainable food consumption behavior. We consider employees of NGOs as suitable for this purpose, assuming the NGO in question strives to promote sustainability in the consumption of food. Alternatively, representatives of companies in the field of food retailing and food production also qualified for inclusion if their supply of goods could be assigned to at least one category of sustainable food. Experts were recruited by phone or e-mail.

The Austrian experts comprise a biological researcher; an officer for sustainability of food distribution in public institutions; a product manager for organic food; an officer for environmental guidance on

[2] We admit this as a limitation of our study because this might cause a selection bias toward more wealthy citizens in Sri Lanka.

[3] Cultural differences concerning timeliness and discussion discipline resulted in a less structured flow of the interviews and in turn longer durations (100–110 min).

nutrition, gardening, and textiles; and two managers employed in retail grocery chains. In Sri Lanka, we identified a founder of a retail shop for organic groceries; an authorized representative for certifying organically produced food; and two producers of organic food. Interview guidelines were used in face-to-face interviews, which were conducted in German and English in Austria and Sri Lanka, respectively, and lasted between 24–48 min. All interviews were audio-recorded.

2.3.2 Results

Audio recordings were transcribed, translated (for interviews from Sri Lanka), and their content analyzed by employing the semantic-content transcription system according to Dresing and Pehl (2013, 20). We use this system because the purpose of the transcript is a pure content analysis; deeper phonetic and phonological information was not needed. By doing so, existing texts are structured, condensed, coded, and assigned to a set of categories according to the respective research objectives (cf. subsection 2.2).[4] Content analysis identified four main categories: sustainable food, values, moderators, and interdependence of consumption drivers. Each main category contains subcategories, for instance, with respect to sustainable, organic, regional, seasonal, or social food,[5] among others. Table 2.3 provides an overview of our category system.

Results concerning O1, role of *biospherical* values: While motives for protecting the environment are present in the mind of consumers, in many cases it may only contribute to a limited extent to the purchase of organic foods. Only a small percentage of customers who are extremely invested in protecting the environment are guided by biospherical values in their purchase decisions; this holds true for both Austria and Sri Lanka. The avoidance of packaging-related considerations is attributed primarily to biospherical values. This issue is of increasing importance

---

[4] We analyzed focus and expert interviews separately but present results simultaneously for reason of clarity. In addition, we abstain from including exemplary verbatim of interviewees because of constraints in space.

[5] We use the term "social food" for food which was produced under fair conditions by neither exploiting workforce nor the environment.

Table 2.3 The four main categories and their subcategories of content analysis

Sustainable food	Values	(Potential) moderators	Interdependence of consumption drivers
Organic	Biospherical	Availability	Purchase barrier
Regional	Altruistic	Awareness	Purchase motive
Seasonal	Egocentric	Convenience	Promotive factors
Social		Health	
Sustainable in general		Issues of production	
No packaging		Knowledge	
		Price	
		Transparency	
		Trust	
		Not relevant[a]	

[a]Includes all text that addresses topics which are not of further interest for the research purpose

in Austria (e.g., zero-waste initiatives). Barriers against this trend, on the one hand, pose logistical challenges for retailers and, on the other hand, reduce shopping convenience and product storage life for consumers. In Sri Lanka, food is commonly sold unpackaged, but with small plastic bags freely available at the checkout. The government and NGOs are working on raising awareness of environmentally sustainable practices (e.g., replacing plastic bags with reusable fabric bags).

The percentage of strict vegetarians is relatively small in Austria; however, the protection of animals is more relevant to consumers. While they usually do not abstain entirely from meat, dairy products, and eggs, they will commonly favor organic foods to salve their conscience because such foods are produced under more stringent animal welfare rules. The situation differs in Sri Lanka given that organic foods are rarely available.

Results concerning O1, role of *altruistic* values: For the purchase of social food in Austria, we clearly notice a positive link with altruistic values, which are also the main aspects considered in purchase decisions. For Sri Lanka, no conclusion can be reached in this respect because social food is rarely available.

In the case of organic food, altruistic values are relevant in families striving for high-quality, health-promoting foods—this is the central motive for the purchase of organic products, especially in Sri Lanka.

Here, food safety is lower than in Austria due to lack of governmental oversight. Target groups for organic foods predominantly consist of parents caring for the elderly, the young, and the sick or injured. Importantly, however, affordability is a central issue. Consumers claiming altruistic motives seem also more likely to buy regionally produced food because they want to support local farmers.

Results concerning O2, role of *egocentric* values: Whereas empirical evidence for **O1** by-and-large coincides with the findings reported in the literature (cf. Table 2.2, column 2), this is not the case for **O2.** Surprisingly, egocentric values were found to be associated more positively (rather than negatively, as proposed by Table 2.2, column 3) with the purchase of sustainable foods. We elaborate on this claim in the sequel.

The image associated with the purchase of ecological foods—and, to a somewhat lesser extent, of social food—is very positive. By purchasing such products, consumers transfer these characteristics onto themselves, thereby increasing their social status (i.e., impression management). Organic foods are more expensive than conventional alternatives. The regular purchasing of organic foods or visiting of health-food stores, therefore, expresses financial prosperity. This is especially true in Sri Lanka, where organic foods are prohibitively expensive and only affordable to a small proportion of its inhabitants. Therefore, ecocentric values in terms of impression management are more important in Austria than in Sri Lanka.

Additional findings :*Availability of organic products.* In Austria, twenty percent of the agricultural land is used for organic farming. The market share for organic food is approximately eight percent and growing steadily; accordingly, the availability of organic foods is high. In Sri Lanka, the market for organic foods remains in its infancy. For example, although producers have been offering organically certified food for several years, these products were largely designated for export to Europe or North America. Thus, the availability of organically produced food for local consumption is poor.

Availability of packaging-free products. Austrian supermarkets offer packaging-free fruits and vegetables only to a very limited extent. Moreover, the concentration of grocery retailing is extremely high, which makes direct supply from organic farmers (who usually deliver unpackaged foods) negligible. In Sri Lanka, the structure of the food market is entirely different. There are many small retailers and markets with regional suppliers and off-farm sales, all of whose products are predominantly packaging-free. Supermarket chains in Sri Lanka are experiencing strong growth rates, but market penetration remains less than ten percent. Large food retailers typically have more sophisticated logistics that allow for a wide range of imported and processed foods, most of which are packaged for logistical reasons and shelf life.

Availability of regional products. Regional foods are available in both countries if consumers are willing to constrain their grocery purchases to seasonal products. Austria faces another barrier due to the extra effort required to visit appropriate suppliers. The lack of labeling indicating the food's origin is detrimental in Sri Lanka in this respect.

Availability of social products. Social foods are available in Austria exclusively for products from developing countries; social foods from local farmers are not available. In Sri Lanka, the availability of social food is scarce.

Awareness of environmental issues. Consumer awareness of environmental issues is present among consumers in both countries.

Convenience. In both Austria and Sri Lanka, we recognize the barrier of convenience to purchasing sustainable products. Despite its ready availability in Austria, regular, long-term nutrition using sustainable food usually requires higher acquisition efforts, and consumers are often unwilling to accept additional monetary or non-monetary costs regardless of the importance they place on sustainability. This also holds true in Sri Lanka because the limited availability of sustainable foods is even more pronounced.

The *health* of oneself and of one's family is the main selling point in Austria and Sri Lanka for the purchase of organically produced foods. Consumers expect these foods to have superior nutritional value relative to conventionally produced food. They expect that organic farmers abstain from using pesticides, non-natural fertilizers, and pollutants. Security in Schwartz's value system is comprised mostly of health; thus, health can be assigned to the conservation supra-dimension (cf. Fig. 2.1; Schwartz 1992). Surprisingly, our literature review did not yield any research reporting a significant association between security and sustainable food purchases; additional research on this topic is warranted.

Labelling and knowledge. Austrians are knowledgeable about understanding various food labels and certifications. Nevertheless, there is a lack of transparency: if non-organic alternatives are on sale, it is often not evident which choice better supports sustainability. Consider the following example: (i) An organic product is packaged in a foil made from corn starch but imported from Greece; (ii) as an alternative, the same organic product is available in plastic packaging but produced in Austria; (iii) yet another alternative is the same product, but it is conventionally and regionally farmed. In this example, it can be difficult to determine which alternative is most objectively beneficial for the environment. In Sri Lanka, choice overload is a rare occurrence given the low availability of sustainable foods and the near complete absence of quality-indicating labels.

Price. In Austria, the price of a certain range of sustainable foods is not a significant barrier for most customers; organic foods and locally produced products are both reasonably priced. This does not apply to those with lower economic prosperity, who are more likely to restrict purchases exclusively to lower-priced items. Certain organic product categories (e.g., meat) and most of the social products are significantly more expensive, and are treated as specialty goods and, consequently, bought only occasionally. Compared to Austria, the prohibitive price of organic products in Sri Lanka poses a much more significant barrier.

Transparency and trust. Not only in terms of certification, but also in general, many Austrians are under the impression that producers might employ deceptive strategies to maximize profit, which applies to both labels and the durability of groceries. Sri Lankans share such skepticism. In the absence of stringent rules for labeling, a lack of transparency arises, with some suppliers distributing organic foods without the oversight of an independent authority.

Sociodemographics. If there are children or sick members in a given family, the purchasing of environmentally friendly foods rises. Higher education also fosters demand for sustainable groceries, on average. In addition, people who do not prepare their meals at home, but rather opt to eat out or purchase convenience food, are less concerned about foods' sustainability profile. These observations apply to both countries.

2.4 Discussion

In accordance with theoretical reasoning, empirical evidence confirms that values of self-transcendence are positively associated with attitudes toward sustainable food. More specifically, a positive association was found between biospheric values and the purchase of food with ecological product characteristics. Supposedly, however, this relation is indirect because environmentally friendly consumption was rarely mentioned by respondents as a main reason for buying organic food—the main reason reported was health for both countries under investigation. Altruistic values were also found to play a positive role for attitudes toward groceries with social properties. In this case, altruistic values are likely to be predominantly relevant, particularly in Austria. Lack of availability of social foods precludes the making of respective statements for Sir Lanka.

Contrary to what has been reported in the literature, empirical evidence suggests a positive link between values of self-enhancement and the inclination toward sustainable food. The favorable image associated with the use ecological or social-friendly products, and the general trend toward sustainability in recent years, may explain this result. Again, this result applies to both countries; but, the comparatively higher price of such products poses a general barrier for purchasing these products in Sri Lanka; on the other hand, such a barrier might also cause such products to be perceived as Veblen goods.

For future research, we will refine our research agenda in two ways. First, we will further delve into the associations between egocentric values and products with sustainable attributes. Second, we will include an **O3**, which will analyze the type of role that values of Schwartz's supra-dimension of conservation—health, in particular—have regarding the purchase of sustainable foods. Finally, we emphasize that our results support the universal concept of Schwartz's value system, because the differences between Austria and Sri Lanka concerning the consumption of sustainable groceries are quite small despite significant differences in culture and economic development.

References

Auger, Pat, and Timothy M. Devinney. "Do what consumers say matter? The misalignment of preferences with unconstrained ethical intentions." *Journal of Business Ethics* 76, no. 4 (2007): 361–383.

Balderjahn, Ingo, Mathias Peyer, Barbara Seegebarth, Klaus-Peter Wiedmann, and Anja Weber. "The many faces of sustainability-conscious consumers: A category-independent typology." *Journal of Business Research* 91 (October 2018): 83–93.

Blok, Vincent, Thomas B. Long, A. Idil Gaziulusoy, Nilgin Ciliz, Rodrigo Lozano, Donald Huisingh, Maria Csutora, and Casper Boks. "From best practices to bridges for a more sustainable future: Advances and challenges in the transition to global sustainable production and consumption: Introduction to the ERSCP stream of the special volume." *Journal of Cleaner Production* 108, Part A (December 2015): 19–30.

Cameron, Linda D., Paul M. Brown, and Judith G. Chapman. "Social value orientations and decisions to take proenvironmental action 1." *Journal of Applied Social Psychology* 28, no. 8 (1998): 675–697.

Chandler, Edward W. *Anthropocentrism: Construct validity and measurement.* PhD diss., Louisiana State University, 1981.

Cordano, Mark, Stephanie Welcomer, Robert F. Scherer, Lorena Pradenas, and Victor Parada. "Understanding cultural differences in the antecedents of pro-environmental behavior: A comparative analysis of business students in the United States and Chile." *The Journal of Environmental Education* 41, no. 4 (2010): 224–238.

Davis, Kyle F., Jessica A. Gephart, and Thushara Gunda. "Sustaining food self-sufficiency of a nation: The case of Sri Lankan rice production and related water and fertilizer demands." *Ambio* 45, no. 3 (2016): 302–312.

De Groot, Judith I., and Linda Steg. "Value orientations to explain beliefs related to environmental significant behavior: How to measure egoistic, altruistic, and biospheric value orientations." *Environment and Behavior* 40, no. 3 (2008): 330–354.

Dissanayake, Dinithi, Carol Tilt, and Maria Xydias-Lobo. "Sustainability reporting by publicly listed companies in Sri Lanka." *Journal of Cleaner Production* 129 (August 2016): 169–182.

Dresing, Thorsten, and Thorsten Pehl. "Praxisbuch Interview, Transkription und Analyse. Anleitungen und Regelsysteme für qualitativ Forschende." 5 (2013): 813–829.

Ewing, Brad, David Moore, Steven Goldfinger, Anna Oursler, Anders Reed, and Mathis Wackernagel. *Ecological footprint atlas 2010*. Global Footprint Network, Oakland, 2010.

Ertz, Myriam. "Proposition of an integrative theory of socially-responsible consumption behavior." *Electronic Green Journal* 1, no. 39 (2016): 1–18.

Flachowsky, Gerhard. "How do we receive CO(2)-footprints for food of animal origin?" *Archives of Animal Breeding*, 51 (2008): 67–82.

Gatersleben, Birgitta, Niamh Murtagh, N., and Wokje Abrahamse. "Values, identity and pro-environmental behavior." *Contemporary Social Science* 9, no. 4 (2014): 374–392.

Hertwich, Edgar G. "Life cycle approaches to sustainable consumption: A critical review." *Environmental Science & Technology* 39, no. 13 (2005): 4673–4684.

Jungbluth, Niels, Olaf Tietje, and Roland W. Scholz. "Food purchases: Impacts from the consumers' point of view investigated with a modular LCA." *The International Journal of Life Cycle Assessment* 5, no. 3 (2000): 134–142.

Karp, David G. "Values and their effect on pro-environmental behavior." *Environment and Behavior* 28, no. 1 (1996): 111–133.

Knaus, Anja, and Ortwin Renn. *Den Gipfel vor Augen. Unterwegs in eine nachhaltige Zukunft*. Metropolis, Marburg, 1998.

Lindeman, Marjaana, and Minna Sirelius. "Food choice ideologies: The modern manifestations of normative and humanist views of the world. *Appetite* 37, no. 3 (2001): 175–184.

MacKinnon, Barbara. *Ethics and contemporary issues*, 5th edition, Thomson/Wadsworth, Belmont, California, 2007.

Merchant, Carolyn. *Radical ecology: The search for a livable world*. Routledge, New York, 1992.

Nordlund, Annika M., and Jörgen Garvill. "Value structures behind pro-environmental behavior." *Environment and Behavior* 34, no. 6 (2002): 740–756.

Oreg, Shaul, and Tally Katz-Gerro. "Predicting pro-environmental behavior cross-nationally: Values, the theory of planned behavior, and value-belief-norm theory." *Environment and Behavior* 38, no. 4 (2006): 462–483.

Peyer, Mathias, Ingo Balderjahn, Barbara Seegebarth, and Alexandra Klemm. "The role of sustainability in profiling voluntary simplifiers." *Journal of Business Research* 70, no. C (2016): 37–43.

Ranganathananda, Swami. *Eternal values for a changing society: Education for human excellence*, Bharatiya Vidya Bhavan: Mumbai, 1995.

Schwartz, Shalom H. "Normative explanations of helping behavior: A critique, proposal, and empirical test." *Journal of Experimental Social Psychology* 9, no. 4 (1973): 349–364.

Schwartz, Shalom H. "Universals in the content and structure of values: Theoretical advances and empirical tests in 20 countries." *Advances in Experimental Social Psychology* 25, no. 1 (1992): 1–65.

Schwartz, Shalom H. "An overview of the Schwartz theory of basic values." *Online Readings in Psychology and Culture* 2, no. 1 (2012): 2307–0919.

Schwartz, Shalom H., and Wolfgang Bilsky. "Toward a universal psychological structure of human values." *Journal of Personality and Social Psychology* 53, no. 3 (1987): 550–562.

Schwartz, Shalom H., and Wolfgang Bilsky. "Toward a theory of the universal content and structure of values: Extensions and cross-cultural replications." *Journal of Personality and Social Psychology* 58, no. 5 (1990): 878–891.

Seegebarth, Barbara. "*Mindful consumption: Essays on sustainable consumption and anticonsumption.*" Habilitation diss., Technical University Braunschweig, Germany, 2020.

Sharma, Rajat, and Mithileshwar Jha. "Values influencing sustainable consumption behavior: Exploring the contextual relationship." *Journal of Business Research* 76 (October 2017): 77–88.

Svensson, Eva. "Achieving sustainable lifestyles? Socio-cultural dispositions, collective action and material culture as problems and possibilities." *Local Environment* 17, no. 3 (2012): 369–386.

Statistik Austria. 2011. "Konsumerhebung 2009/10. Monatliche Verbrauchsausgaben der privaten Haushalte - Hauptergebnisse." Accessed August 31, 2017. http://www.statistik.at/web_de/statistiken/menschen_und_gesellschaft/soziales/verbrauchsausgaben/konsumerhebung_2009_2010/index.html#index1.

Stern, Paul C., and Thomas Dietz. "The value basis of environmental concern." *Journal of Social Issues* 50, no. 3 (1994): 65–84.

Stern, Paul C., Thomas Dietz, and Gregory A. Guagnano. "The new ecological paradigm in social-psychological context." *Environment and Behavior* 27, no. 6 (1995): 723–743.

Tobler, Christina, Vivianne H. Visschers, and Michael Siegrist. "Organic tomatoes versus canned beans: How do consumers assess the environmental friendliness of vegetables?" *Environment and Behavior* 43, no. 5 (2011): 591–611.

Vermeir, Iris, and Wim Verbeke. "Sustainable food consumption among young adults in Belgium: Theory of planned behavior and the role of confidence and values." *Ecological Economics* 64, no. 3 (2008): 542–553.

3

Sustainability and Omnichannel Strategies in the Italian Wine Industry

Marta Galli, Roberta Sebastiani, and Alessia Anzivino

3.1 Introduction

The issue of sustainability is acquiring ever greater importance in the wine business worldwide, being increasingly recognized as a source of competitive advantage in terms of brand image and profit for Small and Medium-sized Enterprises (SMEs) (Broccardo and Zicari 2020). In particular, consumers are progressively more interested in having a quality product with sustainable characteristics, and they are willing to

M. Galli · R. Sebastiani · A. Anzivino (✉)
Department of Management, Catholic University of the Sacred Heart, Milan, Italy
e-mail: Alessia.Anzivino@unicatt.it

M. Galli
e-mail: marta.galli@unicatt.it

R. Sebastiani
e-mail: roberta.sebastiani@unicatt.it

C. Simões et al. (eds.), *Corporate Responsibility, Sustainability and Markets*, Palgrave Studies in Governance, Leadership and Responsibility, https://doi.org/10.1007/978-3-030-79660-0_3

pay a higher price for a bottle that respects these traits (Corduas et al. 2013; Forbes et al. 2009; Iannone et al. 2016; Pomarici and Vecchio 2014; Szolnoki 2013).

Considering the world wine scenario up to the 1980s, the main actors were Italy, France, Spain, and Portugal, and the agricultural sector was the basis of the economy of these countries. In the 1990s, new countries entered the wine market because of a crisis of the consumers in the Old World. Outside the Old World, the USA and Australia were the first to enter the wine industry, followed later by Chile and South Africa (Nelgen and Anderson 1961). Moreover, in the following years, Argentina and New Zealand gained market shares, and the Asian market broke down old barriers and entered the wine industry (Mariani et al. 2012).

To define what sustainability is in the wine industry, it is necessary to understand the definitions, principles, and past and current practices (Flores 2018). In Resolution CST (Scientific and Technical Committee) 1/2004, the International Organization of Vine and Wine (OIV) defines sustainability as "a global strategy on the scale of the grape production and processing systems, incorporating at the same time the economic sustainability of structures and territories, producing quality products, considering requirements of precision in sustainable viticulture, risks to the environment, product safety and consumer health and valuing of heritage, historical, cultural, ecological and aesthetic aspects" (CST 1/2004). In its turn, the resolution of 2008 includes the guidelines, while that of 2016 gives general principles about sustainability (CST 1/2008).

Since viticulture depends heavily on natural resources, such as the composition of the soil, water, and solar energy and how these interact with other ecological processes, a winery must protect and preserve the environment (CST 1/2008). This goal can be achieved thanks to the implementation of the guidelines of OIV resolution CST 1/2008 (CST 1/2008). The mainstays that are contained in the OIV resolution of 2016 refer to the general principles of environmental, social, economic, and cultural issues (OIV-CST 518/2016). The first part of the resolution gives the principles for a sustainable viticulture that respects the environment, such as the selection of the site, soil management, preservation of the biodiversity and landscape, optimization of energy and water use, optimization of the use of technical inputs during the production and processing phases, waste management, management of byproducts, and limitation of noise and air pollution (OIV-CST 518/2016). The second part of the resolution concerns the sensitivity of sustainable viticulture to social and cultural aspects and underlines the fact that "Any sustainable development initiative should take into account the objectives of stakeholders, as well as the entire community. Companies should consider the socio-economic impact of their activities and should consider getting involved in the socio-economic development of regions (or areas)" (OIV-CST 518/2016). Finally, the last part of the resolution concerns the maintenance of economic viability. Indeed, "[t]he ability to innovate and adapt to technological and socio-economic changes and cost management should be especially developed in order to generate sustainable growth that will provide income and employment in times to come" (OIV-CST 518/2016).

In order to support wineries in adopting a sustainable approach in the Old and New World, several programs have been developed with specific aims (Giacomarra et al. 2016; Gilinsky et al. 2016; Hughey et al. 2005; Pullman et al. 2010). New World countries have been the first to implement sustainability programs, with the first one being implemented by the Lodi Wine Grape Commission in 1992, while the first movement to protect the environment was in California in the 1980s. In the following years, several programs for sustainable winegrowing have been developed, but no univocal certification scheme exists. Also the Old World countries have implemented sustainability practices. The European Union, through its Executive Agency for Small and Medium-sized Enterprises (EASME), in the time period 2014–2020, has developed and financed a sustainability program called "LIFE." This program has the aim of reducing resource waste, improving the EU's environmental and climate policies, better managing the environmental governance, and supporting civil society and local actors (LIFE program, EU). What emerges from literature and practice is that in the Old World countries, respect for tradition, culture, and terroir reflects the concept of sustainability as a combination of environmental, cultural, social, and economic aspects (Benedetto 2013; Benedetto et al. 2014; Iannone et al. 2016; Lamastra et al. 2014; Rugani et al. 2013).

One of the main challenges that wineries face concerning sustainability is consumer awareness and the value placed by wine customers on sustainable practices (Benedetto et al. 2014). The literature (Schäufele and Hamm 2017) on consumer perceptions, preferences, and willingness-to-pay regarding wine with sustainability characteristics shows that consumers have low awareness about what "sustainability" really means in the wine industry. In this scenario, producers may play a key role in disseminating information about the different aspects—environmental, social, and economic—that characterize sustainability in the wine industry with the aim of "raising consumers' knowledge of sustainable wine production to create preferences and influence purchase behaviour" (Schäufele and Hamm 2017, 388). In recent years, SME wineries have started to go digital both to enhance their competitiveness and establish a closer relationship with their customers (Szolnoki et al. 2013). The opportunities provided by technology are progressively impacting the experience that wine consumers have in their purchasing processes (Szolnoki et al. 2013).

By adopting an omnichannel perspective that integrates offline and online touchpoints, wineries are moving toward the co-creation of an integrated experience with their consumers able to convey values and information about their sustainable strategies and products (Verhoef et al. 2009). However, little is known about how, in particular, small and medium wineries implement omnichannel strategies and their impact on the communication of sustainability issues to consumers. Thus, this chapter aims to discuss how, in particular, SME Italian wineries are adopting omnichannel strategies for communicating their sustainable strategies and practices to consumers.

This chapter is organized as follows. First, it provides a theoretical framework, drawing together various research studies on sustainability in the wine industry and on omnichannel strategies adopted in the same industry; secondly, it presents the methodology used in this chapter and then presents and discusses the findings. Finally, it summarizes the conclusions and gives some recommendations for managers.

3.2 Theoretical Framework

Great attention is being driven on sustainability issues, both in the New and Old worlds, that not only regard environment and pollution, but also social, cultural, and economic dimensions all over the world (Borsellino et al. 2016; Benedetto et al. 2013). Considering the economic aspects, wineries implement these strategies in order to obtain a competitive advantage and improve efficiency and brand image (stakeholders' concerns). The other categories of drivers for sustainability are internal, and they are linked to ethical and moral concerns (Corbo et al. 2014; Gabzdylova et al. 2009; Giacomarra et al. 2016; Santiago-Brown et al. 2014; Santini et al. 2013). It is essential to underline that the definition of sustainability includes the social aspect, which is also linked to traditions, history, and culture (Flores 2018).

When talking about the wine industry and in particular SME wineries, it is important to underline that in the Old World, countries are linked to geographical characteristics and terroir composition (Flores 2018). For this reason, the activities that a wine firm organizes are connected to the place and history of the region. Moreover, wine is a "cultural commodity," which in the French tradition means that it is linked to the place, soil, and exposure (Fetter 2016). The French word terroir is the combination of these three components of the place, and it is different in every region. The terroir gives to wine recognizability and unique quality characteristics. For this reason, it is difficult for newcomers to emulate these old aspects that are connected to the place and country (Fetter 2016). Due to this particular nature of the product, for Old World countries, sustainability practices are the basis for their success (Fischer 2004). Nevertheless, for big firms, cooperatives, and wine groups, it is more natural to share these values due to the massive amount of financial, physical, and marketing resources. On the other hand, it is difficult for SMEs to communicate sustainability values to consumers, and for this reason, it is necessary that the winery, environment, and consumers co-evolve (Pomarici 2016).

The growth of the wine industry in the last 15 years is based on the enhancement of the relationship between the winery, environment, and consumer (Pomarici 2016). Indeed, the environment can have a double meaning; the first one is related to the environment as an ecological approach and a green strategy, and the second one is the environment as a group of firms that come from the same region or territory that share information, knowledge, and innovation (Pomarici 2016). The sustainable challenge has become a "must have" for all the wineries around the world, and their focus is on the relationship with the final client in a co-definition and co-creation of values. Nevertheless, nowadays, companies have to face knowledgeable consumers who want to buy quality wine at a low-medium price (Goldstein et al. 2008).

Indeed, sustainability practices are also linked to the final sales of the product. In particular, when consumers buy a sustainable bottle of wine, they expect not only a quality product, but they also want to find the values of the sustainability approach. Several authors have conducted research studies about the behavior and reaction of purchasers to sustainable products around the world (Ferrara et al. 2020). In Australia, more than 50% of wine consumers pay more for a bottle of wine if it is sustainable (D'Souza et al. 2006); in contrast, a research conducted in Canada (Berghoef and Dodds 2011) shows that only a small segment of consumers look for a sustainable bottle of wine. Even if Australian consumers will pay more for a sustainable bottle of wine, other studies show that sustainable attributes do not influence consumers' choice either for consumers from Australia or New Zealand (Remaud et al. 2008; Forbes et al. 2009). Mueller and Remaud in 2010 studied purchasing behavior and reaction to sustainability in the US, Canada, France, Germany, and the UK and concluded that in these countries, the awareness of environmental issues and sustainable programs is low; in France in particular, environmental attention is not considered as a valuable attribute by most of the consumers (Bazoche et al. 2008). Moreover, in some countries, including the US, Canada, Ireland, and Sweden, the quality, control, and traceability of wine are more important than sustainability (Loveless et al. 2010). A study conducted by Vecchio in 2013 shows that there is a difference between generations: young people are willing to pay more for a sustainable product than elders (Vecchio 2013).

More recent contributions show that there is increasing attention to environmental problems, even if some segments of consumers are still not able to appreciate the characteristics of a sustainable product (Benedetto et al. 2014; D'Amico et al. 2016; Pullman et al. 2010). These kinds of consumers are not willing to pay a higher price for these wines because they do not recognize their intrinsic value, so wineries need to invest in brand image in order to communicate these values (Corduas et al. 2013; Forbes et al. 2009; Iannone et al. 2016; Pomarici et al. 2014; Szolnoki 2013). Therefore, wineries need to translate their sustainable approach into a competitive advantage, product differentiation, and cost reduction (Christmann 2000).

It is essential to highlight that sustainable agriculture is different from an organic or biodynamic approach (Szolnoki 2013). Indeed, the OIV guidelines and general principles are not for organic or biodynamic production (Boulanger-Fassier 2008; Flores 2018; Pratt 2012; Szolnoki 2013). The reason why it differs from these kinds of production is linked to the intangible aspects that are the basis for quality wine. These aspects are the culture, landscape, history, traditions, and human capital that are contained in a bottle of wine (Christ and Burritt 2013).

Nevertheless, wineries in Old World countries are mainly SMEs, and so it is more difficult to communicate their values and their sustainable innovation to consumers. Indeed, SMEs encounter three main problems implementing innovative strategies, the lack of management capabilities, the lack of physical resources, and the lack of investments in R&D (Narula 2004). Moreover, there are also problems of information asymmetries between wineries and consumers due to difficulties in the communication of values and practices with traditional tools. The quality of the product is the most important thing, and the winemaker produces a product according to traditions and the characteristics of the place and not just to satisfy the trends of the market, but sometimes consumers do not understand this issue (Narula 2004).

Companies ought to create multiple touchpoints with consumers and reduce these information barriers. Baxendale et al. (2015) defined a touchpoint as an "episode of direct or indirect contact with the brand." It is crucial for SME wineries to use several tools, both traditional and non-traditional (the traditional points of contact are traditional media, telephone, salesforce, catalogs, customer service, payments, returns, loyalty programs, and the non-traditional points are e-mail, paid and organic search, display ads, tradeshows, and interactive TV, mobile devices, and social media). Thanks to this multitude of touchpoints, consumers can obtain all the information about the technical characteristics of the product and winery practices, both in terms of production procedures, grape varieties, and sustainable practices. Moreover, touchpoints represent a way for firms to be in contact with consumers during every moment of their routine and create a "one-to-one relationship" between the customer and the brand. That kind of relationship allows companies to go into great detail in the interaction with clients, and so it produces more information for each one (Baxendale et al. 2015).

Customer touchpoints have acquired great importance for brands thanks to five forces (Wind and Hays 2016). These forces are the technological improvement, the proliferation of social media, the presence of more instructed and more skeptical consumers, a hyper-connected world, and new and disruptive business models (Wind and Hays 2016). In an always-connected world, small and medium wineries can use the Internet to share information about their products and their sustainable practices. In that way, the omnichannel customer can buy a bottle of wine in a physical shop while, at the same time, checking the quality characteristics on websites (Verhoef et al. 2009). The experience and intangible aspects have predominance over tangible ones; the brand image is composed of symbolism, emotional values, and history (Charters and Pettigrew 2005). Moreover, according to Holbrook, and Hirschman (1982), "the experiential view of consumer behaviour recognized the special nature of products and services that have a hedonic component such as wine, leisure activities and pleasure travel". The experience-driven approach is the basis of the omnichannel strategy, because, today's consumers want a new shopping experience with a personalized and integrated relationship with the service provider (Carroll and Guzman 2013).

From the analysis of the literature emerges that SME wineries are investing in sustainability and the development of omnichannel strategies, but it is not clear if these could form a link between these two topics. The current literature discusses these two themes separately, and the link between them is poorly investigated, so the aim of this chapter is to discuss how, in particular, SME Italian wineries implement sustainable practices and the impact of omnichannel strategies on the communication of sustainability issues to consumers. In particular this chapter addresses three main questions: do Italian wineries implement omnichannel strategies for the communication of sustainable values to consumers? Why Italian wineries implement sustainability practices? Are there different approaches to the implementation of omnichannel strategies to communicate sustainability practices and values in SME wineries?

3.3 Methodology

The Italian Please confirm the section headings are correctly identified throughout the chapters case study is considered for analysis because it is attractive both for the prevalence of small and medium estates and because it is a traditional market with an old wine history. For these reasons, the Italian market takes a specific approach to the development of new channel strategies, such as the online ones.

Considering the Italian scenario, several programs have been developed toward sustainability, such as "Tergeo," "Magis," "Vino Libero," and "VIVA Sustainable Wine" (Corbo et al. 2014). Most of the programs focus both on the vineyard and company sustainability, except for "Magis" and "Vino Libero," which focus only on the sustainability of the final product. Apart from the Tergeo and Vino Libero protocols, which partially consider the economic aspects, all the programs focus on the environmental, social, and economic points of view. In recent years, the "Unione Italiana Vini" has taken on responsibility for the environmental issue and in 2015 released the first report on sustainable wine growing (Unione Italiana Vini 2015).

In order to unify the separate initiatives and establish a unique vision, a new entity known as "Equalitas" was introduced in 2015. Equalitas gives certification to wineries, wines, and territories that respect environmental, economic, and social sustainability (Environmental Ethical Economical). Moreover, in 2019, during the event "Milano Wine Week," the minister for agricultural policies announced a unique national standard for wine sustainability driven by "Ministero per le Politiche Agricole alimentari e forestali (Mipaaf)" and Equalitas (Environmental Ethical Economical).

UniCredit every year publishes an "Industry Book" about the dynamics and prospects of the wine sector. In 2018, data (UniCredit 2018) showed that the total number of firms in the Italian scenario was 2,000, with a total production of 50.4 million hectoliters of wine. In the world ranking, Italy occupies the first stage with a turnover of 11 billion euros, which represents 8 percent of the national revenues of the food and beverage sector. The wine production in Italy represents 17% of the world's total, with an annual growth rate of 10.5%. Moreover, the Italian scenario is composed mainly of small and medium wineries, most of which are family-owned (Unicredit 2018).

In order to pursue the aim of the study, we adopted a mixed-method approach and proceeded with triangulation of the data. In particular, we used data derived from questionnaires, in-depth interviews with key informants in Italian SME wineries, and researchers' active participation in fairs and conventions. Specifically, we collected data through a survey involving 173 Italian small and medium wineries in order to study how many wineries have developed omnichannel strategies and 15 in-depth interviews with wineries' managers and key informants about sustainability in the wine industry. We also collected qualitative data from active participation in fairs and conventions on the issue of sharing value and co-creating value with consumers.

3.4 Findings and Discussion

Results from our study highlight that three are the main issues for Italian SME wineries when implementing omnichannel strategies to support sustainable issues: "challenges in omnichannel strategies," "experiencing sustainability," and "implementation of omnichannel communication strategies."

3.4.1 Challenges in Omnichannel Strategies

In order to study the implementation of omnichannel strategies for the communication of sustainable values to consumers, it is crucial to underline some answers to the survey. In order to create a new customer experience, the wineries of the sample are starting to implement new strategies both online and offline, and they are starting to integrate the two channels. Considering the importance given to the experiential approach, the wineries of the sample responded that the experience in the cellar is essential. Indeed, 92% ("very much" and "very very much" answers) of the questionnaire sample think that the purchasing experience is essential (Fig. 3.1). These results reflect the consideration explained before, regarding the experience-driven approach in Italian and French wineries.

To create a unique experience for the consumer, wineries can choose different activities (Fig. 3.2). The collected data show that the activities that the interviewees prefer are connected to the terroir and special

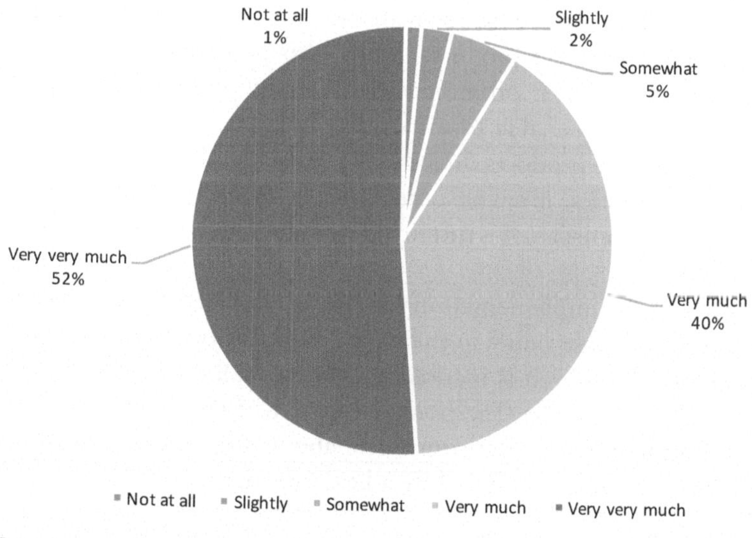

Fig. 3.1 Importance of the experience lived during the purchase in the winery (*Source* Data from the questionnaire)

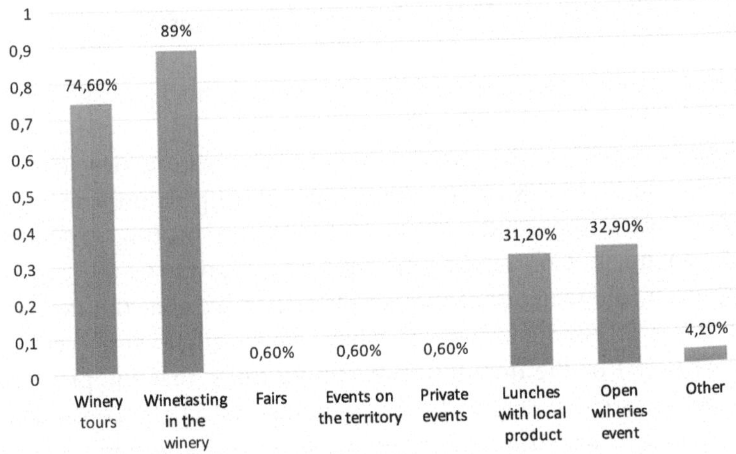

Fig. 3.2 Activities chosen to create a unique experience for the consumer (*Source* Data from questionnaire)

characteristics of the place and the winery's products. Indeed, for 74.6% of respondents, wineries communicate sustainable values during winery tours. They also create activities with the local community and organize lunches featuring local products, while also participating in the event "cantine aperte" that is promoted by the organization *turismo del vino*. This event aims to enable tourists, wine lovers, and consumers to visit wineries and taste products directly. Wineries, thanks to the use of these traditional activities, give consumers the opportunity to touch, see, and taste the characteristics of a sustainable product and appreciate the value of the firm.

Regarding the implementation of new technologies for the communication of sustainable values in the wine sector, the questionnaire revealed that the use of the web is increasing. Moreover, 93% of wineries of the sample use social media (Facebook, Instagram, Twitter, and YouTube) to share information with the consumers about the winery, products, and production practices. As stated by a key informant:

> Thanks to the Use of Social Networks I Can Create a Direct Dialogue with My Community of Consumers and I Can Show Them My Terroir (Winemaker).

The questionnaire data showed that a balance exists between online and physical advertising. Physical advertising is made through traditional channels, fairs, and expositions, and wine tastings, while online advertising is made through online channels (websites, social media, blogs, and influencers) and mailing lists. These data were confirmed during the in-depth interviews:

> The Use of Technologies for the Advertising Has Changed the Way Wineries Interact with Consumers; Now They Can Reach Them from Every Place and in Every Time (Service Provider).
>
> The Integrated Use of Physical and Online Advertising Has Helped Me to Create a Unique Experience for the Consumers (Sales Manager, SME Winery).

Moreover, the use of the website is crucial to communicate sustainability. A total of 93.6% of the respondents answered that they use the website to share information about winery practices and products.

3.4.2 Experiencing Sustainability

Data from both the questionnaire and in-depth interviews show that a lot of attention is being paid to sustainability. Indeed, 93.6% of the respondents answered that they implement sustainability practices to support their place, economy, and social community. As a winery owner explained:

> "For Us Sustainability is not Only the Respect of the Place and Nature but also of the People and the Community" (Winery Owner).

The interviewees from wineries also underline the fact that respect for their place and terroir is the most important thing and the basis of their competitive advantage:

> "We Adopted Sustainability Protocols, Such as the Protocol of the Consorzio Di Tutela Della Valpolicella that Has the Aim to Respect, Retrench and Reduce (RRR)" (Winemaker).

In order to share sustainability practices with the community, 73.4% of the wineries of the sample answered that the omnichannel approach allows direct contact and a simple way of communicating with consumers. From the interviewees' quotes, it is clear that Italian wineries are starting to use both online and offline channels in order to share their practices with the community:

> New online channels allowed me to share with consumers the sustainable practices that I implement and in that way my community can better understand and recognize the values that are contained in a bottle of wine (Winery Owner)

For consumers, recognizing sustainability values can help during their purchasing experience and allow them to choose and prefer the product of one winery over another. Social networks are becoming a fundamental channel to share sustainability for SME wineries, enabling them to translate these practices to consumers like big firms do. A winery marketing manager reported:

> Thanks to social media now consumers easily recognize the quality contained in my wines, connected to the sustainability attention, and moreover they identify the basis of my competitive advantage (Marketing Manager, SME winery).

3.4.3 Implementation of Omnichannel Communication Strategies

Considering the data collected from the questionnaire and the interviews, the wineries of the sample can be divided into two groups, each with a different approach to the implementation of omnichannel strategies to communicate sustainability practices and values. The first approach has been called "advanced" and corresponds to a higher level of implementation of the strategies, and the second approach has been called "on the go." The characteristics of the wineries that have an "advanced" approach include higher investments in personal relationships, a high level of customization, greater attention to sustainability issues, and focus on the offer of a unique experience. These wineries create a unique experience for the consumer, both offline and online. In the second approach, “on the go,” the investment remains only on brand image, customization of the products is still at an initial stage, and little attention is paid to the personal relationship with the client. The results of the first approach show that omnichannel strategies are becoming a must-have for wineries, in order to communicate with their consumers not only the practices that they have adopted but also the values that are contained in a bottle of wine.

3.5 Conclusion

The aim of the chapter was to study SME wineries' approach to omnichannel strategies, how they share their sustainable practices with their consumers, and if there is a link between these two topics. Italian SME wineries seem to be conscious of the need to better value their efforts in terms of sustainable practices among consumers. Aware customers confirm a willingness to pay for sustainable products, as in previous studies, but according to our interviewees, they are increasingly searching for new forms of engagement.

Wineries could achieve new types of engagement by closely following the purchasing processes of their customers both off- and online. They are investing in experiences able to explicitly transfer, for example, the value of the terroir that until now has been somehow taken for granted, especially by small and medium wineries. This issue recalls the challenge of sharing the traditions, cultures, and practices related to wine production, especially in Old World countries with regard to younger generations. These new consumers are always connected and able to exploit the Internet to obtain information about the products they are interested in, but they lack the background deriving from the experiences elder generations lived in the past about the production processes and the link between the product and where it comes from. Wineries are effectively moving in this direction by developing omnichannel strategies able to enhance their competitive advantage and better interact with their customers. However, data reveal that Italian SME wineries have two different paces corresponding to different approaches toward the adoption of omnichannel strategies and the sharing of sustainability issues with consumers: "advanced" and "on the go."

Few of them are exploring the new opportunities that an omnichannel strategy may provide by investing significant resources and integrating offline and online processes, thus sometimes redefining their business models. This effort allows them to co-create effective integrated experiences, enabling them to communicate and share sustainable issues with their consumers. The results emerging from our study confirm that this is a promising line of conduct for SME wineries since it impacts significantly not only on the awareness of the consumers but also on their preferences and willingness to pay higher prices for sustainable wines. However, as highlighted by the research, there is still room for exploring in greater depth the SME wine producers' resistance to overcome the outdated boundaries mainly focused on sharing values and traditions only through direct sales in the cellar. Another possible development of the research could be about the impact of climate change on this analysis, which has not been explored in this study.

References

Baxendale, Shane, Emma K. Macdonald, and Hugh N. Wilson. "The Impact of Different Touchpoints on Brand Consideration." *Journal of Retailing* 91, no. 2 (2015): 235–53. https://doi.org/10.1016/j.jretai.2014.12.008.

Bazoche, Pascale, Christophe Deola, and Louis-Georges Soler. "An Experimental Study of Wine Consumers' Willingness to Pay for Environmental Characteristics." *European Association of Agricultural Economists (EAAE) > 2008 International Congress, August 26–29, 2008, Ghent, Belgium* No. 725–2016–49590 (2008).

Benedetto, Graziella. "The Environmental Impact of a Sardinian Wine by Partial Life Cycle Assessment." *Wine Economics and Policy* 2, no. 1 (2013): 33–41. https://doi.org/10.1016/j.wep.2013.05.003.

Benedetto, Graziella, Benedetto Rugani, and Ian Vázquez-Rowe. "Rebound Effects Due to Economic Choices When Assessing the Environmental

Sustainability of Wine." *Food Policy* 49 (2014): 167–73. https://doi.org/10.1016/j.foodpol.2014.07.007.

Berghoef, Naomi, and Rachel Dodds. "Potential for Sustainability Eco-Labeling in Ontario's Wine Industry." *International Journal of Wine Business Research* 23, no. 4 (2011): 298–317. https://doi.org/10.1108/17511061111186488.

Borsellino, Valeria, et al. "Green Wine Through a Responsible and Efficient Production: A Case Study of a Sustainable Sicilian Wine Producer." *Agriculture and Agricultural Science Procedia* 8 (2016): 186–192.

Boulanger-Fassier, Sylvaine. "La viticulture durable, une démarche en faveur de la pérennisation des territoires viticoles français?." *Géocarrefour* no. 3 (2008): 181–190.

Broccardo, Laura, and Adrian Zicari. "Sustainability as a Driver for Value Creation: A Business Model Analysis of Small and Medium Entreprises in the Italian Wine Sector." *Journal of Cleaner Production* 259 (2020): 120852. https://doi.org/10.1016/j.jclepro.2020.120852.

Bruwer, Johan, and Karin Alant. "The Hedonic Nature of Wine Tourism Consumption: An Experiential View." *International Journal of Wine Business Research* 21, no. 3 (2009): 235–57. https://doi.org/10.1108/17511060910985962.

Carroll, Donald, and Inés Guzmán. "The New Omni-Channel Approach to Serving Customers." *Accenture Consulting* (2013).

Charters, Steve, and Simone Pettigrew. "Is Wine Consumption an Aesthetic Experience?" *Journal of Wine Research* 16, no. 2 (2005): 121–36. https://doi.org/10.1080/09571260500327663.

Christ, Katherine L., and Roger L. Burritt. "Critical Environmental Concerns in Wine Production: An Integrative Review." *Journal of Cleaner Production* 53 (2013): 232–42. https://doi.org/10.1016/j.jclepro.2013.04.007.

Christmann, Petra. "Effects of 'best practices' of environmental maanagement on cost advantage: the role of complementary assets." *Academy of Management Journal* 43, no. 4 (2000): 663–680.

Corbo, Chiara, Lucrezia Lamastra, and Ettore Capri. "From Environmental to Sustainability Programs: A Review of Sustainability Initiatives in the Italian Wine Sector." *Sustainability* 6, no. 4 (2014): 2133–59. https://doi.org/10.3390/su6042133.

Corduas, Marcella, Luciano Cinquanta, and Corrado Ievoli. "The Importance of Wine Attributes for Purchase Decisions: A Study of Italian Consumers' Perception." *Food Quality and Preference* 28, no. 2 (2013): 407–18. https://doi.org/10.1016/j.foodqual.2012.11.007.

D'amico, Mario, Giuseppe Di Vita, and Luisa Monaco. "Exploring Environmental Consciousness and Consumer Preferences for Organic Wines Without Sulfites." *Journal of Cleaner Production* 120 (2016): 64–71. https://doi.org/10.1016/j.jclepro.2016.02.014.

D'souza, Clare, Mehdi Taghian, and Peter Lamb. "An Empirical Study on the Influence of Environmental Labels on Consumers." *Corporate Communications: An International Journal* 11, no. 2 (2006): 162–73. https://doi.org/10.1108/13563280610661697.

Fetter, Joel. "Cultural Commodity, Global Economy: What Does Globalization Mean for the French Wine Business?". MALD Thesis. Tufts University, Medford MA (2016).

Ferrara, Carmen, Veronica Zigarelli, and Giovanni De Feo. "Attitudes of a sample of consumers towards more sustainable wine packaging alternatives." *Journal of Cleaner Production* 271 (2020): 122581.

Fischer, Josie. "Social Responsibility and Ethics: Clarifying the Concepts." *Journal of Business Ethics* 52, no. 4 (2004): 381–90. https://doi.org/10.1007/s10551-004-2545-y.

Flores, Shana Sabbado. "What Is Sustainability in the Wine World? A Cross-Country Analysis of Wine Sustainability Frameworks." *Journal of Cleaner Production* 172 (2018): 2301–12. https://doi.org/10.1016/j.jclepro.2017.11.181.

Forbes, Sharon L., David A. Cohen, Ross Cullen, Stephen D. Wratten, and Joanna Fountain. "Consumer Attitudes Regarding Environmentally Sustainable Wine: An Exploratory Study of the New Zealand Marketplace." *Journal of Cleaner Production* 17, no. 13 (2009): 1195–99. https://doi.org/10.1016/j.jclepro.2009.04.008.

Gabzdylova, Barbora, John F. Raffensperger, and Pavel Castka. "Sustainability in the New Zealand Wine Industry: Drivers, Stakeholders and Practices." *Journal of Cleaner Production* 17, no. 11 (2009): 992–98. https://doi.org/10.1016/j.jclepro.2009.02.015.

Giacomarra, Marcella, Antonino Galati, Maria Crescimanno, and Salvatore Tinervia. "The Integration of Quality and Safety Concerns in the Wine Industry: The Role of Third-Party Voluntary Certifications." *Journal of Cleaner Production* 112 (2016): 267–74. https://doi.org/10.1016/j.jclepro.2015.09.026.

Gilinsky, Armand, Sandra K. Newton, and Rosana Fuentes Vega. "Sustainability in the Global Wine Industry: Concepts and Cases." *Agriculture and Agricultural Science Procedia* 8, no. 1 (2016): 37–49.

Goldstein, Robin, Johan Almenberg, Anna Dreber, John W. Emerson, Alexis Herschkowitsch, and Jacob Katz. "Do More Expensive Wines Taste Better? Evidence from a Large Sample of Blind Tastings." *Journal of Wine Economics* 3, no. 1 (2008): 1–9. https://doi.org/10.1017/s1931436100000523.

Grojean, Michael W., Christian J. Resick, Marcus W. Dickson, and D. Brent Smith. "Leaders, Values, and Organizational Climate: Examining Leadership Strategies for Establishing an Organizational Climate Regarding Ethics." *Journal of Business Ethics* 55, no. 3 (2004): 223–41. https://doi.org/10.1007/s10551-004-1275-5.

Guidlines For The Integration of Sustainable Agriculture and Rural Development into Agricultural Policies, FAO, 1997.

Holbrook, Morris B., and Elizabeth C. Hirschman. "The Experiential Aspects of Consumption: Consumer Fantasies, Feelings, and Fun." *Journal of Consumer Research* 9, no. 2 (1982): 132. https://doi.org/10.1086/208906.

Hughey, Kenneth F. D, Susannah V. Tait, and Michael J. O'Connell. "Qualitative Evaluation of Three 'Environmental Management Systems' in the New Zealand Wine Industry." *Journal of Cleaner Production* 13, no. 12 (2005): 1175–87.

Iannone, Raffaele, Salvatore Miranda, Stefano Riemma, and Iolanda De Marco. "Improving Environmental Performances in Wine Production by a Life Cycle Assessment Analysis." *Journal of Cleaner Production* 111 (2016): 172–80. https://doi.org/10.1016/j.jclepro.2015.04.006.

Lamastra, Lucrezia, Nicoleta Alina Suciu, Elisa Novelli, and Marco Trevisan. "A New Approach to Assessing the Water Footprint of Wine: An Italian Case Study." *Science of The Total Environment* 490 (2014): 748–56. https://doi.org/10.1016/j.scitotenv.2014.05.063.

Loveless, Kellie, et al. *The relative importance of sustainability, quality control standards and traceability for wine consumers: A cross-national segmentation.* Diss. University of Canterbury, 2010.

Mariani, Angela, Eugenio Pomarici, and Vasco Boatto. "The International Wine Trade: Recent Trends and Critical Issues." *Wine Economics and Policy* 1, no. 1 (2012): 24–40. https://doi.org/10.1016/j.wep.2012.10.001.

Merli, Roberto, Michele Preziosi, and Alessia Acampora. "Sustainability Experiences in the Wine Sector: Toward the Development of an International Indicators System." *Journal of Cleaner Production* 172 (2018): 3791–805. https://doi.org/10.1016/j.jclepro.2017.06.129.

Mueller, Simone, and Hervé Remaud. *Are Australian wine consumers becoming more environmentally conscious? Robustness of latent preference segments over time.* Diss. University of Auckland Business School, 2010.

Narula, Rajneesh. "R&D Collaboration by SMEs: New Opportunities and Limitations in the Face of Globalisation." *Technovation* 24, no. 2 (2004): 153–61.

Nelgen, Signe, and Kym Anderson. *Global wine markets, 1961 to 2009: A statistical compendium.* University of Adelaide Press, 2011.

Oiv, "Resolution CST 1/2004-Development of Sustainable Vitiviniculture", Paris, France, 2004.

Oiv, "Resolution CST 1/2008-Oiv Guidelines for Sustainable Vitiviniculture: Production, Processing and Packaging of Products", 2008, Verone/It.

Oiv, "Resolution CST 518/2016-Oiv General Principles of Sustainable Vitivini Culture - Environmental - Social - Economic and Cultural Aspects". Bento Gonçalves, Brazil, 2016.

Pomarici, Eugenio, and Riccardo Vecchio. "Millennial Generation Attitudes to Sustainable Wine: An Exploratory Study on Italian Consumers." *Journal of Cleaner Production* 66 (2014): 537–45. https://doi.org/10.1016/j.jclepro.2013.10.058.

Pomarici, Eugenio. "Recent Trends in the International Wine Market and Arising Research Questions." *Wine Economics and Policy* 5, no. 1 (2016): 1–3. https://doi.org/10.1016/j.wep.2016.06.001.

Pratt, Marlene A. "Comparison of Sustainability Programs in the Wine Industry." *Business Ethics Quarterly* 14, no. 2 (2012): 243–262.

Pullman, Madeleine E., Michael J. Maloni, and Jesse Dillard. "Sustainability Practices in Food Supply Chains: How Is Wine Different?" *Journal of Wine Research* 21, no. 1 (2010): 35–56. https://doi.org/10.1080/09571264.2010.495853.

Remaud, Herve, et al. *Do Australian wine consumers value organic wine?* Diss. AWBR Academy of Wine Business Research, 2008.

Rugani, Benedetto, Ian Vázquez-Rowe, Graziella Benedetto, and Enrico Benetto. "A Comprehensive Review of Carbon Footprint Analysis as an Extended Environmental Indicator in the Wine Sector." *Journal of Cleaner Production* 54 (2013): 61–77. https://doi.org/10.1016/j.jclepro.2013.04.036.

Santiago-Brown, Irina, Andrew Metcalfe, Cate Jerram, and Cassandra Collins. "Transnational Comparison of Sustainability Assessment Programs for Viticulture and a Case-Study on Programs' Engagement Processes." *Sustainability* 6, no. 4 (2014): 2031–66. https://doi.org/10.3390/su6042031.

Santini, Cristina, Alessio Cavicchi, and Leonardo Casini. "Sustainability in the Wine Industry: Key Questions and Research Trends A." *Agricultural and Food Economics* 1, no. 1 (2013): 9.

Schäufele, Isabel, and Ulrich Hamm. "Consumers' Perceptions, Preferences and Willingness-to-Pay for Wine with Sustainability Characteristics: A Review." *Journal of Cleaner Production* 147 (2017): 379–94. https://doi.org/10.1016/j.jclepro.2017.01.118.

Szolnoki, Gergely. "A Cross-National Comparison of Sustainability in the Wine Industry." *Journal of Cleaner Production* 53 (2013): 243–51. https://doi.org/10.1016/j.jclepro.2013.03.045.

Unicredit. "Il settore del vino in Italia: tendenze, dinamiche competitive e prospettive di sviluppo." Industry Book, 2018.

Unione Italiana Vini, 2015 https://www.unioneitalianavini.it/2015/11/.

Vecchio, Riccardo. "Determinants of Willingness-to-Pay for Sustainable Wine: Evidence from Experimental Auctions." Wine Economics and Policy 2, no. 2 (2013): 85–92. https://doi.org/10.1016/j.wep.2013.11.002.

Verhoef, P. C. Lemon, K. N. Parasuraman, A. Roggeveen, A. Tsiros, M., and Schlesinger, L. A. "Customer Experience Creation: Determinants, Dynamics and Management Strategies." *Journal of Retailing* 85, no. 1 (2009): 31–41.

Viva Sustainable Wine. 2013. http://www.viticolturasostenibile.org/Downloads/Bordeaux_VIVA_Poster.pdf.

Wind, Y. J., and Hays, C. F. *Beyond advertising: Creating value through all customer touchpoints*. John Wiley & Sons, 2016.

4

A Social Responsibility Map of Spanish Professional Football League Clubs

Roberto Fernández-Villarino
and José Andrés Domínguez-Gómez

4.1 Introduction: Why a Social Analysis of Football Clubs Is Needed

This paper presents a descriptive analysis of the social performance of the football clubs taking part in the two professional categories comprising the Spanish Professional Football League (from here on LaLiga). The data are presented on the basis of indicators adapted to the sector, drawn from the ISO 26,000 international guidelines for Social Responsibility (SR). Data was gathered during the 2014–2015 season, immediately after the coming into effect of the Economic Control Regulations (ECR from here on). This set of rules was an innovation, since it was designed

R. Fernández-Villarino (✉) · J. A. Domínguez-Gómez
University of Huelva, Huelva, Spain
e-mail: roberto@uhu.es

J. A. Domínguez-Gómez
e-mail: andres@uhu.es

C. Simões et al. (eds.), *Corporate Responsibility, Sustainability and Markets*, Palgrave Studies in Governance, Leadership and Responsibility,
https://doi.org/10.1007/978-3-030-79660-0_4

by the clubs themselves and was therefore self-imposed, with the objective of ensuring the viability of a sector which had begun to manage large economic volumes without the necessary professionalization and financial regulation. The clubs, through LaLiga (the governing body of Spanish professional football), had decided to equip themselves with a compulsory model of economic governance which would regulate the sector and thereby guarantee its financial sustainability. The most serious sanction for lack of compliance with the regulations is expulsion from competition (relegation to non-league status). Five years have now passed since the coming into effect of the regulations and the sector is unanimous in seeing the impact of the ECR as positive, homogenizing their management model, which in turn ensures their financial sustainability and, as the data presented here show, moves them towards social sustainability, enhanced balance and transparency both in sporting competition and other activities (merchandising, external investment, etc.).

There are various reasons for academic interest in the data presented here. The first factor is the theoretical background to the convergence of financial performance and social performance in company management (Franch et al. 2008; Gual and Criado 2008; Mohr et al. 2001; Vivó and Franch 2008). This convergence favours profitability for shareholders in the current social context of strong pressure towards transparency and sustainable behaviour (Ashley et al. 2000). At the same time our study foreshadows more sophisticated research, with longitudinal, inferential or other design models, the need for which will arise in the near future due to the growing importance of professional football as an entertainment industry.

Also, this study is justified by the increasing economic impact of the football sector. What was originally a simple sporting activity has now become a genuine *industry*, providing entertainment every day of the week. Economic figures for professional football are currently at the same level as those of the theatre, cinema, television, etc., with a current annual world turnover of €30,000 million, close to that of the large Hollywood studios (FITS Forum, September 2015, Geneva). Football generates more income than all four large American professional leagues taken together (the NFL, NBA, MLB and NHL), and in 2016 represented 40% of the profits from professional sports worldwide, estimated at €72,000 million (Andrews, M. 2016). In Spain, the total earnings of the football industry for the 2016–2017 season were more than €15,688 million, 1.37% of Spanish GDP. Furthermore, for each euro of the LaLiga's direct activity, €4.2 was generated in additional income in the wider economy (PWC report, based on LaLiga data, 2018).

The third point justifying this study is the importance of football in the cultural, social and educational fields. Football, as a cultural activity, plays a part in the transmission and strengthening of social, geographical and political identities (through the individual's links with the team/group and the group's with the territory). It is also a tool for socialization and education in values (effort, sacrifice, pursuit of the prize, competitiveness, friendship, etc.). From the extensive literature on these topics (among others, Hunt et al. 1999; Melnick 1993; Sutton et al. 1997), it is worth noting research stressing the affective power of supporting a football team, leading to what is currently studied as the 'fan phenomenon' (Walker and Kent 2009). Thus, sport in general and football in particular represent an ideal platform for promoting actions for social change on both local and global levels (Breitbarth et al. 2011). The growing importance of football in the socio-cultural sphere is clearly reflected in the regulations, which have increasingly linked sport with values. In this respect we could mention, for example, the European Parliament Resolution, 29th March 2007, on the future of European professional football (2006/2130 (INI) and the Nice European Council Declaration on Sport (10/12/2000; IP/00/1439).

Thus, here we present a brief yet unprecedented account of the social performance of the Spanish professional football sector, in a context in which recent pressures on the sector towards financial regulation has made its economic production soar, and with this also its importance in society and the media. This context has spurred Spanish football clubs to corporatize and to professionalize their management, with the result that they are increasingly similar to 'normal' companies participating, like any other, in a market which is as complex and exacting as the society it forms part of. The market and society at large expect companies to behave responsibly, and football is beginning to respond to this demand.

4.2 Theoretical Framework: Corporatization, Professionalization and Social Responsibility in Football

Currently, actors in the field of Social Responsibility (SR) in organizations (companies and institutions) increasingly interpret the concept in terms of its complexity and significance for corporate objectives. A company can no longer be understood without taking into account its social, territorial, cultural, political and environmental settings (Martinuzzi and Schönherr, n.d.; Engert and Baumgartner 2016, Engert et al. 2016; Schönherr et al. 2019). Gradually a vision of SR is being adopted which makes it into an overall framework for the company, giving more attention to aspects such as business ethics, policies for compliance with regulations, decent working conditions, taking social risks into account, the leadership model, constant improvement of internal communications, and commitment to the improvement of learning and training (Schönborn et al. 2019).

Furthermore, social sustainability management is gaining importance in political, social and economic agendas as an approach to global agreement for facing the challenges of the future. Management models now have the objective of bringing competitiveness into line with the requirements of a complex concept of sustainability in which social factors become the drivers of integrated, balanced and reasonable development. This means that when SR is properly integrated into the business model it creates trust, improves the reputation of the firm and strengthens the latter's relationships with the community, in pursuit of corporate objectives which are no longer merely based on profit, but rather on the stakeholders themselves within the company's relational context (Herrmann 2004).

This approach to SR has become the norm in many industries and economic activities (McKinsey and Company 2006, 2009), but has arrived late to the professional sports industry in general, and to football in particular (Breitbarth and Harris 2008; Smith and Westerbeck 2007; Walters and Chadwick 2009). Thus, in the mid-1990s football was used by some governments as a key element in promoting their own political objectives (Tacon 2007), instrumentalizing it to boost and increase business generally (Anagnostopoulos and Shilbury 2013).

However, the political economy of football has undergone a major shift in recent decades (Breitbarth and Harris 2008), enabling stakeholders to gain ground on shareholders (Agle et al. 2008). Comparison of sources of clubs' income before and after 1990 fully confirms this change. A model of funding typical to the 1980s, based on the principles of speculation, subsidies, sponsors and localism (SSSL), has given way to one based on appealing to the media, the figure of the magnate, merchandising, markets, and globalism (MMMMG; Andreff's 2000). This shift lies behind the need to develop a more ambitious, more modern strategy, founded on contemporary management values, oriented towards the global market and SR having a fundamental role in communication with stakeholders, through which the firm can demonstrate good governance and alignment with their activities (Bale 2000; Barn and Baines 2004; Szymanski 1998). The soaring volume of business generated by the sector has accelerated its corporatization, a process also fuelled by the scrutiny of regulatory organisms, international NGOs and other community groups (Breitbarth et al. 2011).

Currently the sporting world, and football especially, figure increasingly in studies of corporate economy and management (Bryson et al. 2015), in a clear response to this growing socio-environmental complexity and the tensions involved in their transformation into a fully 'normal' sector (similar to other spheres of economic activity) in both internal aspects (within companies) and external aspects (relationships with their environments). The sector no longer deals with *fans* but *consumers* (whether fans or not), who analyze brands and question their trust in them and approach or avoid them by assessing (intuitively or rationally) their social performance (Lee and Shin 2010). Moving to the centre of management concerns we see factors such as ethical behaviour, integrity, clarity and transparency of the information provided to shareholders, investors and society as a whole. From the historical perspective of SR we could say that, according to the data shown below, football is gradually embracing the classical concept of *corporative citizenship* or the *corporate citizen* (Silvestre et al. 2018), in which the company has a duty to commit itself more thoroughly to facing society's challenges, beyond its purely legal obligations. This duty is nourished by citizens who are concerned about the challenges confronting society as a whole and increasingly committed to tackling them: citizens who participate more in the political community and exert pressure towards convergence with *global corporate citizenship* (Ashley et al. 2000).

At this transitional moment for the sector, as it shifts from a classical profit-based management model to another centred on the actors involved, debate arises around the potential relationship between economic and social performance. Plentiful studies over the last decades have shown that SR is economically positive for organizations, that it can lead to higher profits, and that it can reach more diverse publics, thereby also driving enhanced earnings (Burt 1983; Margolis and Walsh 2001; Pava and Krausz 1996; Roman et al. 1999; Stanwick and Stanwick 1998; Ullman 1985). SR initiatives can influence consumers' intentions to buy (Murray and Vogel 1997; Sen and Bhattachary 2001), and the company's ethical track record is increasingly coming under consumer scrutiny (Creyer and Ross 1997). For some years now the literature has pointed to the impact of new values such as cooperation (versus competition) on the influence of the brand and intentions to buy (Klein and Dawar 2004).

Does the influence of SR on consumer attitudes show itself in the same way in the sports industry as in others? Smith and Westerbeek (2007) conclude that, in terms of SR, there is no distinction between a sports-based organization and other corporations. However, as Walker and Kent (2009) argue, the sports industry cultivates an 'affective bond' which can bestow on it values distinct from other industries. This affectivity has to do with sport's ability to bring together all types of groups on an equal footing in common spaces; to create group identities which enable an extremely diverse range of people to participate with the same excitement, thereby transcending all frontiers (Giulianotti and Robertson 2009). Factors identified as being clearly sensitive to this strong affective bond include reputation, sponsorship and the close identification of football teams with their local communities. Thus there is fertile ground for shaping the perfect consumer: passionate about (or at least identified with) the company, its brand and its symbols, the company in turn being closely associated with a shared territory and cultural register.

4.3 Method

The results shown here stem from fieldwork undertaken throughout Spain, surveying 32 professional football clubs from the total of 42 taking part in competition in the 2014–2015 season (a coverage of 76.2%). The research method adopted was the mixed, semi-structured interview, responded to by the head managers of the clubs and/or their foundations. The data collection was part of the project titled Fair Play Social, an initiative of the Professional Football Foundation (FFP) and LaLiga, which to date is still underway. The overall objective of the project is to promote SR among the member companies (clubs).

The tool used for gathering data was composed of: (1) socio-demographic details of the informants and closed questions on characteristics of the club of interest for SR management; (2) SR indicators adapted from the ISO 26,000 guidelines; (3) open questions on the companies' social activities and projects. The challenge facing the tool was twofold. Firstly, it had to be aligned with the standard international guidelines (ISO 26,000), the criteria of reference both for the FFP-LaLiga's strategic plan for SR in the sector and also for reporting standards for non-financial information (in this case the Global Reporting Initiative in its 4th version, GRI4). Secondly it was the first social analysis of the sector, which meant that it had to be limited to the minimum possible number of indicators; indicators that could also be completed with readily accessible, reliable data, enabling informants to respond to them (bearing in mind the circumstances of the study: participants' high workload—and hence the risk of their not completing the survey—and the originality of the topic).

In Table 4.1 the indicators chosen are shown, with their link to each ISO dimension. These are indicators with an adequate degree of commonality, that is, their data can be collected in all or almost all football clubs, directly accessible on their websites, and therefore can be representative of the particularities of the sector. On the other hand, the fact that the chosen indicators are linked to some of the dimensions of ISO 26,000 helps these or other authors to advance towards the creation of a system for measuring performance in social sustainability in the sector: the problem of Standard and comparable measurement of

Table 4.1 Selection of indicators chosen by each ISO dimension

ISO26000 dimensions	Indicators
Organizational Governance	Number of women in management positions in the club Number of women in management positions in the foundation
Human rights	Accessibility to club facilities for users with reduced mobility Accessibility to club facilities for members and followers Accessibility to interior club facilities or annexes
Working practices	Measures for fostering work-life balance
Environment	Measures for saving supplies (utilities) Waste recycling methods Measuring environmental impacts
Fair operating practices	Prioritizing contracts with SMEs Prioritizing contracts with local suppliers
Consumer affairs	Availability of personnel for attention to clients Procedures for complaints and claims by clients
Active participation and community development	Number of events associated with corporate SR

Source Authors own work

social performance is one of the great challenges of large international sustainability knowledge and reporting projects (GRI, SDGs …).

As indicated above, the open short-answer questions centred on clubs' social activities and projects, gathering information on their type, objectives and geographical scope. The complete set of responses was transcribed, coded and analyzed using content analysis software (Atlas.ti v8.0). Categorization of objectives yielded the following topics: sports schools and campuses, sports-based leisure activities, educational activities, support for NGOs and other bodies, art (culture), gastronomy, grants and awards, activities and actions for vulnerable groups, gender equality actions, alternative football, public relations (club–society), intercultural actions and cooperation with countries of the South, collective agreements and sponsorships, acknowledgements and homages, actions in hospitals and blood donations, benefit events and fund-raising, and lastly a miscellaneous category of 'others.' The field of social action was divided into five levels: local, provincial, county/region, national and international. The complete number of objectives set out in the interview was recoded into a total of 17, whose wording is shown in Table 4.4. Throughout the research process, the Ethics principles were complied. For this, both the LaLiga Foundation and LaLiga's regulatory compliance and data protection body controlled, through their internal compliance protocols, that authors have complied with the key principles (such as confidentiality, data protection, research integrity, etc.) in every stage of data collection, storage and analysis.

4.4 Results

Characteristics of the club of interest for SR management and informants' socio-demographic details (Table 4.2).

Many Spanish football clubs have set up a foundation through which they channel their social actions. Thus, we found that the clubs organized such endeavours in two ways: either through a foundation or without one. At the time of gathering the data 73% of clubs had chosen to set up a foundation. The highest-ranking executives of the clubs were mostly male, with a mean age of 52.80% of club presidents had university degrees. Most had held the position for less than 5 years (60%). The person in charge of the clubs' SR activities (our informant) was also chiefly male (77.8%), although in this role there were more than double the number of women presidents. Overall, these executives were younger, almost all with university degrees and including a large number of postgraduates (37%). The new professional profile of the football club manager responds to these characteristics of youth, highly educated and trained and increasingly female in gender.

Decision-making posts are still mainly occupied by men, although women are represented both on management boards (an average of above 2) and among heads of foundations. Accessibility to club facilities for all actors associated with the company was scored as 'excellent' (from 7 to 9). In the previous decade, and particularly after the ECR came into effect,

Table 4.2 Characteristics of the club of interest for SR management and informants' socio-demographic details

		n	%	Mean
Having a foundation			73	
Gender of club president	Male	27	90.0	
	Female	3	10.0	
Age of club president				52,00
Academic qualifications of club president	None	0	0.0	
	Primary school	2	6.7	
	Secondary school	4	13.3	
	Bachelor's degree	15	50.0	
	Postgraduate degree or PhD	9	30.0	
Time position held by club president	1 to 4 years	18	60.0	
	5 to 8 years	6	20.0	
	9 to 12 years	1	3.3	
	More than 13 years	5	16.7	
Gender of person in charge of club SR activities	Male	21	77.8	
	Female	6	22.2	
Age of person in charge of club SR activities				41,00
Academic qualifications of person in charge of club SR activities	None	0	0.0	
	Primary school	0	0.0	
	Secondary school	1	3.7	
	Bachelor's degree	16	59.3	
	Postgraduate degree or PhD	10	37.0	
Time position held by person in charge of club SR activities	1 to 4 years	15	57.7	
	5 to 8 years	3	11.5	
	9 to 12 years	4	15.4	
	More than 13 years	4	15.4	
Would you say that you know how to explain what Corporate Social Responsibility is? (0–10)		32		8,23

Source Authors own work

clubs had developed their infrastructures in line with the requirements of universal access and other factors related to sustainable performance in terms of the new SR. This was also the case for measures for saving regular supplies (water and energy, essentially) and waste recycling; for both indicators we found percentages of around three-quarters of the clubs interviewed.

In aspects relating to the environmental dimension of the ISO 26,000, the relatively low frequency of measurement of environmental impacts was notable (only one out of every three clubs had carried this out), contrasting with the normally close attention to waste recycling and energy and water savings. Aside from this, the vast majority of clubs prioritized contraction of local providers (93%), preferably SMEs (67%).

The difference between these two figures was explained informally by interviewees in terms of the difficulty of finding certain highly specialized or high-quality services and products in the local market. In consumer affairs, almost all clubs had personnel devoted to attention to clients, in addition to systematic procedures for dealing with complaints and claims. As in the case of waste recycling and regular supply savings, this high frequency is most likely due to the legal obligation to have such procedures. Lastly, the clubs declared an average of over 24 external activities or events seen as SR (Table 4.3).

Table 4.3 SR Indicators (ISO 26,000)

SR indicators	*n*	%	Mean
Number of women in management positions CLUB	32		2,04
Number of women in management positions FOUNDATION	32		1,06
Level of accessibility to club facilities for users with reduced mobility (0–10)	32		6,93
Level of accessibility to club facilities for members and followers (0–10)	32		6,93
Level of accessibility to interior infrastructures or annexes to the stadium (0–10)	32		7,27
Level of accessibility to facilities for workers, suppliers etc. to offices (0–10)	32		8,23
Measures for ensuring work-life balance	32	63	
Measures for savings in regular supplies	32	77	
Methods of waste recycling	32	73	
Measurement of environmental impacts	32	33	
Prioritization contracting services from SMEs	32	67	
Prioritization contracting services from local suppliers	32	93	
Existence of personnel devoted to attention to clients	32	87	
Existence of procedures for complaints and claims from clients	32	100	
Number of SR events	32		24,27

Source Authors own work

Turning to the social activities and projects carried out by clubs in their environments, support for third sector bodies was the most frequent: almost four out of five clubs carried out some kind of investment (economic, with their own resources or provided by the brand) in this category. Educational activities and those oriented towards vulnerable groups were in second place (around 60% of the clubs undertook these). The third-ranking group of projects was in the area of sports schools and campuses and public relations (around 50%). The wide variety of social activities was completed with another seven types, performed by approximately one in four clubs (international cooperation, cultural and leisure activities, collective agreements, sponsorship and homages). Less frequent was the organization of benefit events and actions in favour of gender equality; these were undertaken by only 12.5% of clubs (Table 4.4).

The most frequent objectives of the clubs' social actions were in the area of collaboration with associations, the promotion of social inclusion for vulnerable groups, the transmission of values and boosting the public image of the club. These four groups of objectives were cited by at least

Table 4.4 Club social activities and projects

Club social activities and projects	*n*	%
Sports schools and campuses 14/15	15	46.9
Sports-based leisure activities 14/15	8	25.0
Educational activities 14/15	20	62.5
Support for NGOs and other bodies 14/15	25	78.1
Art, culture and/or gastronomic activities 14/15	9	28.1
Grants and awards 14/15	8	25.0
Activities and actions for vulnerable groups 14/15	19	59.4
Gender equality actions 14/15	4	12.5
Alternative football 14/15	4	12.5
Club-society relationships 14/15	16	50.0
Interculturality actions and cooperation with countries of the South 14/15	9	28.1
Collective agreements and sponsorships 14/15	8	25.0
Acknowledgements and homages 14/15	7	21.9
Actions in hospitals and blood donation 14/15	12	37.5
Benefit events and fund-raising 14/15	6	18.8
Other 14/15	8	25.0

Source Authors own work

half the number of clubs. Transmission of knowledge, awareness-raising and working with the health system made up a second group of objectives often set for the clubs' social actions; at least one in three clubs took part in these (Table 4.5).

Table 4.5 Objectives of activities and projects

Objectives of activities and projects	*n*	%
O1. To transmit positive values related to football and sport 14/15	18	56.3
O2. To work with associations and public bodies by participating in campaigns, fund-raising, and/or other activities 14/15	21	65.6
O3. To promote analysis, reflection and relationships around football and other areas (culture, art, etc.) 14/15	2	6.3
O4. To undertake sports activities in the area of values education and healthy ways of understanding sports 14/15	7	21.9
O5. To foster social inclusion and improve the situation of particularly vulnerable groups (disabled, immigrants, minors, prisoners, etc.) 14/15	19	59.4
O6. To foster and promote the practice of sports 14/15	9	28.1
O7. To boost sports actions with special attention to the gender perspective 14/15	2	6.3
O8. To encourage education and other non-sports fields 14/15	8	25.0
O9. To carry out activities of knowledge transmission and awareness-raising 14/15	15	46.9
O10. To facilitate access to sports practices and/or boost football and sporting values among underprivileged people/areas 14/15	7	21.9
O11. To boost the image of the club and its relationships with society 14/15	18	56.3
O12. To work with the health system through hospital visits and support for campaigns 14/15	12	37.5
O13. To create sports schools and/or infrastructures 14/15	2	6.3
O14. To sign and/or pursue collective agreements, strategic alliances and sponsorships 14/15	6	18.8
O15. To organise leisure, benefit and/or recreational activities 14/15	6	18.8
O16. To ensure or improve club services 14/15	4	12.5
O17. To raise funds for investment in other club projects 14/15	3	9.4
Local area 14/15	19	59.4
Provincial area 14/15	20	62.5
Regional/county area 14/15	13	40.6
National area 14/15	17	53.1
International area 14/15	12	37.5

Source Own authors

The geographical scope of clubs' social actions tended to be local; in general, the data revealed that frequency diminished with physical distance from the club. This held true on all levels except the national, cited by 53.1% of interviewees. This may be related to the scope of the main competitions of the great majority of clubs, covering the whole territory of Spain. On the same topic, it was notable that 12 clubs cited the international arena as interesting for their SR, as a similar number regularly compete internationally (principally in Europe).

4.5 Discussion and Conclusions

The results shown here indicate two factors as the main characteristics of clubs' social performance: (1) the high number and wide variety of initiatives, and (2) the weakness of the strategic approach in SR management and practice. The need for a strategic approach to social performance in professional football was highlighted in 2008 by the G14 (the association of the 14 most important European clubs). The president of this body, Jean-Michel Aulas, set as a specific objective the assessment of social activities, with a clear stress on systematic analysis aimed at maximizing social impact, mainly through 'measuring and evaluating our social performance and investments in the community' (G-14, 2008, p. 62).

It is to be hoped that in the near future the sector will adopt a more strategic approach to social performance. Given its gradual normalization as an economic sector, it may be foreseen that its strategic models will be similar across the board. Thus, social and political concerns common to the whole of society may well increase in importance (for example, gender equality, climate change, etc.). Or, from a more analytical point of view, clubs may evolve towards maximizing their effective social impact, paying attention to the social needs of their environments (in the most local area); or towards the consideration of criteria of growing international importance, such as SDGs and the GRI. In addition, in the Spanish business context, clubs are subject to increasingly strict regulation in terms of positive socio-environmental impacts and risk control. The most recent example in Spain is the 11/2018 Law on Non-Financial

Information and Diversity, which is also fully consistent with the above-mentioned international criteria. Some of the data we have discussed may corroborate this hypothesis, such as the arrival of a new generation of professionals, young people with a high level of education and training which, in the majority of cases, come from other economic sectors (as the fieldwork for this study revealed). Normally the youth of people occupying executive positions is related to better social performance of companies (De Pelekais and Aguirre 2008).

Football, as an economic sector, shares corporate social risks with all other sectors, but also involves risks of its own. These are linked to close contradictions between the positive values sport in itself transmits (comradeship, teamwork, health, sportsmanship, links with the local community, identity, etc.) and corruption, match-fixing, scandals, frauds and other types of malpractice which become news (Mendelewitsch and Jessel 2007). However, these risks could be mitigated or diminished by an RS strategy that encompassed a culture of risk assessment, impact measurement and communication/interaction with stakeholders (Breitbarth et al. 2011). As a strategic factor to take into account in risk management, we should add the proven emotional bond fans have with football in general and their club in particular; the fan´s 'affective bond' with his club (Walker and Kent 2009) as we underlined. Some decades ago, it was demonstrated that fans show absolute loyalty and faithfulness to their team's stock of values, regardless of the negative effects of other factors or events. It could be said that the club forms part of their way of life (Branston et al. 1999). A factor of strength is thereby generated which, managed strategically, could multiply the social impact of SR programmes. These are strengths which can only with great difficulty be reproduced in other industries either close to sport (leisure and entertainment) or far from it (Yang and Sonmez 2005).

However, at the time of completing the fieldwork for this study, it could not credibly be argued that the G14's 2008 message had made appreciable impact on Spanish football. Blumrodt et al. (2012) have underscored that the fact that managers of sporting bodies in general underestimate the importance of SR, and hence it would be difficult for them to adopt a strategic approach. For similar reasons, Breitbarth and Harris (2008) advocate launching SR regulations for the professional football world. From a socio-structural point of view, and as highlighted in the theoretical framework of this work, the top management and organizational institutions linked to the professional football sector nowadays host a debate that, in the light of what has happened in other economic sectors, will be resolved through pressures from the top down (regulations) but mainly from the bottom up (consumer demand). Despite the delay in incorporating football industry into corporatization and professionalization, our data and grey literature review seem to point out that it has maintained a progressive commitment to society, since, as we have seen in our results, it has set up a large corpus of social programmes with stable financial backing, mainly devoted to strengthening the associative fabric (two out of every three clubs defined precisely this as their SR objective). On the one hand, this indicates a clear orientation towards social action for the benefit of the community (Marquis et al. 2007), particularly groups in a clear situation of vulnerability (almost 60% of clubs addressed their social project objectives to these groups) from the same geographical area, or when they are further away, within the company's range of operations (almost two out of three clubs devoted their social action to the local or provincial area). Otherwise strengthen the argument pointed out in the background and theoretical framework of a greater approach of the world of football to the concept of the citizen company, business citizenship or corporate citizenship (Silvestre et al. 2018).

The last note of interest in the analysis of the data presented here is that SR in Spanish football is mainly carried out under the aegis of the foundations set up by the clubs. This is a classic format, common to all the large European leagues, which externalizes and differentiates the company's social activities from that which is its main object or purpose (in this case, their economic performance deriving from football). It is generally accepted, however, that this differentiation does not facilitate the implementation of a modern, strategic form of SR (Anagnostopoulos and Shilbury 2013). On the other hand, our data revealed social performance with a certain amount of 'modernity' in the pattern of SR, in line with the indicators from the ISO 26,000 guidelines, such as the preference for contracting local SMEs, measures for promoting work-life balance, universal accessibility to facilities, measures for recycling and energy saving, etc. Also, clubs' project objectives tended towards this mixed model. For example, there were very frequent references to promoting the image of the club through social relations, and some clubs (12.5%) stated that their social projects aimed to ensure or improve their own services. This coexistence of old and new SR factors suggests a model in a period of transition, which, as we remarked previously, will probably evolve in the medium term towards embracing the socio-environmental dimension as a core part of the business.

The shift in models may have been facilitated by economic restructuring resulting from the coming into effect of the ECR in the season in which our data were gathered. Finding conclusive evidence of the link between social and economic performance would be particularly interesting in the area of sports companies, a field in which there is as yet little research. Some studies, however, have investigated this relationship, for example Inoue et al. (2011), which adopts 'benefit spending' as a variable indicating good financial performance among the clubs of the four big US professional leagues (basketball, American football, baseball and hockey). Recent studies have shown the positive link between greater attention paid to the social actors in the club/company's local networks and the positive impact of such community interaction on club reputation (Walker and Kent 2009), which is a progressive reality in Spanish professional football clubs, as can be contrasted in our results. Reputation is a highly interesting driver of financial performance, which again indicates that financial restructuring and social action are indirectly connected. Therefore, a field of academic work of high social interest emerges which, given the economic, political, cultural and even emotional importance of football, should be approached from a transdisciplinary perspective.

References

Agle, Bradley R., Thomas Donaldson, R. Edward Freeman, Michael C. Jensen, Ronald K. Mitchell, and Donna J. Wood. 'Dialogue: Toward Superior Stakeholder Theory'. *Business Ethics Quarterly* 18, no. 2 (2008): 153–190.

Anagnostopoulos, Christos, and David Shilbury. 'Implementing Corporate Social Responsibility in English Football: Towards Multi-Theoretical Integration'. *Sport, Business and Management: An International Journal* 3, no. 4 (2013): 268–284.

Andrews, Matthew, and Peter Harrington. 'Off Pitch: Football's Financial Integrity Weaknesses, and How to Strengthen Them', 2016.

Araújo, Rafaela Garcia. 'FGV-EBAPE E-Mail: Helio.Irigaray@fgv.Br', n.d., 11.

Ashley, Patrícia Almeida, Renata B. G. Coutinho, and Patrícia A. Tomei. 'Responsabilidade Social Corporativa e Cidadania Empresarial: Uma Análise Conceitual Comparativa'. *Encontro Anual Da Anpad* 24 (2000).

Bale, John. 'The Changing Face of Football: Stadiums and Communities'. *Soccer & Society* 1, no. 1 (2000): 91–101.

Barn, S.S., and Baines, P.R. Fulham FC: Club-Supporter Relationship 'Come All ye Faithful'. In Harris, P & McDonald, F. (eds.), *European Business & Marketing*, 184–194. London: Sage, 2004.

Blumrodt, Jens, Douglas Bryson, and John Flanagan. 'European Football Teams' CSR Engagement Impacts on Customer-Based Brand Equity'. *Journal of Consumer Marketing* 29, no. 7 (2012): 482–493.

Branston, J. Robert, Keith Cowling, Nestor Duch Brown, Jonathan Michie, and Roger Sugden. 'Modern Corporations and the Public Interest'. In *The Business of Football: A Game of Two Halves?*, 180. mainstream, 1999.

Breitbarth, Tim, and Phil Harris. 'Conceptualising the Role of Corporate Social Responsibility in Professional Football', n.d., 10.

———. 'The Role of Corporate Social Responsibility in the Football Business: Towards the Development of a Conceptual Model'. *European Sport Management Quarterly* 8, no. 2 (2008): 179–206.

Breitbarth, Tim, Gregor Hovemann, and Stefan Walzel. 'Scoring Strategy Goals: Measuring Corporate Social Responsibility in Professional European Football'. *Thunderbird International Business Review* 53, no. 6 (2011): 721–737.

Bryson, Alex, Bernd Frick, and Rob Simmons. 'Sports Economics: It May Be Fun but What's the Point?' *National Institute Economic Review* 232, no. 1 (2015): R1–R3.

Burt, Ronald S. 'Corporate Philanthropy as a Cooptive Relation'. *Social Forces* 62, no. 2 (1983): 419–449.

Creyer, Elizabeth H. 'The Influence of Firm Behavior on Purchase Intention: Do Consumers Really Care about Business Ethics?' *Journal of Consumer Marketing* 14, no. 6 (1997): 421–432.

De Pelekais, Cira, and René Aguirre. *Hacia Una Cultura de Responsabilidad Social*. Pearson Educación, 2008.

Engert, Sabrina, and Rupert J. Baumgartner. 'Corporate Sustainability Strategy—Bridging the Gap Between Formulation and Implementation'. *Journal of Cleaner Production* 113 (February 2016): 822–834. https://doi.org/10.1016/j.jclepro.2015.11.094.

Engert, Sabrina, Romana Rauter, and Rupert J. Baumgartner. 'Exploring the Integration of Corporate Sustainability into Strategic Management: A Literature Review'. *Journal of Cleaner Production* 112 (2016): 2833–2850.

'European Parliament Resolution, 29th March 2007, on the Future of European Professional Football (2006/2130 (INI). Accessed 13 January 2020. https://www.google.com/search?ei=dJUcXqXNGv3Kgweo16qYAw&q=European+Parliament+Resolution%2C+29th+March+2007%2C+on+the+future+of+European+professional+football+%282006%2F2130+%28INI%29&oq=European+Parliament+Resolution%2C+29th+March+2007%2C+on+the+future+of+European+professional+football+%282006%2F2130+%28INI%29&gs_l=psy-ab.3...31029.765519..765959...0.1..0.47.50.2......0....1j2..gws-wiz.....0..0i71.fNmZdBuLg74&ved=0ahUKEwil1_-7-oDnAhV95eAKHairCjMQ4dUDCAs&uact=5.

Franch, Maria Rosario Balaguer, Maria Angeles Fernandez Izquierdo, and Maria Jesus Munoz Torres. 'The Role of Fund Management Institutions in the Development of Socially Responsible Investments: An Analysis of the Spanish Case'. *International Journal of Electronic Finance* 2, no. 3 (2008): 314–329.

Giulianotti, Richard, and Roland Robertson. *Globalization and Football*. Sage, 2009.

'Global Reporting Initiative'. Accessed 20 January 2020. https://www.globalreporting.org/Pages/default.aspx.

'Gual & Criado 2008 Financial Performance and Social...—Google Académico'. Accessed 13 January 2020. https://scholar.google.es/scholar?hl=es&as_sdt=0%2C5&q=Gual+%26+Criado+2008+financial+performance+and+social+performance&btnG=.

Gual, Jordi Truñó I., and Josep Rialp Criado. 'La Responsabilidad Social Corporativa: Gestión Empresarial de Un Activo Intangible'. *Revista de Contabilidad y Dirección* 7 (2008): 163–184.
Herrmann, Kristina K. 'Corporate Social Responsibility and Sustainable Development: The European Union Initiative as a Case Study'. *Indiana Journal of Global Legal Studies* 11 (2004): 205.
Hunt, Kenneth A., Terry Bristol, and R. Edward Bashaw. 'A Conceptual Approach to Classifying Sports Fans'. *Journal of Services Marketing* 13, no. 6 (1999): 439–452.
ICSS. 'FITS FORUM Closes With Call For Integrity Body', 4 September 2015. http://theicss.org/2015/09/04/fits-forum-closes-with-call-for-integrity-body/.
Inoue, Yuhei, Aubrey Kent, and Seoki Lee. 'CSR and the Bottom Line: Analyzing the Link Between CSR and Financial Performance for Professional Teams'. *Journal of Sport Management* 25, no. 6 (2011): 531–549.
Jessel, Jérôme, and Patrick Mendelewitsch. *La Face Cachée Du Foot Business.* Flammarion, 2007.
Klein, Jill, and Niraj Dawar. 'Corporate Social Responsibility and Consumers' Attributions and Brand Evaluations in a Product–Harm Crisis'. *International Journal of Research in Marketing* 21, no. 3 (2004): 203–217.
Lee, Ki-Hoon, and Dongyoung Shin. 'Consumers' Responses to CSR Activities: The Linkage Between Increased Awareness and Purchase Intention'. *Public Relations Review* 36, no. 2 (2010): 193–195.
Margolis, Joshua Daniel, and James P. Walsh. *People and Profits?: The Search for a Link Between a Company's Social and Financial Performance.* Psychology Press, 2001.
Marquis, Christopher, Mary Ann Glynn, and Gerald F. Davis. 'Community Isomorphism and Corporate Social Action'. *Academy of Management Review* 32, no. 3 (2007): 925–945.
Martinuzzi, P. D., Dr André, and Norma Schönherr. 'Corporate Impact Measurement and Management at the Dawn of a New Global Sustainable Development Agenda', n.d.
Melnick, Merrill J. 'Searching for Sociability in the Stands: A Theory of Sports Spectating'. *Journal of Sport Management* 7, no. 1 (1993): 44–60.
Mohr, L. A, Webb, D. J., and Harris, K. E. 'Do Consumers Expect Companies to Be Socially Responsible? The Impact of Corporate Social Responsibility on Buying Behavior'. *Journal of Consumer Affairs* 35 (2001): 45–72.
Murray, Keith B., and Christine M. Vogel. 'Using a Hierarchy of Effects Approach to Gauge the Effectiveness of CSR to Generate Goodwill Towards

the Firm: Financial Versus Nonfinancial Impacts'. *Journal of Business Research* 38, no. 2 (1997): 141–159.

Pava, Moses L., and Joshua Krausz. 'The Association Between Corporate Social-Responsibility and Financial Performance: The Paradox of Social Cost'. *Journal of Business Ethics* 15, no. 3 (1996): 321–357.

'Pwc Impacto Economico y Social Laliga 2018—Buscar Con Google'. Accessed 13 January 2020. https://www.google.com/search?q=pwc+impacto+economico+y+social+laliga+2018&oq=pwc+impacto+economico+y+social+laliga+2018&aqs=chrome..69i57j69i60.4328j0j4&sourceid=chrome&ie=UTF-8.

Roman, Ronald M., Sefa Hayibor, and Bradley R. Agle. 'The Relationship Between Social and Financial Performance: Repainting a Portrait'. *Business & Society* 38, no. 1 (1999): 109–125.

Ruhanen, Lisa, and Michelle Whitford. 'Indigenous Sporting Events: More Than Just a Game' 6, no. 1 (2011): 19.

Schönborn, Gregor, Cecilia Berlin, Marta Pinzone, Christoph Hanisch, Konstantinos Georgoulias, and Minna Lanz. 'Why Social Sustainability Counts: The Impact of Corporate Social Sustainability Culture on Financial Success'. *Sustainable Production and Consumption* 17 (2019): 1–10.

Sen, Sankar, and Chitra Bhanu Bhattacharya. 'Does Doing Good Always Lead to Doing Better? Consumer Reactions to Corporate Social Responsibility'. *Journal of Marketing Research* 38, no. 2 (2001): 225–243.

Silvestre, Winston Jerónimo, Paula Antunes, and Walter Leal Filho. 'The Corporate Sustainability Typology: Analysing Sustainability Drivers and Fostering Sustainability at Enterprises'. *Technological and Economic Development of Economy* 24, no. 2 (2018): 513–533.

Smith, Aaron C. T., and Hans M. Westerbeek. 'Sport as a Vehicle for Deploying Corporate Social Responsibility'. *Journal of Corporate Citizenship* 25, no. 1 (2007): 43–54.

Stanwick, Peter A., and Sarah D. Stanwick. 'The Relationship Between Corporate Social Performance, and Organizational Size, Financial Performance, and Environmental Performance: An Empirical Examination'. *Journal of Business Ethics* 17, no. 2 (1998): 195–204.

Sutton, William A., Mark A. McDonald, George R. Milne, and John Cimperman. 'Creating and Fostering Fan Identification in Professional Sports'. *Sport Marketing Quarterly* 6 (1997): 15–22.

Szymanski, Stefan. 'Why Is Manchester United so Successful?' *Business Strategy Review* 9, no. 4 (1998): 47–54.

Tacon, Richard. 'Football and Social Inclusion: Evaluating Social Policy'. *Managing Leisure* 12, no. 1 (2007): 1–23.

Ullmann, Arieh A. 'Data in Search of a Theory: A Critical Examination of the Relationships Among Social Performance, Social Disclosure, and Economic Performance of US Firms'. *Academy of Management Review* 10, no. 3 (1985): 540–557.

Vivó, Laura Albareda, and María Rosario Balaguer Franch. 'La Responsabilidad Social de La Empresa y Los Resultados Financieros'. *Revista de Contabilidad y Dirección* 7 (2008): 11–26.

Walker, Matthew, and Aubrey Kent. 'Do Fans Care? Assessing the Influence of Corporate Social Responsibility on Consumer Attitudes in the Sport Industry'. *Journal of Sport Management* 23, no. 6 (November 2009): 743–69. https://doi.org/10.1123/jsm.23.6.743.

Walters, Geoff, and Simon Chadwick. 'Corporate Citizenship in Football: Delivering Strategic Benefits through Stakeholder Engagement'. *Management Decision* 47, no. 1 (2009): 51–66.

Yang, Deli, and Mahmut Sonmez's. 'Forethought'. *Business Strategy Review* 16, no. 2 (2005): 1.

5

Investigating the Effectiveness of Banks' Non-financial Reporting in Portugal

Aldina Lopes Santos and Lúcia Lima Rodrigues

5.1 Introduction

Governments, consumers and investors have been gradually pressing companies to be strictly transparent on the economic, environmental and social impact of their business (Maravić 2019). Non-financial reports have been significant sources of information used in decision-making processes. Thus, it is crucial that they meet qualitative criteria to ensure comparability and faithful presentation. However, Corporate Social Responsibility (CSR) reports have shown qualitative deficiencies preventing effective comparability (Lament 2016). Those reports are being considered as non-comparable and unclear; therefore, the introduction of sectoral reporting standards are being required, to improve

This chapter is financed by National Funds of the FCT – Portuguese Foundation for Science and Technology within the project UIDB/03182/2020.

A. L. Santos (✉) · L. L. Rodrigues
NIPE, School of Economics and Management, University of Minho, Braga, Portugal

C. Simões et al. (eds.), *Corporate Responsibility, Sustainability and Markets*, Palgrave Studies in Governance, Leadership and Responsibility, https://doi.org/10.1007/978-3-030-79660-0_5

clarity and comparability of the non-financial information (Lament 2016).

Sustainable development has gained momentum with the Directive 2014/95/EU about non-financial reporting. The Directive was published in 2014, amending Directive 2013/34/EU regarding disclosure of non-financial information by certain large undertakings and groups (EU—European Parliament and the Council 2014). Decree-Law 89/2017 transposed the Directive 2014/95/EU into the Portuguese legislation. Decree-Law 89/2017 establishes that all large companies (which are public-interest entities and exceeding an average of 500 employees during the year) should include a "non-financial statement" in their management report (República Portuguesa 2017). Thus, the objective of the Directive is to improve CSR information that can promote sustainable development. The increase in transparency will improve markets efficiency. Sustainability risks and their impact on society are expected to be disclosed, reinforcing investor and consumer confidence (República Portuguesa 2017), (EU—European Parlament 2016). Thus, mandatory non-financial reporting is considered important for a sustainable global economy, by combining long-term profitability with social justice and environmental protection (EU—European Parliament and the Council 2014).

Non-financial reporting practices have become an integral part of the business operations of most companies (Perrini 2006). Therefore, social and environmental responsibilities should be integrated into the companies relations with stakeholders, and simultaneously looking for strategic diversification in terms of specific modes of development (Perrini 2006).

According to Hart (1997, p. 67), "corporations are the only organizations with the resources, the technology, the global reach, and ultimately, the motivation to achieve sustainability". Thus, by taking adequate account of relevant non-financial information, investors can contribute to a more efficient allocation of capital, leading to better longer-term investment achievements (EU—European Commission 2011a), contributing to social progress and employment, improving the environment and fighting climate change (EU—European Commission 2011b). The financial sector's role is unquestionably crucial in modern economies

(Anagnostopoulos et al. 2018). Thus, it is expected that they contribute for better non-financial reporting.

This chapter aims to evaluate non-financial reporting of financial institutions operating in Portugal, in the first year of application of the Directive 2014/95/EU (2017). This study addresses three research questions: (i) To what extent did Portuguese banks complied with the Directive, in the first year of adoption (2017)? (ii) Was the non-financial information comparable and detailed? and (iii) How regulations should be revised to improve the non-financial statement?

5.2 Mandatory Non-financial Information and Guidelines in the EU

The Directive 2014/95 is the first European regulation that requires undertakings to provide mandatory non-financial information (Carini et al. 2018). However, there is a concern that this regulation may lead only to more reporting, not better reporting (Maravić 2019). The non-financial statement requires information concerning environmental, social and employee-related, human rights, anti-corruption and bribery matters. Additionally, it requires the disclosure of information regarding the diversity policies in relation to the administrative, management and supervisory bodies (enhancing aspects such as age, gender, educational and professional backgrounds) (EU—European Parliament and the Council 2014).

The disclosure of non-financial information has been extensively promoted in the EU (Szabó and Sørensen 2015). The Directive 95/2014/EU made mandatory non-financial reporting, bringing CSR disclosure regulation to the levels of current best practices (Szabó and Sørensen 2015). The Directive is considered a step forward in non-financial reporting, imposing a more regulated concept, for better compliance with the sustainability needs (Georgiana-Loredana 2018). Being the disclosure regime quite comprehensive, undertakings are facing serious obstacles towards the directive implementation, due to more specific requirements (Szabó and Sørensen 2015). The new Directive perhaps will not affect the quantity of information disclosed but it is expected to increase the consistency and comparability of the CSR report. Thus, to ensure reporting quality, further measures should be taken (Szabó and Sørensen 2015), namely in terms of guidelines and assurance. According to the Decree-Law 89/2017, the auditor must certify whether the non-financial statement appears in the annual management report or is presented in a separate report (República Portuguesa 2017).

In 2017, a methodology for reporting non-financial information (guidelines) emerged to support non-financial information:

> [T]he aim of these guidelines is to help companies to disclose high quality, relevant, useful, consistent and more comparable non-financial (environmental, social and governance-related) information in a way that fosters resilient and sustainable growth and employment, and provides transparency to stakeholders.
>
> EU—European Commission 2017, P. C 215/4

The content of those guidelines includes: business model, policies and due diligence, outcome, principal risks and their management, key performance indicators, and thematic aspects (EU—European Commission 2017).

In 2018, the European Commission appointed the Technical Expert Group on Sustainable Finance (TEGSF) to develop recommendations on climate-related disclosures, leading to the guidelines on non-financial reporting. These guidelines include a supplement on reporting climate-related information (2019) and further guidance for banks and insurance companies (EU—European Commission 2019). This document states that banks can exacerbate climate-related risks if banks support economic activities that contribute to climate change via Greenhouse Gas (GHG) emissions, including deforestation, forest degradation or land-use change. Banks can promote the transition to a low-carbon and climate resilient economy and increase awareness of the transition by integrating an evaluation of the potential impact on climate change of their prospective investments, loans and insurance contracts into their policies and procedures (EU—European Commission 2019).

5.2.1 Highlights and Trends

A study in Italy reveals that the EU Directive enhanced the disclosure of non-financial disclosure, confirming the role of EU regulations in improving the quality of non-financial information (Venturelli et al. 2017). However, according to Venturelli et al. (2017), the Public Interest Entities (PIEs) pathway towards Environmental, Social and Governance (ESG) reporting needs action in the field of sustainability policy, risk assessment and diversity; and in the field of social and environmental accounting, specifically Key Performance Indicators (KPIs). In terms of non-financial information (NFI) score, the best results were obtained by companies that were already involved in CSR practices before the Directive, and that already issued voluntary and assured sustainability reports (Venturelli et al. 2017). Additionally, there is also a good correlation between these variables: firm size, experience in preparing a sustainability report, adoption of GRI rules and assurance of the quality of non-financial information. Therefore, firms and countries already proactive in CSR reporting will not have significant benefits with the application of the Directive; but it is expected that firms and countries that are less compliant will have the opportunity to improve the quality of non-financial information (Venturelli et al. 2019).

CSR reporting has been increasing worldwide and especially in Europe in the last decades (Arraiano and Hategan 2019). In spite of that, the practice of preparing and submitting non-financial reports in Central and Eastern European countries are substantially different, mainly due to different government policies and cultures (Arraiano and Hategan 2019). Popescu (2019)studied non-financial reporting in Romania, in 2018. The author concludes that there was an improvement in the quality of non-financial reporting. However, more emphasis should be placed on transparency and information free access. This could be achieved by introducing this requirement in regulations. A study published by Maj (2017) suggests that in Polish energy industries, the diversity of information disclosed by organizations is quite narrow. Furthermore, generally, organizations do not disclose much general information on social issues; neither discloses any information on human rights. Reporting on labor practices and decent work has been rather modest (Maj 2017).

Companies have preferred annual reports to communicate voluntary CSR disclosures, yet they have placed little emphasis on reporting about human rights and anti-corruption measures (Matuszak and Rózańska 2017). In general, the new reporting obligation is expected to increase the extent and quality of non-financial disclosure (Matuszak and Rózańska 2017). However, the establishment of common rules for firms that operate in different sectors can impede an effective harmonization (Caputo et al. 2019). A case study in the oil and gas sector by Carini et al. (2018) revealed a fair level of completeness of non-financial information, although some areas (where financial and sustainability reports overlap) have to be improved to achieve the requirements of the Directive. The introduction of sectoral reporting standards has been considered important to improve clarity and comparability of the reports (Lament 2016).

5.2.2 The Directive 2014/95/EU and Banks' Non-financial Reporting

Some large banks seem to follow a trend to issue annual combined reports where non-financial and financial information are disclosed together, while other banks report the non-financial disclosures as a stand-alone report; the non-financial information that is being disclosed is most often descriptive or descriptive-quantitative. The most transparent way to present data is by disclosing quantitative information (Zabawa 2018). Bank managers should convince the board to be involved

> in different CSR activities as an important part of their strategic initiatives, and to allocate more resources to those that have significant positive relationships with FP [Financial Performance] and less to others, thereby improving overall stakeholder wellbeing and thus creating positive social change.
>
> Matuszak and Rózańska 2019, 17

Additionally, regulators should encourage banks to report CSR information, which improves reputation (Branco and Rodrigues 2006) and consequently increases the safety and soundness of the banking system (Matuszak and Rózańska 2019). Furthermore, engaging in CSR can increase social welfare, by focusing on the needs of employees, clients and communities (Matuszak and Rózańska 2019).

According to the new legislation, the non-financial statement should contain enough information for an understanding of the evolution, performance, position and impact of the company's activities, with at least environmental, social and worker issues; but also promoting equality between women and men, non-discrimination, respect for human rights, anti-corruption and bribery (República Portuguesa 2017). Disclosed non-financial information is also required to include: (i) a brief description of the business model of the company; (ii) sustainability policies followed by the company, including due diligence procedures applied; (iii) results of such policies; (iv) associated risks; and, (v) key performance indicators relevant to company's specific activity (República Portuguesa 2017). Furthermore, Law no. 148/2015 of the Portuguese Republic classifies credit institutions [Banks] as entities of public interest (República Portuguesa 2015).

5.3 Banks' Non-financial Reporting in Portugal

5.3.1 Analysis and Evaluation Methodology

According to Banco de Portugal (Portuguese Central Bank) there are thirty banks and two saving banks in Portugal (Banco de Portugal 2018); however, only nine entities (eight banks and one saving bank) are required to comply with the Directive 2014/95/EU. Our sample is composed by these nine entities.

Data presented in this paper is the result of a detailed analysis of non-financial reporting disclosed by those nine selected entities. The study aims to evaluate the quality and quantity of the disclosed information for 2017. Data were collected from annual reports, standalone sustainability reports and banks' websites. Research limitations are associated with the sample size, although it accounts for all the Portuguese banks that are required to comply with the Directive.

In terms of auditing, all auditors confirm that all banks comply with the non-financial statement. Three banks, which follow GRI guidelines, present an independent report of limited reliability assurance regarding the information on the sustainability report, prepared by an independent external entity. Baret and Helfrich (2019) advocate the importance of social and environmental assurance, stating that the growing pressure of stakeholders requires transparency about CSR practices, that is essential to know how reliable disclosures are.

The study aims to verify whether banks comply with the Directive and to compare non-financial reports, in terms of: location, denomination of the non-financial statement, volume of information, content, topics covered in the annual report, environmental matters, social and employee matters, equality between women and men and non-discrimination, respect for human rights, fighting corruption and bribery attempts, and some detailed information (where possible). We also present an adapted correlation table based on the content of the Directive, using as a working basis a correlation table already presented by two banks.

5.3.2 Results

5.3.2.1 Non-financial Statement Location

An exhaustive reading across the available information reveals that there is no uniformity regarding the location of non-financial information. We identified three different locations (Fig. 5.1): in the annual report (67%), in the annual report but complemented with the sustainability report (22%) and in the stand-alone sustainability report (one bank). Furthermore, it is remarkable that two banks have prepared integrated reports, one of them in accordance with the International Integrated Reporting Council (IIRC). Previous studies also came to similar conclusions, mainly regarding the location of the non-financial statement (Zabawa 2018), as well as about overlapping information (Carini et al. 2018).

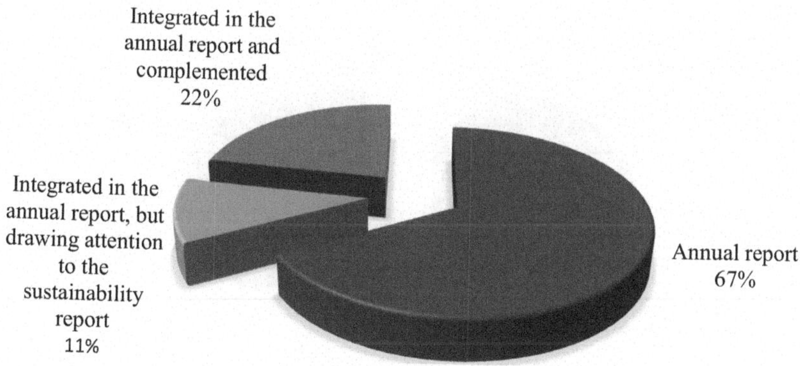

Fig. 5.1 Non-financial reporting location (n = 9)

The variety of locations makes it difficult to find non-financial information, and the comparison between companies. Matuszak and Rózańska (2019) also found that the different locations of non-financial information were a problem. An integrated or combined report should systematize the location of non-financial information, avoiding the present dispersion. Previous studies point out that better and more concise reports (Tiron-Tudor et al. 2019) would require the standardization of the location of non-financial information (Caputo et al. 2019; Carini et al. 2018).

5.3.2.2 Non-financial Information Denomination

Non-financial information was disclosed under five different denominations (Fig. 5.2):

- "Non-financial statement" (56%)—the most common denomination, and:
- "Non-financial indicator table"; "Disclosure of non-financial information in accordance to the Decree-Law No. 89/2017, July 28"; "Sustainability accounts"; and "Non-financial and diversity information".

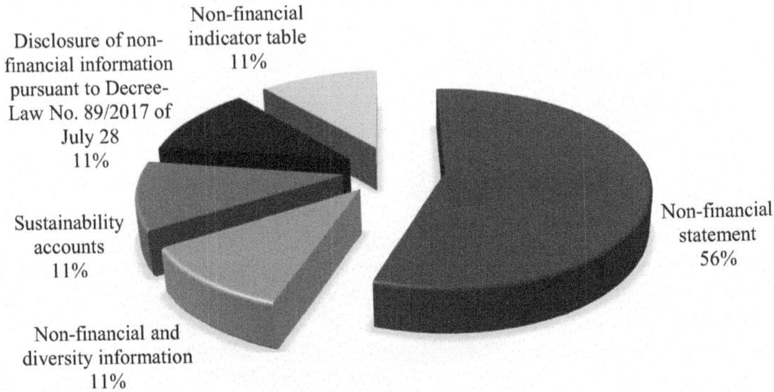

Fig. 5.2 Denominations given to the non-financial information ($n = 9$)

The lack of a systematic approach makes it difficult for the reader to understand whether non-financial information was disclosed. Thus, standardization would help stakeholders. As stated by Maravic (2019), the gradual development of international non-financial reporting standards will help to compare business results.

5.3.2.3 The Volume of Non-financial Information Disclosed

The number of pages dedicated to non-financial reporting was quantified to evaluate the volume of non-financial information, considering: the total number of pages (financial + non-financial) (AR); the number of pages dedicated to non-financial information (either integrated in a chapter of the annual report or dispersed in the annual report) (NF); the number of pages in the sustainability report (SR); and AR-NF, the number of the pages dedicated to financial information. Figure 5.3 illustrates the diversity of non-financial reporting volume in terms of number of pages.

Some annual reports have only a few sentences and others provide detailed information. Some banks only mention in the annual report that non-financial information is disclosed in the sustainability report. Figure 5.3 shows that in general, non-financial information is a small percentage of the total information disclosed. We found duplicated

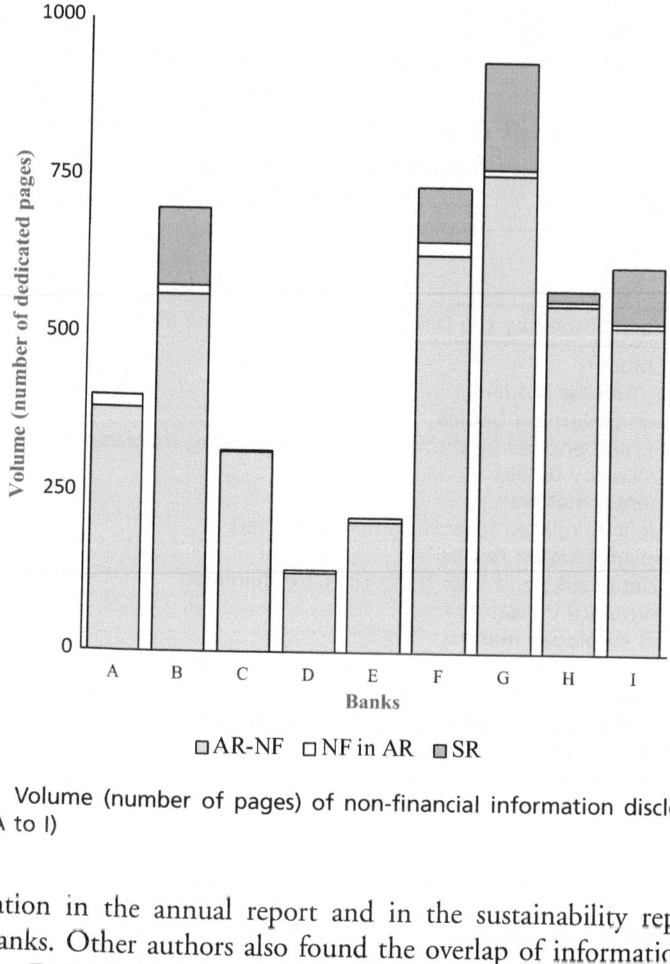

Fig. 5.3 Volume (number of pages) of non-financial information disclosed by banks (A to I)

information in the annual report and in the sustainability report in some banks. Other authors also found the overlap of information. For example, Carini et al. (2018) pointed out that the main difficulty is to evaluate the relations between quantity and quality of the disclosure. In this context, "drowning in information" should be avoided because large volumes of information can hamper accessibility.

5.3.2.4 Non-financial Information Content

Two of the analyzed banks presented the correlation table with Decree-Law No. 89/2017, as an attempt to make the information comparable, indicating its location. Considering the correlation table presented by those two banks, we evaluate the non-financial information content of our sample (Table 5.1) verifying and quantifying the percentage of entities that have referred to a specific content item (or sub-items) in the disclosed information (in compliance with the Directive and Decree-Law 89/2017).

Table 5.1 Compliance with the Directive and Decree-Law No. 89/2017

Contents established by the Directive and Decree-Law 89/2017	(%)
Business Model	
Company Business Model	100
Diversity in governing bodies	
Diversity policy applied by the company in relation to its management and supervisory bodies	56
Environmental matters	
Specific policies related to environmental matters	100
Policy implementation results	100
Key associated risks and how these risks are managed	100
Key performance indicators	100
Social and employee matters	
Specific policies related to social and employee matters	100
Policy implementation results	100
Key associated risks and how these risks are managed	100
Key performance indicators	100
Gender equality and non-discrimination	
Specific policies related to gender equality and non-discrimination matters	100
Policy implementation results	100
Key associated risks and how these risks are managed	100
Key performance indicators	100
Respect for human rights	
Specific policies related to respect for human rights	78
Policy implementation results	33
Key associated risks and how these risks are managed	100
Key performance indicators	33
Anti-**corruption and bribery matters**	
Specific policies related to combating corruption and bribery attempts	89
Policy implementation results	89
Key associated risks and how these risks are managed	100
Key performance indicators	78

Source Adapted from Santander Totta (2018) and Montepio (2018) ($n = 9$)

"Diversity in governing bodies" only achieved 56% of the analyzed companies. Mainly, this item was disclosed by public entities that are required to comply with it. "Respect for human rights" was mentioned by all considered entities, by referring the "Key associated risk and how these risks are managed" (100%), but "Policy implementation results" and "Key performance indicators" were sub-items only provided by 33% of the analyzed sample. The "Specific policies related to respect for human rights" were mentioned and disclosed by 78% of the analyzed entities.

The "Anti-corruption and bribery matters" were disclosed but only briefly mentioned in the analyzed reports. A similar study performed in Poland also reported that companies placed little relevance on reporting about human rights and anti-corruption matters (Matuszak and Różańska 2017).

5.3.2.5 Non-financial Information Topics

Data reveal that all the 29 non-financial information topics are mentioned at least by one bank. Table 5.2 illustrates the heterogeneity observed among banks. "Framework" was mentioned by 3 banks (A, B and I); "Social responsibility", "Environment" and "Correlation Table between the Annual Report and Decree-Law 89/2017" were reported by 2 entities. Table 5.2 points out the topics addressed by each bank. Data show that there is a large disclosure diversity, leading to the heterogeneity of the non-financial information reports. This is contrary to what the Directive's aims to achieve (EU—European Parliament and the Council 2014).

5.3.2.6 Non-financial Statement Matters (Items and Sub-Items)

In the non-financial statement, there is a variety of items and sub-items covering themes under Decree-Law 89/2017:

Table 5.2 Diversity of topics addressed by analyzed banks

Non-financial information topics disclosed in the annual reports	Non-financial Information in the annual reports (A, B, … I)									Number of annual reports
	A	B	C	D	E	F	G	H	I	where the topic was observed
Framework		☐					☐			3
Brief description of the business model										1
Environmental responsibility										1
Social responsibility			☐							
Total tax contribution										1
Business value creation		☐								1
Value creation for employees		☐								1
Value creation for society		☐								1
Environment			☐		☐					
Labor issues			☐							1
Equality and diversity			☐							1
Corruption prevention and bribery			☐							1
Overall rating			☐							1
Resources and organization				☐						1
Social and environmental responsibility				☐						1
Risk management				☐						1
Company governance model				☐						1
Deontology and ethics in the exercise of activity					☐					1
Security and health					☐					1
Employee social support policies					☐					1

Non-financial information topics disclosed in the annual reports	Non-financial Information in the annual reports (A, B, … I)									Number of annual reports
Talent retention and gender equality					□					1
Regional development and social responsibility					□					1
Stakeholder engagement						□				1
Value created for each stakeholder group						□				1
Environmental impact						□				1
Correlation table between the annual report and Decree-Law 89/2017		□				□				
Other disclosures of non-financial information pursuant to Decree-Law 89/2017							□			1
Reading guide for sustainability information								□		1
Non-financial indicator table									□	1
	5	5	6	4	6	4	1	1	2	
	Non-financial information topics observed in bank's annual reports									

> The non-financial statement [...] shall contain sufficient information for an understanding of the evolution, performance, position and impact of [...] company's] activities concerning, at a minimum, environmental, social and worker issues, equality between women and men, non-discrimination, respect for human rights, the fight against corruption and attempts to bribery.
>
> República Portuguesa (2017, p. 4269)

In this study, the following variety of items and sub-items were assessed: "Environmental matters", "Social and employee matters", "Equality between women and men and non-discrimination", "Respect for human rights", "Fighting corruption and bribery attempts".

Environmental matters (Fig. 5.4)—the most discussed topics in the theme were: "paper consumption reduction and paper recycling" (being addressed by all banks), closely followed by "energy consumption, energy efficiency renewable energy" and "waste management and treatment" (>85%). The least addressed issues were "volunteering (tree planting)" and "environmental impact studies of funded projects" (<25%), or even "credit granting process and project finance", "community environmental projects", "awareness raising and environmental responsibility

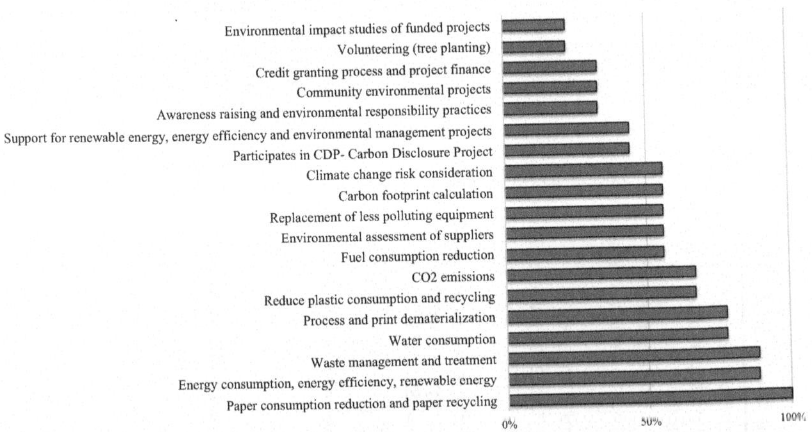

Fig. 5.4 Environmental matters ($n = 9$)

practices" (33%). These results reveal a very humble and mostly "inside" bank's vision concerning environmental matters.

Social and employee matters (Fig. 5.5)—the most discussed topics in this theme were "employee training", "retention and talent development" and "ethics and integrity", addressed by all banks (mainly related to self-interests and reputation); while the least addressed were "parenting support", "social responsibility commission/sustainability committee established" and "tax contribution" (<35%).

Equality between women and men and non-discrimination (Fig. 5.6)—"gender equality (male/female)" and "diversity in age" are addressed by all banks, probably because of the easy access to this information; while "non-discrimination based on ancestry, family status, genetic background and language" (around 10%) is the least disclosed item.

Respect for human rights (Fig. 5.7)—the most addressed sub-items were "workers' rights" and "protection of workers' health" (100%), probably due to worker unions pressure; while "training in human rights policies and practices", "integration and development of employees with special needs" (22%), "degree of accessibility to facilities by people with disabilities" and "human rights in supplier contracts" (33%) are the less addressed.

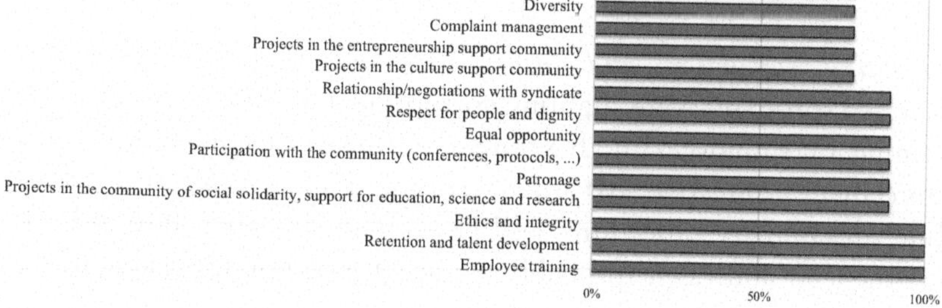

Fig. 5.5 Social and employee matters ($n = 9$)

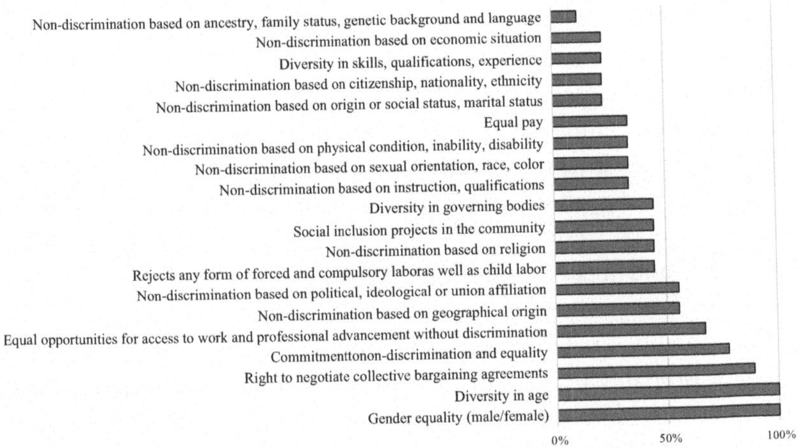

Fig. 5.6 Equality between women and men and non-discrimination (n = 9)

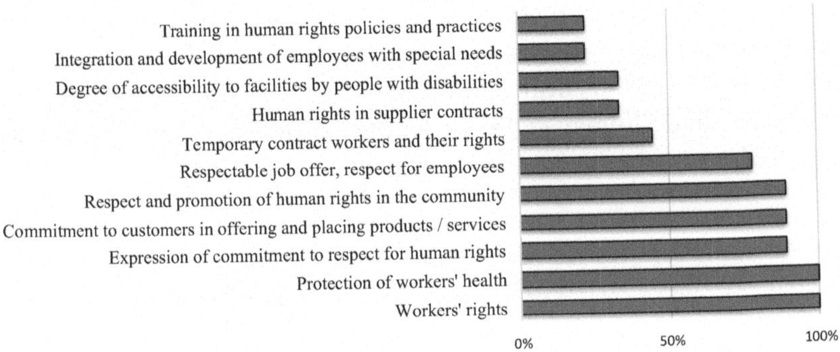

Fig. 5.7 Respect for human rights (n = 9)

Fighting corruption and bribery attempts (Fig. 5.8)—the most addressed sub-items were "fighting corruption and bribery attempts" and "training of employees in these areas" (100%), due to additional law enforcement (Directive 2015/849/UE and Directive 2016/2258/UE); while "disciplinary procedures and lawsuits in this area" (around 10%) were the least addressed (probably because it was not applicable in some cases).

Detail of the information.

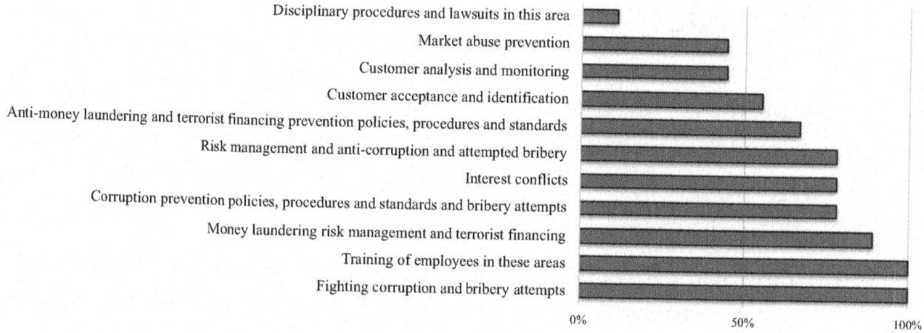

Fig. 5.8 Fighting corruption and bribery attempts ($n = 9$)

"Social, environmental and reputational risks: - The implementation of Sustainability Policies in the analysis and decision of credit operations and the application of the Equator Principles (referred to in the chapter on the Environment and Climate Change) are particularly relevant in the management of these risks".
"Analysis of social and environmental risk in credit operations".

(Santander Totta 2018)

"The Bank also manages indirect environmental risks, during the process of assessing and granting credit and project finance, and can carry out environmental impact studies, in accordance with the applicable legislation in force".
"Sensibly company clients, from sectors of activity with greater exposure to risks and environmental regulation, to the theme of climate change".
"Identify and classify Corporate Customers with greater social and environmental risks."

(Millennium BCP 2018)

"The credit risk assessment of companies and project finance already includes environmental and social aspects:
• **The** project finance credit risk assessment includes, in the analysis of each project, a category referring to the project's Sustainability and Socio-environmental Impact, where it is intended to analyze different domains of project finance intervention supported on four essential positioning axes: economically profitable, financially viable, socially fair, environmentally friendly;
• **The credit risk assessment of companies also considers the dimensions related to the** company's credibility in social and environmental terms".

(CGD 2018a)

"The CGD Group's project finance portfolio is mainly concentrated on projects in the Iberian Peninsula. The safeguarding of a set of obligations at an environmental and social level is a prerequisite of the legislation in these countries, being mandatory compliance by the respective economic agents. Confirmation that the environmental licensing of a given project has been properly established is a precondition for obtaining financing".

"For the assessment of environmental and social risks, CaixaBI uses an independent technical consultant. Only when justified in terms of risk, is an audit carried out exclusively focused on the social and/or economic dimension of a given project. In the context of a greater involvement of Multilateral Institutions as potential financiers of projects advised by CaixaBI, the Bank, anticipating the information needs of those institutions, requests the projects to analyze the sustainability of the project, with description/evaluation of its social and environmental impact".
"The following criteria are taken in account: the project's impact on local job creation; sharing the management practices associated with the project with the local community - spillover effects; and human resource hiring practices in **line with the promoter's country of origin** practices. This is due to mandates related to projects in countries such as Angola, Mozambique and Brazil".

(CGD 2018b)

Fig. 5.9 Degree of details regarding environmental matters in credit granting process and project finance (*Source* Adapted from Santander [2018], Millennium BCP [2018] and CGD [2018a, b])

The detail of non-financial information varies among banks. Figure 5.9 illustrates the information on the item regarding environmental matters in "credit granting process and project finance" disclosed by three banks. One bank just referred to the topic; another one disclosed that the bank manages the environmental risk in the lending process; only one bank provides a more detailed disclosure.

5.4 Discussion

In this chapter, we have addressed three questions. Considering the first question: (i) *To what extent did Portuguese banks complied with the Directive, in the first year of adoption (2017)?* Data indicates that in 2017 all banks provided non-financial information and disclosed core requirements. However, some information is less addressed, such as, policy implementation results and key performance indicators, both associated with "respect for human rights". Additionally, concerning the more specific information in the reports, disclosures on "environmental impact studies of funded projects" or "integration and development of employees with special needs" are almost not addressed.

Concerning the second question: (ii) *Was the non-financial information comparable and detailed?* Data reveal that non-financial information is not comparable and there are substantial differences in terms of detail among banks. Thus, comparability of banks' non-financial statements is difficult not only due to different presentation format (including different denominations), but also because of the number of pages and topics covered. The annual report is the privileged source for presenting the non-financial statement, but some banks complement this statement with some more information that is disclosed in the sustainability report and on the website. However, usually the information overlaps. Thus, some banks present a combined report presenting financial and non-financial reporting together. Some banks devote a chapter to the "non-financial statement" in the annual report, while others prefer to use other denominations to disclose the non-financial information. Some banks also present a stand-alone sustainability report. Regarding the detail, there is no uniformity: some banks only refer to some topics, others detail them.

Finally, regarding the last question: (iii) How regulations should be revised to improve *the non-financial statement*? The findings of this study suggest that regulations should advance with the standardization of the non-financial information, to improve comparability between banks. Thus, we suggest regulators should define the specific topics that banks ought to disclose and its depth; we also believe that the indirect effects on the environment should not be ignored (for example, information about how banks assess environmental matters in credit granting process and project finance is important). Some banks present tables to make the correspondence between the themes, to help to identify the topics covered. We believe that this table is useful and should be required. The "non-financial statement" should be a chapter of the annual report or included in the Integrated Report (IR), thus avoiding scattered information. Finally, the non-financial statement should have an additional theme about climate change with a clear and precise definition of policies, risks, results and indicators.

As several authors have mentioned in previous studies, the legislation will need to provide greater harmonization based on detailed rules and standards to collect and disclose non-financial information (Szabó and Sørensen 2015), establishing a set of common rules for firms that operate in similar sectors (Caputo et al. 2019; Lament 2016). As it was stated by Romoli et al. (2014), more comparable mandatory rules can improve transparency in CSR reporting. These rules will permit to reveal the real intention of the corporations towards stakeholders. When there is greater standardization, there is more comparability and it will be easier to observe the evolution, performance, position and impact of the company's activities.

Currently, regulations prompt banks to disclose non-financial information; however, comparability is not yet promoted. Data suggest that major differences are related to diversity of topics and volume of reporting. As Carini et al. (2018) and Lament (2016), we also found that the existing regulations and the reporting practices do not ensure the comparability of the non-financial information.

5.5 Conclusions

Banks' non-financial reports aim to respond to stakeholders' concerns regarding a better society and a better environment. The Directive 2014/95/EU fills a regulatory gap. It aims to be a contribution to the dissemination or improvement of CSR reports' quality. Thus, the Directive 2014/95/EU contains regulations that aim to contribute not only to extend non-financial reporting but also to improve the comparability and usefulness of information presented in non-financial statements.

The Directive is a decisive step in reporting non-financial information. The guidelines that were issued to help the implementation of the Directive reinforce what is necessary to include in the non-financial statement. However, our study reveals that the lack of uniformity does not permit to compare banks' disclosure. With the issuance of the Directive, the EU drew a path to non-financial reporting. But it is now necessary to issue standards that permit to increase the comparability of this information. The EU needs to go on helping banks to improve non-financial reporting. Gradually, the EU should extend mandatory non-financial reporting to all banks.

5.6 Limitations and Future Research

This chapter has several limitations. Firstly, the sample is small, we only analyzed nine banks. But, as mentioned before, only these nine banks are required to adopt the EU Directive. Secondly, we assumed that the information was reliable and faithful. As auditing of non-financial reporting is not required in Portugal, the integrity of the non-financial information is not confirmed.

Future research should develop studies that permit: to establish specific topics, items and sub-items that banks could present in the non-financial statement; to evaluate whether banks are making a detailed analysis of the indirect environmental and social risks (such as those that are related to lending and project finance); to analyze the disclosure of information associated with climate change in the non-financial statement in Portugal or other countries. Additionally, since the UE Directive does not require assurance and auditing, studies that could assess the integrity of non-financial reporting are necessary. It is important to understand whether what is being disclosed matches with the CSR activities of banks since organizational façades and lack of transparency may happen (see, for example, Andrade et al. 2020).

References

Anagnostopoulos, Theodosios, Antonis Skouloudis, Nadeem Khan, and Konstantinos Evangelinos. 2018. "Incorporating Sustainability Considerations into Lending Decisions and the Management of Bad Loans: Evidence from Greece." *Sustainability* 10 (4728): 1–16. https://doi.org/10.3390/su10124728.

Andrade, Eurídice Mamede de, Lúcia Lima Rodrigues, and José Paulo Cosenza. 2020. "Corporate Behavior: An Exploratory Study of the Brazilian Tax Management from a Corporate Social Responsibility Perspective." *Sustainability (Switzerland)* 12 (11). https://doi.org/10.3390/su12114404.

Arraiano, Irene Guia, and Camelia Daniela Hategan. 2019. "The Stage of Corporate Social Responsibility in EU-CEE Countries." *European Journal of Sustainable Development* 8 (3): 340–53. https://doi.org/10.14207/EJSD.2019.V8N3P340.

Banco de Portugal. 2018. "Instituições Autorizadas." https://www.bportugal.pt/entidades-autorizadas.

Baret, Pierre, and Vincent Helfrich. 2019. "The 'Trilemma' of Non-financial Reporting and Its Pitfalls." *Journal of Management and Governance* 23 (2). Springer US: 485–511. https://doi.org/10.1007/s10997-018-9430-z.

Branco, Manuel Castelo, and Lúcia Lima Rodrigues. 2006. "Corporate Social Responsibility and Resource-Based Perspectives." *Journal of Business Ethics* 69 (2): 111–32. https://doi.org/10.1007/s10551-006-9071-z.

Caputo, Fabio, Rossella Leopizzi, Simone Pizzi, and Virginia Milone. 2019. "The Non-financial Reporting Harmonization in Europe : Evolutionary Pathways Related to the Transposition of the Directive 95 / 2014 / EU within the Italian Context." *Sustainability* 12 (92): 1–13. https://doi.org/10.3390/su12010092.

Carini, Cristian, Laura Rocca, Monica Veneziani, and Claudio Teodori. 2018. "Ex-Ante Impact Assessment of Sustainability Information-the Directive 2014/95." *Sustainability (Switzerland)* 10 (560): 1–24. https://doi.org/10.3390/su10020560.

CGD. 2018a. "Relatório de Gestao e Contas 2017." https://www.cgd.pt/Investor-Relations/Informacao-Financeira/CGD/Relatorios-Contas/2017/Documents/Relatorio-Contas-CGD-2017_Proposta-AG.PDF.

———. 2018b. "Relatório Institucional e de Sustentabilidade 2017." https://www.cgd.pt/Institucional/Sustentabilidade-CGD/Reporting-Desempenho/

Relatorios-Sustentabilidade/2017/Documents/Relatorio-Sustentabilidade-CGD-2017.pdf.

EU—European Commission. 2011a. "A Renewed EU Strategy 2011–14 for Corporate Social Responsility." https://www.europarl.europa.eu/meetdocs/2009_2014/documents/com/com_com(2011)0681_/com_com(2011)0681_en.pdf.

———. 2011b. "Single Market Act Twelve Levers to Boost Growth and Strengthen Confidence 'Working Together to Create New Growth.'" https://eur-lex.europa.eu/LexUriServ/LexUriServ.do?uri=COM:2011:0206:FIN:EN:PDF.

———. 2017. "Guidelines on Non-financial Reporting (Methodology for Reporting Non-financial Information)." *Official Journal of the European Union* 60 (C 215): 1–68.

EU—European Comission. 2019. "Communication from the Commission Guidelines on Non-financial Reporting: Supplement on Reporting Climate-Related Information." *Oficial Journal of the European Union* C 209: 1–30.

EU—European Parliament. 2016. "Corporate Social Responsibility : Accountable , Transparent and Responsible Business Behaviour." *Official Journal of the European Union* C 24: 28–33.

EU—European Parliament and the Council. 2014. "Directive 2014/95/EU of the European Parliament and of the Council—Of 22 October 2014—Amending Directive 2013/34/EU as Regards Disclosure of Non-financial and Diversity Information by Certain Large Undertakings and Groups." *Official Journal of the European Union* L 330: 1–9. http://eur-lex.europa.eu/legal-content/EN/TXT/PDF/?uri=CELEX:32014L0095&from=EN.

Georgiana-Loredana, Frecea. 2018. "Legal or Discretionary CSR: The Directive 2014/95/EU Analysis." *Ovidius University Annals: Economic Sciences Series* XVIII (1): 17–21.

Hart, Stuart L. 1997. "Beyond Greening: Strategies for a Sustainable World." *Harvard Business Review*, 66–76. https://www.info.psu.edu.sa/psu/fnm/ymelhem/psu.courses/business/ethics/ethicsandgreen/Beyond/greening-Strategies-for/aSustainableWorld.1.pdf.

Lament, Marzanna. 2016. "Quality of Non-financial Information Reported by Financial Institutions: The Example of Poland." *The 10th International Days of Statistics and Economics*, 1031–40. https://doi.org/10.24136/ceref.2017.023.

Maj, Jolanta. 2017. "Diversity and Corporate Social Responsibilty Reporting in Enterprises from the Energy Industry Listed on the Warsaw Stock

Exchange." *International Multidisciplinary Scientific GeoConference: SGEM* 17 (53): 159–66. https://doi.org/10.5593/sgem2017/53/S21.018.

Maravić, Ljiljana. 2019. "Why Nonfinancial Reporting Matters ?" *Advances in Economics, Business and Management Research* 108 (Senet): 171–74. https://doi.org/10.2991/senet-19.2019.27.

Matuszak, Łukasz, and Ewa Rózańska. 2017. "CSR Disclosure in Polish-Listed Companies in the Light of Directive 2014/95/EU Requirements: Empirical Evidence." *Sustainability* 9 (2304): 2–18. https://doi.org/10.3390/su9122304.

———. 2019. "A Non-Linear and Disaggregated Approach to Studying the Impact of CSR on Accounting Profitability: Evidence from the Polish Banking Industry." *Sustainability* 11 (183): 1–21. https://doi.org/10.3390/su11010183.

Millennium BCP. 2018. "Relatório e Contas' 17." https://ind.millenniumbcp.pt/pt/Institucional/investidores/Documents/RelatorioContas/2017/2017_RelatorioContas.pdf.

Montepio. 2018. "Relatório e Contas 2017." *Grupo Caixa Económica Montepio Geral*. https://www.montepio.org/wp-content/uploads/2018/03/AMM_RelatorioSustentabilidade2017.pdf.

Perrini, Francesco. 2006. "The Practitioner's Perspective on Non-financial Reporting." *California Review Management* 48 (2): 73–103. https://doi.org/10.2307/41166339.

Popescu, Cristina Raluca Gh. 2019. "Corporate Social Responsibility, Corporate Governance and Business Performance: Limits and Challenges Imposed by the Implementation of Directive 2013/34/EU in Romania." *Sustainability* 11 (5146): 1–31. https://doi.org/10.3390/su11195146.

República Portuguesa. 2015. "Lei n.º 148/2015 - Aprova o Regime Jurídico Da Supervisão de Auditoria, Transpondo a Diretiva 2014/56/UE, Do Parlamento Europeu e Do Conselho, de 16 de Abril de 2014, Que Altera a Diretiva 2006/43/CE Relativa à Revisão Legal Das Contas Anuais e Consolidad." *Diário Da República: I Série*, 7501–16. https://dre.pt/application/file/70236404.

———. 2017. "Decreto Lei No 89/17 de 28 de Julho Do Ministério Das Finanças." *Diário Da República, 1.ª Série - n.º 145 - 28 de Julho de 2017* 145: 4267–71. http://data.dre.pt.

Romolini, Alberto, Silvia Fissi, and Elena Gori. 2014. "Scoring CSR Reporting in Listed Companies—Evidence from Italian Best Practices." *Corporate Social Responsibility and Environmental Management* 21 (2): 65–81. https://doi.org/10.1002/csr.1299.

Santander Totta. 2018. "Relatório de Sustentabilidade 2017." https://www.santander.pt/institucional/banca-responsavel/relatorios-banca-responsavel.

Szabó, Dániel Gergely, and Karsten Engsig Sørensen. 2015. "New EU Directive on the Disclosure of Non-financial Information (CSR)." *Nordic & European Company Law Working Paper*. Vol. 15. https://doi.org/10.1017/9781316875469.

Tiron-Tudor, Adriana, Diana Lavinia Martin, Diana Lavinia Martin, and Gianluca Zanellato. 2019. "Integrated Reporting Framework Application: A European Case Study in the Financial Sector." *Proceedings of the 13th International Conference on Business Excellence 2019* 13: 227–40. https://doi.org/10.2478/picbe-2019-0021.

Venturelli, Andrea, Fabio Caputo, Simona Cosma, Rossella Pizzi, and Leopizzi Simone. 2017. "Directive 2014/95/EU: Are Italian Companies Already Compliant?" *Sustainability* 9 (1385): 1–19. https://doi.org/10.3390/su9081385.

Venturelli, Andrea, Fabio Caputo, Rossella Leopizzi, and Simone Pizzi. 2019. "The State of Art of Corporate Social Disclosure before the Introduction of Non-financial Reporting Directive: A Cross Country Analysis." *Social Responsibility Journal* 15 (4): 409–23. https://doi.org/10.1108/SRJ-12-2017-0275.

Zabawa, Justyna. 2018. "Reporting of Environmental Information in the Largest Banks in Poland: Scope, Measurement, Formal and Legal Conditions." *Prace Naukowe Uniwersytetu Ekonomicznego We Wrocławiu*, no. 520: 150–57. https://doi.org/10.15611/pn.2018.520.13.

6

Taming Wolves: The High Risk of Unethical Behavior in the Polish Financial Sector and Possible Solution

Marta Kightley

6.1 Introduction

Multiple studies show that financial knowledge within Polish society is not only self-reported as very low, but is indeed one of the lowest in OECD countries. At the same time surveys carried out by the Polish Bank Association reveal that around 80% of respondents trust banks, with even more trusting financial advisors within their banks. International comparisons place Poles as being the citizens most trusting of the banking sector in Europe. Against this backdrop, both research and real-life cases show an increasing problem of unethical behavior in the financial sector. Behavioral studies help here by both giving good insight into the mechanisms of such conduct, as well as understanding the reasons why certain customers of financial services are more likely

M. Kightley (✉)
Warsaw School of Economics, Warsaw, Poland
e-mail: msora@sgh.waw.pl

C. Simões et al. (eds.), *Corporate Responsibility, Sustainability and Markets*, Palgrave Studies in Governance, Leadership and Responsibility,
https://doi.org/10.1007/978-3-030-79660-0_6

to fall prey to ill-advised financial decisions. Poland repeatedly experiences scandals within the financial sector. Since the financial crisis in 2008 there were numerous cases of ill-advised or mis-sold financial products: currency options, Swiss franc denominated mortgages, unit-linked insurance policies, investment funds or regular Ponzi schemes disguised as investment in gold. While in general trust in the viability of the financial sector is vital for a strong economy, there are many cases when a high level of trust can be misused and in turn it may adversely affect the financial system as a whole. Misused trust may eventually erode financial markets and prevent the financial system from developing in depth. Multiple national and international financial sector supervisory authorities aware of the problem have introduced new regulations to limit the impact of possible conflicts of interest as well as the sale of inadequate products. The Polish Financial Supervision Authority focuses on the stability of the financial sector and doesn't have a strong mandate to prevent or act on unethical behavior by financial institutions or indeed outright scams. The combination of high trust and low financial knowledge in Poland and a strong predisposition to unethical behavior in the sector will keep resulting in serious problems unless the state takes it seriously.

The aim of this study is to show that the magnitude of unethical behavior in the financial sector is subject to both universal mechanisms as well as specific local conditions. Financial sector is built on trust therefore "Corporate Responsibility, Sustainability and Markets" meet there more intensely than anywhere else. A close look at the financial sector shows very precisely that the marriage of ethical behavior, trust and markets requires the right design on the regulatory framework.

The study is based on literature review and analysis of secondary data. The mechanisms behind relatively high occurrence of unethical behavior in the financial sector are explained based on literature review. In order to assess the scope and character of unethical behavior in the Polish financial sector the author analyzes examples of high-profile cases of unethical behavior of financial sector employees towards retail clients based on fielded literature, official financial sector documents such us annual activities reports, legal documents, transcripts from official inquiries into malpractices of banks, investigative documents published by government organizations as well as media reports. Comparative method is used to assess the financial system regulatory framework and practices.

6.2 Low Level of Financial Literacy and High Trust in Banks

According to a survey of Poles' financial knowledge (GPW and WIB 2019), the self-reported knowledge of those surveyed is low or very low. Only 9% of those surveyed believe their financial knowledge to be good or very good. 44% of respondents consider the topic of bank loans difficult. The lowest belief in their own financial knowledge exists among 18–34-year-old and the elderly. Nearly 60% of those groups believe that their grasp of financial matters is not sufficient.

A grim picture of the financial knowledge, behavior and attitudes of Poles emerges from the *OECD/INFE International Survey of G20/OECD Infe Core Competencies Framework on Financial Literacy for Adults, Adult Financial Literacy Competencies* (OECD and INFE 2016). It confirms the results of the GPW WIB self-assessment survey of 2019. Out of thirty nations surveyed Poles scored the lowest in the combined ranking taking into account financial knowledge, behavior and attitudes. Other Central or Eastern European countries with a similar GDP per capita and similar experiences with transformation of the economic system scored much higher in the comparison. The survey shows that Poles struggle to compare financial products and services and make appropriate, well-informed financial decisions. Poles also have a strong preference for short-term spending, do not watch their spending carefully and do not set or pursue long-term financial goals.

In Poland low financial knowledge accompanies a fairly high and growing trust in financial institutions. A recent survey carried out for the Polish Bank Association, focusing on Banking Sector Reputation (ZBP 2019) shows that trust in the banking sector has reached 72% and even stronger is 87% trust in "your own bank", with an 83% level of trust in "your bank adviser". Over the last few years these numbers have grown yearly. Within the last seven years the reputation of banks has increased from the borderline between a bad and average reputation to a "good" level. Compared to last year's survey the level of trust towards one's own bank has increased by 3 ppt and one's own bank's financial advisor by 4 ppt. The number of respondents declaring trust in the Polish banking sector has risen by 9 ppt over the same period of time. The group distrusting the sector has shrunk to 19% down from 26% in 2018. A growing level of trust in financial services in Poland is also confirmed by the Edelman Trust Barometer (2018), which compared trust in 28 different markets. It shows that even though Poles generally distrust institutions with one of the lowest levels of trust among 28 surveyed countries in 2017 (35% of the general population trusts institutions) they display a high level of trust in financial services (50% of the general population in 2018) with a remarkable growth of 10 ppt in trust in financial services between 2017 and 2018.

6.3 Examples of Unethical Behavior in the Polish Financial System

Against this backdrop it is unsurprising that there have been repeated scandals originating from the abuse of clients' trust by Polish banks and other financial institutions such as: the mis-selling of currency options by banks in Poland which led to numerous bankruptcies after 2008, the mis-selling of Swiss franc based mortgages and passing the currency risk to under-informed customers, scandals around unit-linked insurance policies, cases of mis-selling of corporate bonds and numerous Ponzi schemes.

The mechanism of unethical behavior of highly trusted representatives of the banking sector was revealed in an investigation into a recent scandal involving the mis-selling of corporate bonds. One of the key players in the scandal was a Polish bank called Idea Bank and its subsidiary Lion's Bank. They are accused of mis-selling corporate bonds of GetBack, a debt collecting company, to around 10,000 retail clients. As a result, the bank's clients lost approximately the equivalent of 600 million Euros. The debt collecting company and the bank were linked by their founder, the current owner of Idea bank.

The Office of Competition and Consumer Protection (UOKiK) inquiry into the practices of the bank (UOKiK 2019) revealed scandalous practices towards the bank's clients. They involved bank advisers persistently approaching retail customers (often by phone, email or text message) and offering them corporate bonds as a risk-free investment with a high 5.5% return. The clients were misled to believe that the offer was made exclusively to a very limited, carefully selected group of loyal bank customers whereas in fact it was made to almost all clients including new ones who were known to possess a sum of money exceeding a certain threshold. The clients were pressured to make a decision quickly with the bank's financial advisors filling in the documents for them. The financial advisors were trained to assuage any concerns with regards to risk and used specially prepared prewritten scripts to divert the clients' attention when they asked for time to read the documents. The clients were made to believe that if they took more time, they would lose their chance and were pressured to make transfers on the same day.

Statements given by Idea Bank clients confirm both their very low financial knowledge and their high trust in the bank's financial advisors. The scripts the bank's financial advisors followed and the way they pressured and manipulated the clients indicated premeditated unethical behavior towards trusting individuals. This abused trust led to catastrophic consequences with many of the clients losing their life savings.

Low financial knowledge and high trust in the banking sector played an important role behind other scandals such as the Amber Gold Ponzi scheme in 2018 in Poland. Nearly 20,000 retail clients lost 200 mln Euros. The collapse of the scheme resulted in such public outrage that a special parliamentary committee to investigate it was launched and this was covered live on national television. The scheme started in 2009 and over a period of 3 years lured 50,000 clients with "guaranteed" returns of 10–14% on their investment. The claim was that the money was invested in gold. For three years Amber Gold bank-like branches mushroomed across Poland, even though soon after it was set up the Polish Financial Supervision Authority put Amber Gold on their warning list for performing bank-like activities without authorization and informed prosecutors. The owner of the scheme heavily invested in a local airline which won him credibility and favors from politicians on a local and national scale.

The problem which affected the largest number of households resulting from unethical behavior in the financial sector, high trust and flawed financial consumer protection in the last two decades was Swiss franc mortgages. This type of mortgages were widely recommended by bank advisors to people who not only did not earn in Swiss francs but also were often not eligible for a similar value of loan in Polish zloty. In 2008, just before the financial crisis Swiss franc mortgages made up 76% of all mortgages taken out that year, with approximately one million such contracts concluded over the previous decades in Poland. Problems began when foreign exchange risk started to materialize. For some debtors, the principal of the mortgage increased substantially, the exact amount depending on when the loan was taken out as the CHF/PLN rate doubled between early 2008 and 2015, when the Swiss National Bank removed its currency cap. It left many debtors with negative equity.

The problem resulted in a major public outcry with politicians pledging to find a systemic solution. No such solution was found with every attempt criticized by the Financial Supervision Authority as costing too much cost for the banks (estimated at up to 14 billion Euros depending on the solution) which could translate to a substantial risk for the banking sector. The only way for Swiss franc mortgage holders to enforce a remedy was by suing banks for illegal or abusive clauses used in mortgage agreements.

In selling CHF mortgages, the banks passed the entire risk of such products onto their clients by backing them with financial instruments designed to neutralize the risk for themselves. The agreements contained illegal provisions regarding, for example, instalment conversion rates or low down payment insurance. Transcripts from court cases against the banks reveal malpractice (Frankowicz 2018). A former bank employee testified that using different manipulation techniques towards clients was standard procedure as both his own commission as well as the bank's was higher for CHF mortgages. Financial advisors used a battery of arguments to convince clients that Swiss franc mortgages were cheaper and better, downplaying the risk involved. Clients' testimonies confirm that their decisions were often strongly influenced by advice given by a bank they trusted. The testimonies show that bank's financial advisors themselves did not understand the currency risk involved.

At the same time, awareness of the potential toxicity of such products was present among the top decision-makers in the banks. One ex-top executive of a major bank in Poland and the current prime minister admitted that even though his bank was against such products because of the risk, it ultimately decided to offer them so as not to lose market share (Money.pl 2018). Also in 2005, the Polish Bank Association, aware of the problem, was unsuccessfully petitioning the General Inspectorate for Banking Supervision to ban the selling of foreign currency loans to earners of Polish zloty.

Figure 6.1 illustrates high risk environment for the Polish retail financial sector customers. Low financial knowledge paired with high level of trust in the financial system and possible high level of unethical behavior make the environment conducive for mis-selling products which are profitable but not suitable for the clients. Misusing trust, offering unsuitable products, taking advantage of the low financial knowledge of customers and other forms of unethical behavior is not in the least a uniquely Polish problem. Notorious scandals such as Madoff's Ponzi scheme, the Enron scandal, the Payment Protection Insurance scandal in

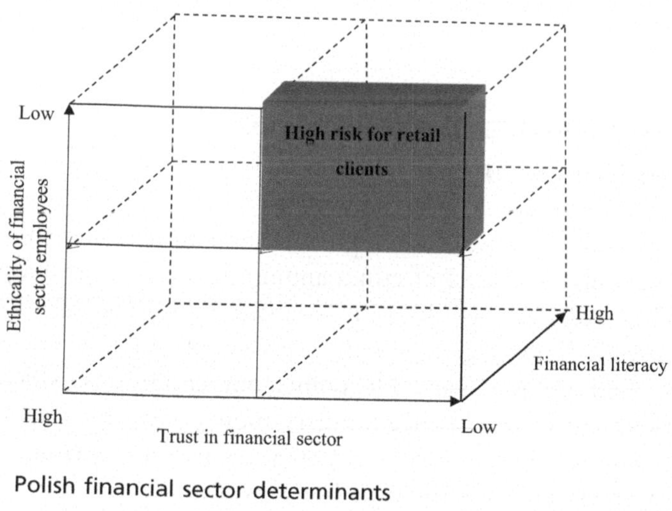

Fig. 6.1 Polish financial sector determinants

the UK and numerous cases of mis-selling of financial products around the world are just a few examples.

An international survey (Labaton 2015) carried out among employees of the financial sector in the US and UK showed that the problem of unethical behaviors and attitudes is widely spread across the industry. The respondents were asked to judge the likelihood of engaging in unethical behavior by their competitors. An alarming 47% of respondents found it likely that their competitors have engaged in unethical or illegal activity in order to gain an edge in the market. The number is even higher among high earners, including high-level decision makers. A substantial percentage of them (34%) have witnessed or have firsthand knowledge of wrongdoing in the workplace. A quarter of respondents admitted that they would likely use non-public information to make a guaranteed $10 million if there was no chance of getting arrested for insider trading. The numbers are twice as high among employees with less than 10 years' experience. Nearly 20% of the respondents believe that financial services professionals must occasionally engage in illegal or unethical activity to be successful. Nearly 40% of the high earners do not believe that financial services are guided by the best interests of clients. Nearly half the respondents from this group consider their country's supervisory authorities ineffective in dealing with serious violations (Labaton 2012).

6.4 The Nature of Weak Ethics in the Financial Industry

Psychology and behavioral studies provide some insight into the reasons for the particular low level of ethics among financial sector employees. Marko Pitesa (2015a, 344–369) in *The Psychology of Unethical Behavior in the Finance Industry* gives a wide overview of different experiments shedding light on the issue. He points out conditions which make the environment of the finance industry more conducive for unethical behavior, among others: a focus on money, a sense of power and wealth, competitiveness and impersonal, technical work.

One of the key factors contributing to the unethical behavior of financial sector employees is simply the focus of the industry on money. In a series of experiments Kouchaki et al. (2013) showed that by exposing participants to money-related words even simple framing decisions with money can trigger unethical intentions and behavior. Vohs Kathleen et al. (2006, 1154–1156) demonstrated that a focus on money may affect the way people engage in social interactions. They concluded that, similar to power, money makes people less dependent on others but also reduced helpfulness towards others.

Pitesa states that on average employees of the financial sector both in the US and the UK earn twice as much as workers from other sectors of the economy. The same ratio applies to Poland (GUS 2018). He refers to psychological research showing that high earnings give people a sense of power that results in more self-interested behavior. Studies show that the powerful are on average more concerned with their own interest and less attentive to others and others' interests. It is argued that the reason is that the powerful are less dependent on others for their own outcomes. In a study by Van Kleef et al. (2008, 1315–1322) in which participants who reported a higher sense of power felt less distress and less compassion while hearing about an experience of suffering by another person. Experiments conducted by Galinsky et al. (2008, 1450–1466) show that those in power have more freedom to pursue their personal goals at the expense of others. However, the same study shows that for highly moral individuals the sense of power may lead to even more moral behavior.

Pitesa (2015b, 344–369) also draws attention to the consequences of high competitiveness in the financial sector. He argues that it leads to a very high use of time and energy in some segments of the industry such as investment banking. This area was described in detail by Michel Alexandra (2011, 325–368). The author conducted a nine-year ethnographic study on investment bankers which revealed an extreme depletion of energy and shortage of leisure within this group. Research by Mead et al. (2009, 594–597) shows that the depletion of energy leads to lower self-control and in turn more unethical behavior. As Hon (2017, 30–36) shows, crucially in this context, a sense of agency is dependent on attentional resources.

The last two commonly given arguments regarding a stronger inclination towards unethical behavior among financial sector employees focus on the rather technical and impersonal character of the majority of the work in the financial sector. Also, important here is the fact that it is often carried out within large organizations. Paul Dembinski (2017) in his book *Ethics and Responsibility in Finance: What next?* stresses that work with numbers and no immediate link to individual clients for high-level decision-makers creates an environment more conducive to unethical behavior. Similarly, the employees of the financial sector who have direct contact with individual clients often follow instructions from their superiors thus greatly reducing their personal agency and the scope of ethical choices. In a different study Schwepker and Good (1999, 38–58) show that a simple motivational tool such as sales quotas can adversely impact moral judgment of financial sector employees.

6.5 The Difficulty of Financial Decisions and Reliance on a Bank's Financial Advisors

The difficulty of taking informed financial decisions and over-relying on a bank's financial advisors is shown in the *Consumer Decision-Making in Retail Investment Services: A Behavioral Economics Perspective* report (Chater et al. 2010). The report provided behavioral insights which informed the EU regulation on Key Information Documents for Packaged Retail and Insurance-based Investment Products. One of the issues the report focuses on is the trust people place in advice provided by sellers of financial products without realizing potential conflicts of interest. The report presents results from two types of experiments: an online study carried out in eight European countries with 6,000 participants and a laboratory one with 480 subjects from three European countries. The results show that retail investors are often confused about the true nature of their investment. At the same time the majority of them trust financial advisors, unaware of potential conflict of interest. The online study reveals that nearly 80% of investment decisions by retail investors are made in a face-to-face setting, usually with an employee of the investment provider or a professional advisor. The majority of those surveyed admit that their final investment choice was influenced by a financial advisor.

The complexity of finance makes it very difficult for an average consumer to take fully informed rational decisions. This is confirmed by behavioral economics, which shows that consumers' decisions are often far from rational. Experiments reveal that investment decisions are subject to all sorts of biases; they are context dependent and driven by emotions. Those biases are used by firms including financial institutions to sell products the clients wouldn't have bought rationally. In order to boost profits, they use techniques which rely on errors studied by behavioral economics.

6.6 Financial Regulators' Response to Unethical Practices

Understanding of the need for closer attention to the problem of unethical practices in the financial sector has increased after 2008. Post-crisis EU regulations such as the Market Abuse Regulation (MAR) prohibit insider dealing, disclosure of inside information and market manipulation, and contain provisions to prevent and detect these. The Markets in Financial Instruments Directive II (MIFID II) makes investing more transparent and safer for individual investors. Among other things, it also tackles the issue of remuneration policies to ensure that staff are not just incentivized to sell products but also act in the best interests of clients.

Post-crisis regulations make a clear distinction between retail clients with limited financial knowledge and professional investors. The newly adopted regulatory approach stems from a deeper understanding of the objective limitations of retail customers who are often unable to process all relevant information and to calculate risk while making financial decisions (Kern 2018). A good example of a more protective stance towards more vulnerable retail investors is the European Securities and Markets Authority's (ESMA) product intervention decision (ESMA

2018). ESMA banned the marketing and sale of contracts for differences (CFDs) and seriously restricted the marketing and sales of binary options to retail investors. The authors of the decisions refer to studies in behavioral economics to explain the harmful effects of marketing those products to retail clients of limited financial knowledge which almost invariably results in big losses for those clients.

Behavioral insights were used in designing key information documents (KID) introduced by the Packaged Retail Investment and Insurance-Based Products regulation (PRIIPs) (EU 2014). PRIIPs regulation introduced a mandatory simple, standardized KID document for retail investors which contains clear information about the character of the product, the risk and return involved under different scenarios and cost. It also recommends a minimum investment period and explains how to file a complaint about the product.

It is not the responsibility of regulatory bodies to stop people from making mistakes, but financial regulators should make sure that the mistakes made by retail clients are not reinforced by unfair practices of financial product providers. The 2008 financial crisis showed that trust in the financial system can erode very quickly. Mis-selling financial products can be very profitable but in the long run can adversely affect the profitability and proper functioning of the whole sector. Ethical behavior is very much an example of coordination failure. It is in everyone's interest that the financial sector behaves in an ethical way but individual gains from unethical behavior are high. Unless there is a central body which coordinates actions of all the players they will end up in a low, Pareto subefficient equilibrium with everyone misusing trust. As a result the financial system will be seriously damaged, and profits will be low. This was clearly demonstrated in the case of selling Swiss franc mortgages in Poland. When the Polish banking lobby ZBP, aware of the risk involved, petitioned the banking sector supervisory body to ban this type of product, individual banks continued selling the mortgages in order to keep their market share. Years after Polish banks stopped selling CHF mortgages they still constitute 20% of all mortgages in the system. Resolving the problem may cost them up to 14 billion Euros.

In the case of the financial sector, national and international supervisory and regulatory bodies are responsible for making sure coordination failure does not happen. Part of this work should be setting rules for consumer protection. In Poland the protection of financial consumers is scattered among three governmental bodies: the Office of Competition and Consumer Protection (UOKiK), the Financial Ombudsman and the Polish Financial Supervision Authority (KNF). Efficient protection of financial customers has to involve deep sectoral knowledge, appropriate tools and has to be implicit in the goals and mission of the organization responsible for it. Meanwhile the only organization which combines the knowledge and possibly the tools—KNF—is not explicitly responsible for consumer protection thus the office allocates very few resources to it (KNF 2018). On top of that, KNF's main focus is on financial sector stability which means that it will always put it above consumer protection if such a conflict occurs.

A good example of a much broader and deeper coverage of consumer protection is the British model of financial supervision. The "twin peaks" model where prudential supervision is separated from conduct control allows the Financial Conduct Authority to include consumer protection among its top operational objectives. Unlike KNF, it involves itself in preventing the mis-selling of financial products or the purchase of unsuitable products, as well as poor customer service. It is also a leading example of approaching the problem of low ethics in the financial sector on three main levels: educating consumers, fining entities which are involved in mis-selling products and working with the industry to prevent mis-selling from happening by establishing a strong new industry ethos.

Figure 6.2 illustrates current Polish financial sector supervision architecture in terms of expertise in the field and focus on consumer protection. It shows that a body focused on market integrity would be better fit for the role. Such organization with a much broader and deeper coverage of consumer protection is a part of the "twin peaks" model where prudential supervision is separated from conduct control. It allows the authority supervising conduct to include consumer protection among its top operational objectives

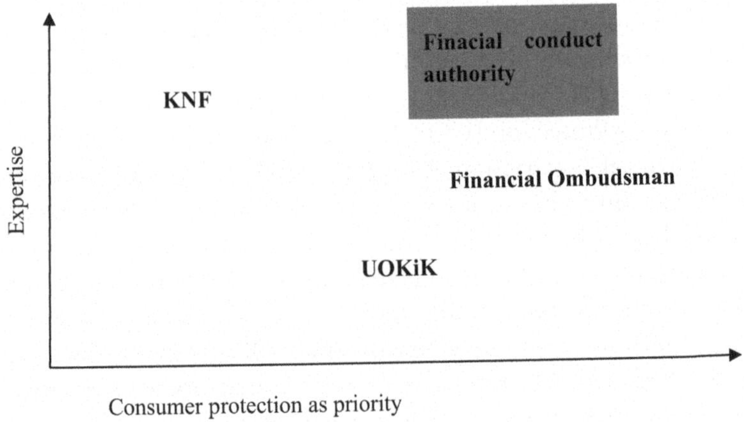

Fig. 6.2 Financial supervision architecture in Poland possible solution

6.7 Conclusions

The financial sector plays a vital role in the economy. A downturn in this sector transmits very quickly to other sectors and a lack of credit leads to bankruptcies and high unemployment. The smooth and efficient functioning of the financial industry is based to a great extent on trust. Clients have to trust banks to deposit money and investors have to trust financial entities to buy investment products.

One of the most important characteristics of this sector is a high level of information asymmetry. Financial products are complex and very hard to understand for the average consumer. In addition to that, behavioral studies show that people's decisions are often far from rational due to various biases. The combination of trust, complexity and bias makes it easy for financial institution to missell products which are profitable but not suitable for clients. A particularly low level of ethics among financial sector employees is confirmed by recent surveys as well as psychological and behavioral studies. As a result the financial sector is prone to scandals which in the long run undermine trust in the system and make customers unwilling to invest or even to save. International and national financial authorities are aware of the problem and are implementing new regulations and policies. A short review of post-crisis financial sector regulations reveals that they rightly take a behavioral approach. Scandals in the financial sector are often results of poor enforcement.

Multiple surveys confirm high trust in financial institutions and a low level of financial knowledge among Poles. At the same time the financial knowledge of retail clients is perceived as much higher by the bank employees. In such an environment the likelihood of misusing trust is even greater. It has been confirmed repeatedly by recurring scandals affecting many retail clients. The similar character of prominent financial scandals as well as the subsequent investigations reveals that the Polish system of protecting financial consumers is flawed. The only authority which possesses the necessary sectoral knowledge and could be equipped with the right tools does not include consumer protection in its priorities. The Swiss francs mortgages problem shows that the "twin peaks" model might be the right solution. Separating prudential from conduct supervision is more likely to ensure that the interests of financial consumers are protected even in situations when there is a possible conflict between protecting consumers and the financial stability of the financial sector.

References

Chater Nick, Steffen Huck and Roman Inderst. 2010. "Consumer decision-making in retail investment services: A behavioural economics perspective." *European Commission Policy Papers*. https://ec.europa.eu/info/sites/info/files/retail_investment_services_2010_en.pdf.

Dembinski Paul. 2017. *Ethics and responsibility in finance: What next?* Routledge.

Edelman Trust. 2018. Edelman Trust Barometer Financial Services 2018. https://www.edelman.com/sites/g/files/aatuss191/files/2018-10/Edelman_Trust_Barometer_Financial_Services_2018.pdf.

ESMA. 2018. "Notice of ESMA's product intervention decisions in relation to contracts for differences and binary options." https://www.esma.europa.eu/sites/default/files/library/esma35-43-1135_notice_of_pi_decisions_on_cfds_and_binary_options.pdf.

EU. 2014. "Regulation (EU) No 1286/2014 of The European Parliament and of the Council of 26 November 2014 on key information documents for packaged retail and insurance-based investment products (PRIIPs)." http://data.europa.eu/eli/reg/2014/1286/oj.

Frankowicz. 2018. Zeznania bankiera pogrążają bank. https://frankowicz.info/zeznania/.

Galinsky Adam D., Joe C. Magee, Deborah H.Gruenfeld, Jennifer A. Whitson and Katie A. Liljenquist. 2008. "Power reduces the press of the situation: Implications for creativity, conformity, and dissonance", *Journal of Personality and Social Psychology*, no 95: 1450–1466.

GPW, WIB. 2019. *Wyniki badania „Poziom wiedzy finansowej Polaków 2019". Kongres Edukacji Finansowej i Przedsiębiorczości, Fundacja GPW, Warszawski Instytut Bankowości.*

GUS. 2018. *Zatrudnienie i wynagrodzenia w gospodarce narodowej w I–III kwartale 2018 r.*

Hon Nicolas. 2017. "Attention and the sense of agency: A review and some thoughts on the matter." *Consciousness and Cognition,* no 56: 30–36.

Kern Alexander. 2018. "Mis-selling of financial products: Marketing, sale and distribution." *Econ Committee European Parliament.*

KNF. 2018. „Sprawozdanie z działalności Urzędu Komisji Nadzoru Finansowego oraz Komisji Nadzoru Finansowego w 2018 roku." https://www.knf.gov.pl/knf/pl/komponenty/img/Sprawozdanie%20z%20dzia%C5%82alno%C5%9Bci%20UKNF%20oraz%20KNF%20w%202018%20roku_66979.pdf.

Kouchaki Maryam, Kristin Smith-Crow, Arthur P. Brief and Carlos Sousa. 2013. "Seeing green: Mere exposure to money triggers a business decision frame and unethical outcomes." *Organizational Behavior and Human Decision Processes*, no 121: 53–61.

Labaton. 2012. US & UK Financial Services Industry Survey. http://www.labaton.com/en/about/press/upload/US-UKFinancial-Services-Industry-Survey-July-2012-Report.pdf.

Labaton. 2015. The Street, The Bull and The Crisis: A Survey of the US & UK Financial Services Industry. https://www.secwhistlebloweradvocate.com/pdf/Labaton-2015-Survey-report_12.pdf.

Mead Nicole, Roy Baumeister, Francesca Gino, Maurice E. Schweitzer and Dan Ariely. 2009. "Too tired to tell the truth: Self-control resource depletion and dishonesty." *Journal of Experimental Social Psychology*, no 45: 594–597.

Michel Alexandra A. 2011. "Transcending socialization a nine-year ethnography of the body's role in organizational control and knowledge workers' transformation." *Administrative Science Quarterly*, no 56: 325–368.
Money.pl. 2018. Premier Morawiecki tłumaczy się z kredytów frankowych. Jego bank jednak ich udzielał. https://www.money.pl/gospodarka/wiadomosci/artykul/kredyty-frankowe-frankowicze-morawiecki-bz,72,0,2414408.html.
OECD, INFE. 2016. OECD/INFE International Survey of Adult Financial Literacy Competencies. www.oecd.org/finance/OECD-INFE-International-Survey-of-Adult-Financial-Literacy-Competencies.pdf.
Pitesa Marko. 2015a. The psychology of unethical behavior in the finance industry. In: *The philosophy, politics and economics of finance in the 21st century: From hubris to disgrace*, ed. Patrick O'Sullivan, Mark Esposito and Nigel Allingto. Research Collection Lee Kong Chian School of Business: 344–369.
Pitesa Marko. 2015b. "The psychology of unethical behavior in the finance industry." 344–369. https://ink.library.smu.edu.sg/lkcsb_research/5030/.
Schwepker Jr Charles H. and David J. Good. 1999. "The impact of sales quotas on moral judgment in the financial services industry." *Journal of Services Marketing*, no 13: 38–58.
UOKiK. 2019. Decyzja częściowa NR RBG - 13/2019. https://www.uokik.gov.pl/download.php?plik=23621.
Van Kleef Gerben A., Christopher Oveis, Ilmo van der Loewe, Alexandr LuoKogan, Jannifer Goetz and Dacher Keltner. 2008. "Power, distress and compassion: Turning a blind eye to the suffering of others." *Psychological Science*, no 19: 1315–1322.
Vohs Kathleen, D., Nicole L. Mead and Miranda R. Goode. 2006. "The psychological consequences of money." *Science*, no 5802: 1154–1156.
ZBP. 2019. *Wybrane obserwacje w zakresie oceny reputacji i zaufania do banków w Polsce w 2019 r.*

Part II

Stakeholders, Sustainability and Ecosystems

7

Interconnectedness and Vulnerabilities of Markets from Climate Change Pressures and Organized Activism: Lessons from an Emerging Market

Kamala Vainy Pillai

7.1 Introduction

Emerging markets are developing countries with sturdy economic expansion and regarded as key drivers of global growth. As they become advanced through rapid industrialization, emerging markets present a wealth of investment opportunities for businesses. Heightened engagement with global markets over time, inextricably exposes them to global market dynamics. This chapter delves into a less explored domain of corporate responsibility (CR), specifically, the implications of superficial CR in relation to 'unsalient' stakeholder issues. Quite often, companies fail to realize the unrelenting growth of business into new markets precipitates a labyrinthine of stakeholder relationships even to the most remote areas (Pillai et al. 2016). This longitudinal study (2012–2017) reticulates the transition from stakeholder 'unsaliency' to dangerous/definitive

K. V. Pillai (✉)
Curtin University, Sarawak, Malaysia

C. Simões et al. (eds.), *Corporate Responsibility, Sustainability and Markets*, Palgrave Studies in Governance, Leadership and Responsibility,
https://doi.org/10.1007/978-3-030-79660-0_7

stakeholder through the interplay of organized activism; and the consequential impact on incognizant companies operating in an emerging market, Malaysia. Malaysia is one of the most open economies in the world with a trade to GDP ratio averaging over 130% since 2010 and ranked in the top 10 emerging markets listing between 2016 and 2019 (World Bank 2020).

The 'unsalient' stakeholder under study is the Indigenous Peoples (IP), who face continued onslaught from economic-related developments through the encroachment of their territories by companies knowingly or unknowingly. While the lackadaisical approach to CR did not pose problems to business-as-usual (BAU) in the past, heightened narratives on grand challenges on mass media has ignited a plethora of challenges. A rising phenomenon from climate change pressures is the emergence of organized transnational social movement networks. These organized transnational movements are geared towards empowering marginalized, vulnerable and unsalient stakeholder(s) with strategic advocacy and activism support, from ideation to execution. From visually savvy, multi-mode advocacy tactics at local and global levels, backed with strong research insights, to well-planned activism campaigns. These movements epitomize the changing dynamics of global advocacy, with impacts on markets. Inadvertantly, compelling organizations to respond judiciously in CR and sustainability practices.

The motivation of this study is tri-fold. First, activism scholarship in CR has not been fully explored in an emerging market context. Second, limited application of primary research in CR studies which facilitate rich authentic insights (Finger and Princen 2013). Finally, scholarly discourse (Jamali and Karam 2018) asserts for more investigations on moderators and unique contextual settings driving CR thinking in emerging markets. The study addresses two primal inquiries: (i) to what extent can activism impact stakeholder saliency? and (ii) identification of unique contextual setting(s) at play in an emerging market context. Finally, insights from the mixed methods longitudinal study elucidate implication of cultural and activism dynamics for theoretical consideration for stakeholder body of knowledge.

7.2 Literature Review

This section expounds on a review of literature on (1) 'unsalient' stakeholder: Indigenous Peoples (IP) and theoretical perspective on stakeholder salience; (2) transnational social movements and non-governmental organizations (NGOs) activism; and (3) cultural dynamics in emerging markets.

7.2.1 Unsalient Stakeholder: Indigenous Peoples (IP) & theoretical perspective

According to World Bank (2019), IP represents just over 6% of global minority population and account for approximately 15% of the extreme poor. The report asserts (i) IP often face impediments to access basic services, natural resources and the formal economy; (ii) international and national laws on IP rights are often violated and rarely enforced. Further, exploitation of natural resources by extractive industries viz. logging and mining has adversely impacted IP territories, fundamental for sustaining their lives, cultures and identity (United Nations 2018). In the United Nations UNDESA report (n.d.), dispossession of traditional native lands, forced assimilation and marginalization are regarded as major, long running problems facing IP globally. Contributory factors include the relentless search for natural wealth and rich agricultural areas; development policies enacted by the state; and rapid globalization (UNDESA, n.d.).

According to Mitchell et al. (1997) stakeholder salience model, the extent of power, legitimacy and urgency determines the level of stakeholder salience. Power perceived in a stakeholder means the ability to influence corporate behavior through economic/financial, political influence or social power. Legitimacy implies legal rights or a desirable social good based at individual, societal or organizational level. Urgency describes the extent stakeholder issues are deemed pressing and demand immediate corporate attention. Higher level of urgency signifies stakeholder's strong 'media attention-grabbin' capacity, forcing hastened corporate responsiveness. In contrast, weak stakeholder salience means inadequate or absence of power, legitimacy and/or urgency. Saliency, therefore, shapes managerial discretion on stakeholder prioritization and allocation of resources to address stakeholder issues. While CR discourse continues to gain traction in emerging markets, studies assert CR primarily revolves around key stakeholders viz. customers, shareholders and employees (Wright and Nyberg 2017). Malaysia has been a signatory to the United Nations Declaration on the Rights of Indigenous Peoples [UNDRIP] since 2007. Findings from a special national inquiry report by Human Rights Commission of Malaysia (SUHAKAM 2013) affirm the state of IP in the Malaysian context is analogous to the weak salience experienced by IPs at the global level.

7.2.2 Climate Change Pressures, NGOs and Transnational Activism

Meanwhile, climate change pressures are triggering the rise of heterogenous, multi-issue interest groups and the emergence of a new spectrum of organized transnational social movement networks. Activism 2.0 in a 'globally connected world' has revolutionized the stage for these non-state actors (Tombleson and Wolf 2017; Ali 2011) to address issues often neglected by corporate giants. Seen as counter-weights to global market capitalism, studies (Pillai 2013; Moksnes and Melin 2012; Bartley and Child 2011; Newell 2000) concur they are increasingly becoming powerful agents of change in CR context with the potential to reverberate substantial reform in governance.

The sophisticated advocacy capability and strong constituency-base invoked by transnational networks (Smith et al. 2017; Batliwala 2002) such as Greenpeace, 'People's Global Action' (PGA), 'Friends of the Earth International', 'Bruno Manser-Fond' (BMF) and 'Rainforest Action Network' are indicative of the pervasiveness of the transnational activism trajectory. These transnational networks create 'boomerang effect' (Keck 2010; Keck and Sikkink 1998) by deploying a series of tactics, namely, (1) information politics: generation and dissemination of salient information; (2) symbolic politics: use of symbols, narratives, etc. to connect with multiple audience; (3) leverage politics: alliances with stronger actors; and (4) accountability politics: holding actors to promises and avowed principles (Hirsch 2010; Nilsen 2010) to exert change. A good example is the artful 'Kill-Kat' global campaign by Greenpeace in 2010. The campaign inevitably forced Nestle, the biggest European multinational food company in the world, to reevaluate its supply chain and source palm oil more responsibly from Indonesia, another emerging market. Further, the relentless pursuit by these movements in the European Union (EU) broke new ground in January 2018 when the European Parliament, as part of its climate change commitment to mitigate deforestation, sanctioned reformation plans for its renewable energy market. The decision to ban the use of palm oil as biofuel in motors from 2021 sent shock waves, particularly, Indonesia and Malaysia, two leading emerging markets which contribute to almost 90% of global supply of palm oil.

7.2.3 Cultural Dynamics of Emerging Markets

The influence of cultural dynamics of markets on institutional logics in CR requires more understanding, especially, in emerging markets. In Asia, home to the largest number of emerging and developing markets, culture is deeply intertwined into the fabric of its society. Contemporary research asserts over time as businesses get accustomed to a cultural context, were inadvertently bound to institutionalize the idiosyncrasies of its settings (Jamali and Carroll 2017). An examination of Hofstede's cultural dimensions theory and an analysis of Hofstede Power Distance Index (PDI) delineate majority of countries in developing and emerging markets have a PDI score above 50 (Hofstede 2017). Power distance (PD) dimension expounds on the strength of social hierarchy and its influence on the relationship between those in power and subordinates in society. Malaysia recorded the highest PDI score of 100. High PDI suggests the level of inequality in society is endorsed by both followers as well as leaders; and challenges to leadership are not well-accepted (Hofstede 2017). Ultimately, the inherent cultural context influences the tendency to accept power coming from institutional hierarchy without deliberation. Concomitantly, studies on the influence of

PD found the lack of stakeholder integration in planning as contributory to 'governance gap' and failure to meet citizens' expectations in socio-development initiatives (Adelopo et al. 2015).

7.3 Methodology

The mixed methods applied in this longitudinal study (2012–2017) is guided by the Pragmatism paradigm which emphasizes on the importance of adopting diverse approaches to derive knowledge (Creswell 2013; Morgan 2014; Tashakkori and Teddlie 2010). A longitudinal study approach was undertaken to examine the effectuation of IP salience by organized activism as part of climate change mitigation and its impact on organizational behavior.

7.3.1 Data Collection and Analysis

Three phases of data collection and analyses were undertaken from 2012 to 2017.

7.3.2 Phase 1: Online Survey—Understanding Managerial Perception

This phase involved collection of primary data using quantitative approach. A Likert-scale survey was applied to assess managerial perception on stakeholder prioritization and level of engagement. Reliability and validity of instrument was established with Rasch analysis using Winsteps version 3.49 for pilot study and final data collection. After establishing 'goodness of fit', the online survey was administered from March to July 2012, with senior executives responsible for CR in public-listed companies on the Malaysia Exchange (ME). In order to pull information-rich data points, random purposeful sampling was adopted. The study focused on companies listed on the Main Market since 2006, when the mandatory requirement for the inclusion of CR report was enacted. This meant 634 companies shortlisted had at least five years of CR implementation and reporting experience (2006–2012). In total, primary data from 100 companies was collected. To establish sufficiency of the sample size of 100, Power analysis was applied. The results confirmed the size was in line with Cohen's (1998) argument as noted in other primary data-related studies that when the assumed effect size was medium, i.e. $R^2 = 0.15$ and the desired power is 0.95, the minimum sample size required to establish sufficiency is 67 (see Nkundabanyanga and Okwee 2011; Pandya and Narendar 1998). Next, a sequence of Rasch modeling analyses enumerated items measured reliability ($r = 0.93$) and persons measured reliability ($r = 0.97$). According to Bond and Fox (2010), the item reliability index of 0.93 indicates confidence in replicability of item placement across other samples. Further, the high person reliability demonstrated the study was able to expect consistency of inferences. For external validity, data was collected from multiple industries representing 12 major industries. Overall, companies fell into four categories: 53% wholly owned Malaysian companies; 27% joint-ownership (Malaysian & foreign partnership); 15% government-linked companies (GLC); and 5% foreign companies. In terms of market orientation, 64% targeted domestic and international markets; 32% purely domestic market and remaining 4% purely international market.

Data analyses on stakeholder prioritization affirmed top five stakeholders among companies: (1) local resident community 79%; (2) local employees' 78%; (3) customers 73%; (4) government agencies 71% and (5) NGOs 71%. In contrast, foreign workers and IP received lower scores, with IP ranking the bottom most. In terms of stakeholder engagement, companies in general were more inclined towards one-way and two-way communication. One-way communication includes reports, newsletters and website; while two-way communication includes face-to-face meetings and surveys. In contrast, multi-way communication involving series of proactive meetings with stakeholder(s) with a win–win focus, was not a common undertaking among companies. A critical exposition from this phase, IP ranked the bottom most in stakeholder prioritization with minimal engagement. The results corroborate with Mitchell et al. (1997) Stakeholder Salience model, where the absence or lack of stakeholder saliency significantly influenced managerial perception on IP, prioritization and extent of CR engagement.

7.3.3 Phase 2: Semi-structured Interview—Influence of NGOs on IP Salience

For this phase, a semi-structured interview was deployed to investigate influence of NGOs. The inquiry aimed to elucidate NGO's role in ameliorating IP salience. Semi-structured questions developed were based on power, legitimacy and urgency attributes expounded in the theory of stakeholder identification (Mitchell et al. 1997; Agle et al. 1999) to extrapolate insights on (i) challenges confronting IP; (ii) role of NGOs; and (iii) motivation(s) for change.

Seven prominent NGOs, representing local and international organizations, actively involved in IP issues in Malaysia were contacted for face-to-face interview. Purposive sampling was adopted for this qualitative phase. The criteria, rationale and validity of NGO selection are expounded in detail here: First, the sample study represented independent, non-state related NGOs with direct involvement in IP issues. The sampling did not include two groups: (a) state-level based civil society groups or village community NGOs, as their views were limited to isolated localities; and (b) state and federal government welfare agencies as their inputs were deemed biased towards the state and its policies. Next, the NGO has established reputation both in Malaysia and internationally on IP advocacy, which enabled it to speak knowledgeably. The objective was to allow for particularizing during data analysis. Therefore, seven NGOs were shortlisted for the purpose of study, namely, (1) Centre for Orang Asli Concerns (COAC); (2) Human Rights Commission of Malaysia (SUHAKAM); (3) United Nations Development Programme (UNDP—Malaysia office); (4) Network of Indigenous People Villages in Peninsular Malaysia (JKOASM); (5) Lariche Community; (6) Malaysian Bar Council—Committee for Orang Asli [IP]; and (7) Amnesty International Malaysia. Out of which five NGOs participated.

Validity of qualitative data was established in line with Creswell (2013). First, through the selection of 'experienced' participants in order to establish information accuracy. NGO representative(s) that partici pated had minimum 5 to over 10 years extensive experience with IP. The assimilation of expert views facilitated the development of valid, well-substantiated consensus for coding and delineation of themes and concepts. Secondly, consistency. All interviews were conducted at the respective NGO's premises, between 45 minutes to an hour, and transcribed within three days of the interview. The adherence to time constraint ensured inconsistencies or gaps did not emerge due to time laps between interview and transcribing process. A copy of the transcript was emailed to the respective participant for vetting, feedback on any inaccuracies in the transcription and final approval. Thirdly, a peer review of transcripts to facilitate substantiated consensus on coding and themes delineated; and finally, triangulation of qualitative data with secondary sources to address any weaknesses or intrinsic biases in terms of measurement bias, sampling bias and procedural bias. Findings in Phase 2 corroborated insights from Phase 1 as follows:

Absence of power in IP: Critical analyses of interview commentaries delineated IP lacked power be it economic, political or social influence. This was clearly exhibited, viz., (1) 'there are a lot of rights but not recognized'; (2) '....don't have the numbers....'; (3) 'the poor'; (4) 'no economic power....Political and economic power are related'.

Absence of urgency in IP: Companies took a lackadaisical approach as IP are deemed as state responsibility. Often referred as '...ignorant, uneducated and powerless community...', managers felt discussions were unwarranted and took a philanthropic approach when dealing with IP issues viz. cash donations or in kind, like school books or basic provisions. When juxtaposed with Hofstede's Power Distance cultural dimension, the insights endorse the interplay of high PDI as IP were expected to accept decisions undertaken by higher authorities with little or no contention.

NGO and IP empowerment: In the absence or inability to voice out due to impeding cultural dynamics at play, IP reached out to NGOs to address grievances overlooked by the state and companies, particularly in relation to land encroachments, loss of livelihood and long term survival. One of the significant initiatives undertaken by NGOs was organizing capacity building 'empowerment' workshops. A striking revelation from the qualitative data analyses epitomized a different nature of empowerment. As the existing CR literature does not offer much, a cross examination into management and organizational development literature offered fresh insight. Following an extensive literature review, the characteristics of empowerment extrapolated from Phase 2 correlated with Meyerson and Kline's (2008) study on 'psychological empowerment (PE)' conceptualized from the widely recognized works of Spreitzer (1995) and Spreitzer et al. (1997). PE is defined as 'a motivational construct manifested in four cognitions: meaning; competence; self-determination; and impact'. PE reverberated a deeper meaning and change in an individual or group facilitating self-independence. Traditionally, empowerment was focused on the provision of financial aids and basic necessities which inadvertently made beneficiaries more dependent. A juxtaposition with UNESCO's stance on empowerment: 'no one can empower another; only the individual can empower herself or himself to make choices or to speak out...institutions...can support processes that can nurture self-empowerment of individuals or community' offered endorsement to the study's proposition. Through capacity building workshops, NGOs trained IP understand their rights in relation to UNDRIP, how to write official complaint letters, where to send them and how to make police reports on land violations. Here, psychological empowerment rendered clarity within IP mindsets and fostered confidence, which axiomatically influenced the level of activism initiated by IP to address their concerns. This included deployment of various local activism tactics by empowered IPs viz. initiating legal challenges; protests and blockades. Triangulation with secondary sources revealed that as time passed, companies who had taken a lackadaisical approach to IP issues inadvertently encountered serious implications. Legal suits initiated by IP on land violations and ensuing international media exposé served as 'coup the grâce' on companies. Further, legal suits meant projects had to be stalled until the case was settled in court, ultimately threatening corporate bottom line and sustainability. Evidence of strengthened IP salience was cited from annual report(s) of affected public-listed companies, such as, prompt affirmative managerial responses, implementation of IP grievances handling procedures availed on corporate website(s) and remedial actions undertaken.

Motivation for Phase 3 of study: While evidence of companies initiating responsible business practices as a direct result of IP activism was noted, this trajectory was not coherent in relation to mega economic-development projects awarded to companies by the state. As these projects were for greater good and critical for socio-economic development of an emerging economy, companies involved were unsusceptible to legal action. IP activism fell short and IP became un-salient or weak again. NGOs also reported superficial CR and sustainability practices in mega development project areas. Companies instinctively discounted local IP issues and overlooked developments on transnational activism movements. This led to Phase 3 of inquiry which examined the influence of transnational activism on IP saliency in an emerging market context.

7.3.4 Phase 3 Case Study (2012–2017): Making a Business Case: Connecting the Dots Artfully—Deforestation, IP Rights and Climate Change Mitigation

Based on the limitation of critical and empirical studies on contemporary transnational activism in CR literature, a case study approach was undertaken. Case study facilitates collection of 'rich' qualitative data from multiple sources across a wide range of platforms, to initiate in-depth investigation into a specific phenomenon in its natural context (Finger and Prince 2013; Ridder 2017; Daymon and Holloway 2011). The case study was Baram hydro-electric mega dam in East Malaysia. East Malaysia shares its borders with Indonesia and Brunei and is located in Borneo Island. Borneo is the third largest island in the world and home to the oldest tropical rainforest in the world, over 130 million years old. Rainforest regions axiomatically have higher congregation of IPs and has been IP communal dwellings for generations. Tropical rainforests also serve as the earth's carbon sink, holding more than 210 gigatons of carbon. Deforestation of tropical rainforest continues to draw global attention as it directly accounts for over 15% of greenhouse gas emissions (GHGs), posing a grand challenge to climate change mitigation.

On one hand, hydro-electric dams are categorized as renewable energy and contribute towards sustainable development; however, research findings elucidate otherwise (Pillai 2014). A report endorsed by IP and NGOs (Business and Human Rights Resource Centre 2014) assert while mega hydro-electric dam projects appear to follow World Dam guidelines, investigations reveal superficial implementation of free, prior and informed consent (PIC) process, social and environmental impact assessment (SEIA), and limited avenues for remedial negotiations and self-determination by affected IPs. While companies involved categorically deny allegations, hydro-electric mega dam project(s) inadvertently meant loss of thousands of hectares of tropical rainforest due to inundation; and loss of land, cultural heritage, livelihood and forced assimilation for IPs.

For this phase, secondary data was extrapolated by tracking (i) local and transnational activism campaign tactics viz. 'Save Sarawak Rivers', 'Jaringan Orang Asal SeMalaysia' (JOAS), 'Borneo Resources Institute Malaysia Sarawak' (BRIMAS); 'International Rivers', 'Bruno Manser Fond' (BMF), 'The Borneo Project' and (ii) institutional responses over a period of five years from 2012 to 2017 (see Fig. 7.1). Data collection was deployed using Keck and Sikkink's (1998) 'boomerang effect' that expounds on four categories of activism tactics: information politics; symbolic politics; leverage politics; and accountability politics.

Findings from Phase 3: According to Keck and Sikkink (1998), the boomerang effect 'occurs in instances when the local campaign faces some barriers, either because of repression or lack of social response, then it throws a boomerang towards the rest of the world'. Here, seeking help from a third party in a different national setting. This may involve 'naming and shaming' the target of the campaign. The higher the boomerang goes is indicative of the level of 'influencers' reached. For the Baram mega dam campaign, transnational networks targeted international funding agencies such as Asian Development Bank (ADB), World Bank; organized public protests in Europe; garnered green politician endorsement in Australia to pressure Australian partner in the project. The Australian company, inevitably, withdrew from the Baram mega dam project. The boomerang effect, therefore, transfers agency from the claimants to cosmopolitan elites that have no direct or personal stake in the matter, hitting its target through international pressure.

In High Power Distance cultures like Malaysia, 'naming and shaming' is shunned. Further, negative publicity is detrimental to an emerging economy. Strong positive reputation is critical to facilitate international

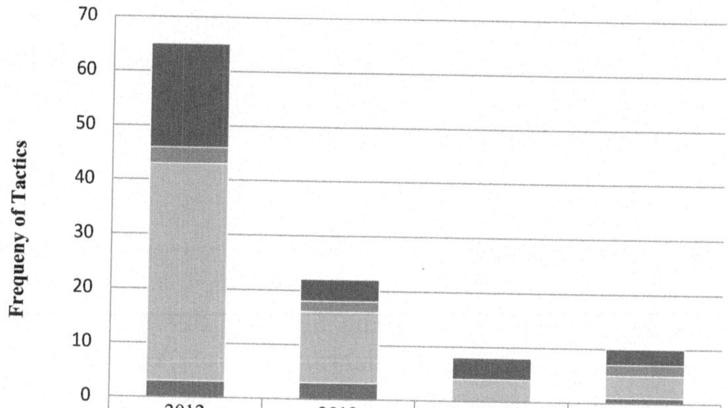

	2012	2013	2014	2015
Accountability Politics	19	4	4	3
Leverage Politics	3	2	0	2
Symbolic Politics	40	13	4	4
Information Politics	3	3	0	1

Fig. 7.1 Transnational activism: 'boomerang effect' tactics
Note (1) *Accountability politics* tactics drawn include official complaints to government agencies, political institutions, petitions and referendums; (2) *Leverage politics*: viz. local and international campaign tours by IP delegation to Asian Development Bank headquarters in Philippines; mega dam project partners' head office in Switzerland and Norway (Europe); public protest in front of the Tasmanian Parliament, Australia; meeting with green politicians in Australia to garner international political endorsement, (3) *Symbolic politics*: viz. social media postings, TV news, video documentaries, satire website, exposé photos, 'shaming' event viz. International Award for worst company of the year, mass mailing to delegates attending international renewable energy conference, public protests in cities during these event(s), and blockades at project sites; (4) *Information politics*: viz. empirical study reports by Institution of higher learning in United States on socio-environmental impacts and in UK on cost-inefficiency implications of mega dam projects to the State

funding support for its large-scale development projects. The well-coordinated, multi-mode transnational activism campaign strategy, led to the cessation of a seven-year IP struggle since 2010. On April 27th, 2016, the Chief Minister of Sarawak, Datuk Patinggi Tan Sri Adenan Satem announced a moratorium on the project. In November 2016, the US$1 Billion mega project was officially cancelled. Early 2017, the Chief Minister took a step further and renamed the project site 'Baram Peace

Park', enabling affected IP communities and NGOs to initiate socio-economic programmes based on IP terms. The unprecedented decision by the state leader broke new ground for IP struggles globally in relation to mega hydro-electric dam projects.

7.4 Discussion

Following a deliberation on the findings, this section highlights two striking expositions on: (i) Identification of 'Vulnerable' stakeholder; and, (ii) Cultural dynamics and leadership: Inclusive leadership.

7.4.1 Identification of 'Vulnerable' Stakeholder

As climate change pressures are expected to propel the intensity of transnational activism and shape sociopolitical thrusts on markets, one of the major challenges for business is identifying stakeholder(s) arising from this context. The insights elucidate a divergent stakeholder disposition. Referred as 'vulnerable' stakeholders by United Nations (UN), they represent different groups in society who experience social exclusion than the general population and are at higher risk as a result of climate change pressures. From a business perspective, this group can be considered an anomaly. Firstly, they don't fall into mainstream stakeholder categories viz. key, primary or secondary stakeholder groups nor do they fit in any of the seven stakeholder classifications in Mitchell et al.'s (1997) model. Secondly, the underlying rationale of stakeholder analysis models is to facilitate strategic managerial decision for effective stakeholder management, based on 'who and what really counts' for stakeholder mapping and prioritization. Hence, while an omission or oversight of this group was unintended, but at what price? The findings elucidate actors, both in the emerging market and developed markets were caught off guard by the onslaught of organized transnational activism and were brought to their knees. This not only indicates a gap in the existing stakeholder literature, but elucidates the interconnectedness and growing vulnerabilities of market actors in the advent of grand challenges.

7.4.2 Inclusive Leadership and Cultural Dynamics

Another compelling elucidation is on leadership. While research on leadership is not new in CR, revelations from the study offer a fresh proposition. The stance taken by the Chief Minister of Sarawak, Datuk Patinggi Tan Sri Adenan Satem, on the Baram Mega Dam project, delineated a new construct at play in terms of leadership, which is contradictory to the benevolent leadership style typical to high Power Distance cultures. A review of CR literature found little evidence on this construct. A cross-examination into management literature offered an exposition on the concept of 'inclusive leadership'. According to Bourke and Espedido (2019); Bourke (2016), inclusive leadership encapsulates six attributes: courage; cultural intelligence, cognizance; commitment and collaboration. The decision by the Chief Minister to terminate the mega-dam project and officially gazette the site into Baram Peace Park with its development dictated by IP was novel in an emerging market context. Following a query on leadership in emerging markets, the author found inclusive leadership traits in India. In 2014, under the leadership of Prime Minister Manmohan Singh, India became the first nation in the world to legally mandate CR under its Companies Act, making it mandatory for companies with minimum turnover and profitability to allocate two percent of net profit for CR. With clear guidelines for CR 'project/program' with a focus on (1) socio-environmental issues; (2) implemented within a set radius of the business operations; and (3) explicit categories viz. addressing hunger and poverty, education, health, gender equality and women empowerment, skills training, environment and social enterprise projects (CSR India 2016).

In extending the insights on cultural dynamics, the author juxtaposed the Borneo case study to a similar project in Brazil, another fast emerging market, the insights were in collusion. In the case of the multi-billion-dollar Belo Monte mega hydroelectric dam project in the Amazon, the largest tropical rainforest in the world, the 20-year struggle of the Kayapos, an IP community, continues to hit the wall despite innumerable transnational activism campaign tactics (Carrington 2010; Cerqueira 2010; Embassy of Brazil in London 2010). Studies found the effectiveness of transnational coalitions depended on the domestic structure of the 'target state' (Adelopo et al. 2015). Cultural dynamics may facilitate or hinder NGO access to the domestic policy and the ability to build 'winning coalitions' within that polity and international institutions, form transnational coalitions and legitimatize efforts to change policy. 'Lack of openness of political institutions and participation, respect of civil liberties, transparency of government, and freedom of the press' are cited as conditions that negate a desired outcome by transnational networks (Adelopo et al. 2015).

7.5 Contributions and Implications of the Study

While there are arguments on the limitation of case studies, empirical insights from this study affirm the pervasiveness of burgeoning international sociopolitical emphasis on climate change mitigation on market logics. Further, the externalization of negative impacts from emerging/developing market to developed markets and vice versa, is indicative of blurring boundaries, growing interconnectedness as well as vulnerabilities of market actors. Fundamentally, challenging the traditional approach to stakeholder thinking in CR. These elucidations contribute a valid argument for theoretical consideration in stakeholder literature.

7.5.1 Theoretical Implication

The theoretical proposition calls for an inclusive approach in stakeholder(s) discernment. Here, the framework (Fig. 7.2) outlines 'macro socio-environmental analyses' as precursor to stakeholder analysis and mapping. Macro socio-environmental analyses has two levels: global level and market level. The global level involves scanning global advocacy/activism narratives on climate change, and identifying any specific environmental and social [stakeholder(s) viz. vulnerable stakeholder] issues connected to an industry/sector and business. Next, at market level, requires assessing inherent cultural dynamics at play viz. power

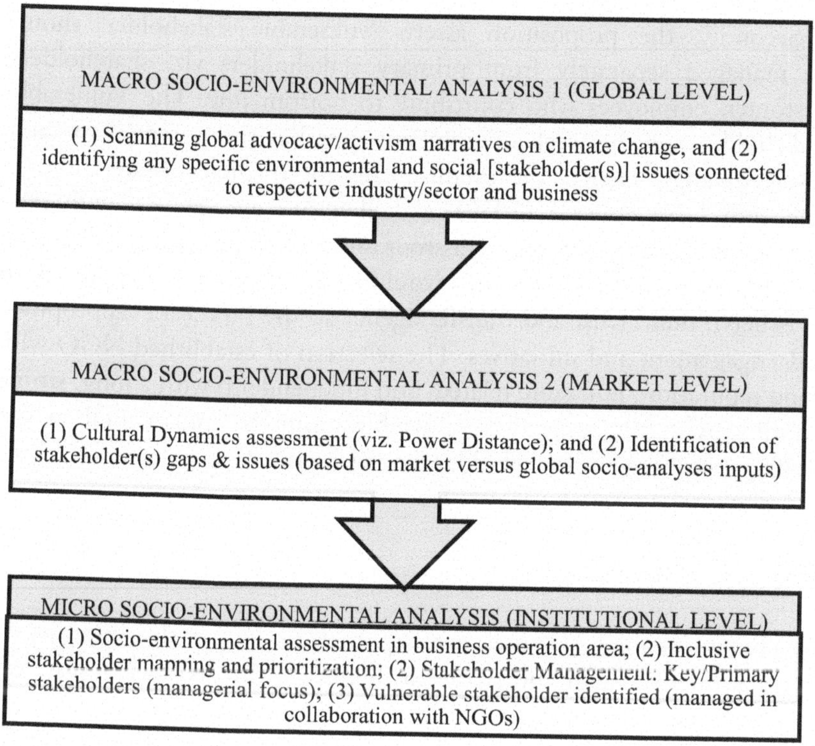

Fig. 7.2 Conceptual framework on 'inclusive stakeholder analysis approach in an emerging market context' (*Source* Authors own work)

distance, in the relevant emerging market. The objective is to determine if any 'vulnerable' stakeholder(s) identified at the global level is exigent in the emerging market of interest; and establish if this group has been overlooked due to cultural context. Essentially, the macro socio-environmental analyses enable actors to determine any gaps in 'stakeholder' identification linked to its business operations based on glocal [global and local] assessment. Next, at the institutional level, the insights from the macro socio-environmental analyses would facilitate an inclusive stakeholder(s) mapping and prioritizationss. Here, managerial discretion based on the traditional application of appropriate stakeholder analysis models would be undertaken for onward strategic stakeholder management planning.

Secondly, the proposition asserts 'vulnerable stakeholder' should be managed separately from primary stakeholders viz. shareholders, customer, employees who contribute to bottom line. The 'vulnerable' stakeholder may be weak or unsalient, but has the potential to cause severe damage. Hence, the premise calls for further consideration, in line with UN's Agenda (2030), a deliberative engagement with relevant, established NGOs with grassroot understanding of the 'vulnerable' stakeholder predicaments. This would facilitate grounded appreciation of issue(s), build trust and transfer agency to the NGO for appropriate CR engagement and initiatives. The selection of established NGO with good reputation, non-state related, and independent; with a long, strong standing with the respective vulnerable group is fundamental in CR strategy planning and stakeholder management.

7.6 Conclusion

As climate change pressures are expected to propel the intensity of transnational activism and shape sociopolitical thrusts on markets, one of the major challenges for business is identifying stakeholder(s) and implementing CR judiciously. The influence of cultural dynamics in an emerging market requires deeper appreciation and discernment. Furthermore, the ripple effects of the externalization of negative impacts from emerging/developing market to developed markets and vice versa, is indicative of blurring boundaries and vulnerabilities of market actors, challenging the traditional CR approach to stakeholder thinking. Hence, an inclusive socio-environmental stakeholder analysis approach is needed to facilitate strategic CR and strengthen corporate resilience. Finally, cultivating an inclusive leadership approach could prove to be efficacious as businesses embrace diverse markets and tackle grand challenges issues concurrently.

7.6.1 Future Research

Application of the framework in other developing/emerging market settings would shed more light on its robustness for CR practice. While the study explored Power Distance cultural dimension, inquiry into other dimensions viz. long term versus short term orientation may offer added insights on the influence of cultural dynamics on managerial discretion in emerging markets on CR thinking and stakeholder management. Finally, delineation of inclusive leadership construct presents another area of inquiry for future research consideration.

References

Adelopo, I, Yekini, K and Raimi, L. Political corporate social responsibility and development. In D. Jamali, C. Karam, and M. Blowfield (Eds.), *Development-oriented corporate social responsibility* (Greenleaf Publishing 2015), 29–49.

Agle, BR, Mitchell, RK and Sonnenfeld, JA. "Who matters to CEOs? An investigation of stakeholders attributes and salience, corporate performance and CEO values." *Academy of management Journal*, 42 No 5 (1999): 507–525.

Ali, AH. "The power of social media in developing nations: New tools for closing the global digital divide and beyond." *Harvard Human Rights Journal*, 24 (2011): 185–241.

Bartley, T and Child, C. "Movements, markets and fields: The effects of anti-sweatshop campaigns on U.S. firms, 1993–2000." *Social Forces*, 90 (2011): 425–451.

Batliwala, S. "Grassroots movements as transnational actors: Implications for global civil society." *Voluntas: International Journal of Voluntary and Nonprofit Organizations*, 13 No 4 (2002): 393–409.

Bond, TG and Fox, CM. *Applying the Rasch model: Fundamental measurement in the human sciences*. 2nd ed. (Routledge Taylor & Francis Group, New York 2010).

Bourke, J. The six signature traits of inclusive leadership: Thriving in a diverse new world. *Deloitte Insights* (2016). https://www2.deloitte.com/us/en/insights/topics/talent/six-signature-traitsof-inclusive-leadership.html.

Bourke, J and Espedido, A. Diversity: Why Inclusive Leaders Are Good for Organizations, and How to Become One. *Harvard Business Review digital* (March 29, 2019).

Business and Human Rights Resource. Special Report on Mega Dam (2014). [Accessed 18/3/2016]. https://www.business-humanrights.org/en/malaysia-save-rivers-report-on-baram-dam-alleges-indigenous-rights-abuses-by-sarawak-energy-state-govt-company-responds.

Carrington, D. "First Amazon bridge to open world's greatest rainforest to development." *The Guardian*. Thursday 5 August 2010. [Accessed 14/8/2010]. http://www.guardian.co.uk/environment/2010/jul/29/manaus-bridge-amazon-rainforest.

Cerqueira, C. "The fight is not only against Belo Monte!" *Indigenous Missionary Council website*. [Accessed 19/7/2010] http://www.cimi.org.br/?system=news&action=read&id=4865&eid=402.

Cohen, J. *Statistical Power Analysis for the Behavioral Sciences*. 2nd Ed. (Lawrence Erlbaum Associates Publishers, New York 1988).

Creswell, John W. *Qualitative inquiry & research design: Choosing among five approaches*. 3rd ed. (Sage, Thousand Oaks, CA 2013): 28–29.

CSR India. [Accessed 20/7/2019]. https://bthechange.com/csr-in-india-is-now-a-law-2502aa6d0daa (2016).

Daymon, C and Holloway, I. *Qualitative research methods* (Routledge, New York 2011).

Embassy of Brazil in London. "Belo Monte Power Plant." *Embassy of Brazil in London*. [Accessed 24/7/2010]. http://www.brazil.org.uk/environment/belomonte.html (2010).

Finger, M and Princen, T. *Environmental NGOs in the world politics: Linking the local and the Global* (2013). [Accessed 10/2/2017]. https://books.google.com.my/books?hl=en&lr=&id=Xb3_fuTskHQC&oi=fnd&pg=PT6&dq=press+conference+and+NGOs&ots=IiIo7PSAgt&sig=ISjZmFoAEoRu2XNFMT3HZu8xUrk&redir_esc=y#v=onepage&q=press%20conference%20and%20NGOs&f=true.

Hirsch, E. in Moore, D, Dore, J and Gyawali, D. "The World Commission on Dam+10: Revisiting the large dam controversy." *Water Alternatives*, 3 No 2 (2010): 3–13.

Hofstede Country Comparison: Power Distance. [Accessed 15/11/2017]. https://www.hofstede-insights.com/country-comparison/malaysia/ (2017).

Jamali, D and Carroll, A. "Capturing advances in CSR: Developed versus developing country perspectives editorial." *Business Ethics: A European Review*, 26 (2017): 321–325.

Jamali, D and Karam, C. "Corporate social responsibility in developing countries as an emerging field of study." *International Journal of Management Reviews*, 20 (2018): 32–61. https://doi.org/10.1111/ijmr.12112.

Keck, Margaret. *Activists beyond borders* (Cornell University Press 2010).

Keck, Margaret E and Sikkink, Kathryn. *Activists beyond borders* (Cornell University Press 1998).

Meyerson, SL and Kline, TJB. "Psychological and environmental empowerment: Antecedents and consequences." *Leadership & Organization Development Journal*, 29 No 5 (2008): 444–460.

Mitchell, RK, Agle, BR and Wood, DJ. Toward a theory of stakeholder identification and salience: Defining the principle of who and what really counts. *Academy of Management Review*, 22 No 4 (1997): 853–886.

Moksnes, H and Melin, M. *Global civil society: Shifting powers in a shifting world* (Uppasala Centre for Sustainable Development, Sweden 2012).

Morgan, D. "Pragmatism as a paradigm for social research." *Qualitative Inquiry*, 20 No 8 (2014): 1045–1053. https://doi.org/10.1177/1077800413513733.

Newell, P. *Climate for change: Non-state actors and the global politics of the greenhouse* (Cambridge University Press, Cambridge, 2000).

Nilsen, HR. "The joint discourse 'reflexive sustainable development': From weak toward strong sustainable development." *Ecological Economics*, 69 (2010): 495–501.

Nkundabanyanga, KS and Okwee, A. "Institutionalizing corporate social responsibility (CSR) in Uganda: does it matter?" *Social Responsibility Journal*, 7 No 4 (2011): 665–680.

Pandya, AM & Narendar, VR. Diversification and Firm performance: An Empirical Evaluation. *Journal of Finance and Strategic Decisions*, 11 No 2 (1998).

Pillai, KV. *The influence of corporate conduct and stakeholder empowerment on corporate citizenship in Malaysia: A mixed methods research*. PhD Diss. Open University Malaysia (2013).

Pillai, KV. *Is renewable energy really clean?* Forbes Capital Flow (2014). [Accessed 18/4/2016]. https://www.forbes.com/sites/realspin/2014/09/24/is-renewable-energy-really-green/#35b514ae6466.

Pillai, KV, Slutsky, P, Wolf, K, Duthler, G and Stever, I. Companies' accountability in sustainability: A comparative analysis of Sustainable Development Goals (SDGs) in five countries. In J. Servaes (Eds),*Communication, culture and change in Asia: Sustainable development goals in the Asian context* (2016).

978-981-10-2814-4, 418881_1_En (Springer) http://www.springer.com/in/book/9789811028144.

Ridder, HG. "The theory contribution of case study research designs." *Business Research*, 10 (2017): 281. https://doi.org/10.1007/s40685-017-0045-z.

SUHAKAM. Report on the national enquiry into the land rights of indigenous peoples. Human Rights Commission of Malaysia (SUHAKAM) (2013). [Accessed 22/4/2013]. www.suhakam.org.my.

Smith, J, Plummer, S and Hughes, MM. "Transnational social movements and changing organizational fields in the late twentieth and early twenty-first centuries. Global networks." *Journal of Transnational Affairs*, 17 No 1 (2017): 3–22.

Spreitzer, G. "Individual empowerment in the workplace: Dimensions, measurement, validation." *Academy of Management Journal*, 38 No 5 (1995): 1442–1465.

Spreitzer, G, Kizilos, M and Nason S. "A dimensional analysis of the relationship between psychological empowerment and effectiveness, satisfaction, and strain." *Journal of Management*, 23 No 5 (1997): 679–704.

Tashakkori, A and Teddlie, C. *SAGE handbook of mixed methods in social & behavioral research* (Sage, Thousand Oaks, CA, US, 2010).

Tombleson, B and Wolf, K. Rethinking the circuit of culture: How participatory culture has transformed cross-cultural communication. *Public Relations Review*, 43 No 1 (2017): 14–25.

UN Agenda 2030. Transforming our world: The 2030 agenda for sustainable development. [Accessed 20/7/2020]. https://sustainabledevelopment.un.org/post2015/transformingourworld.

UNDESA. n.d. [Accessed 20/9/2018]. https://www.un.org/development/desa/indigenouspeoples/mandated-areas1/environment.html.

United Nations. *State of the world's Indigenous peoples* (2018). 3rd ed. https://www.un.org/development/desa/indigenouspeoples/wp-content/uploads/sites/19/2017/12/State-of-Worlds-Indigenous-Peoples_III_WEB2018.pdf.

World Bank. Indigenous peoples. Article updated on September 24, 2019 https://www.worldbank.org/en/topic/indigenouspeoples.

World Bank. (April 2020) .https://www.worldbank.org/en/country/malaysia/overview.

Wright, C and Nyberg, D. "An inconvenient truth: How organizations translate climate change into business as usual." *Academy of Management Journal*, 60 No 5 (2017): 1633–1661.

8

Trans-sustain: Transversal Competency Management for Integrating Sustainability in the Vocational Education of German Butchers

Carolin Ermer, Julia Schwarzkopf, and Kai Reinhardt

8.1 Introduction

Companies in general face the challenge of coping with new and disruptive changes in their environment on an ecological, economic, and social level (Tulder 2003). These circumstances are widely reflected in the concept of the Sustainable Development Goals (SDGs) of the United Nations, which also call for action from businesses to address these SDGs (United Nations 2019). To achieve the SDGs, in addition to acquiring new sustainability skills and competencies, employees responsible for implementing the SDGs also need to develop new and innovative instruments at the organizational-structural level to develop skills from a corporate perspective. This requirement was explicitly proclaimed by the United Nations (2019) in the "Decade of Action" for the implementation of the SDGs. The present article was written for the special issue

C. Ermer (✉) · J. Schwarzkopf · K. Reinhardt
University of Applied Sciences - HTW Berlin, Berlin, Germany
e-mail: Carolin.Ermer@HTW-Berlin.de

C. Simões et al. (eds.), *Corporate Responsibility, Sustainability and Markets*, Palgrave Studies in Governance, Leadership and Responsibility,
https://doi.org/10.1007/978-3-030-79660-0_8

of Palgrave Chapters on "Corporate Responsibility, Sustainability and Markets" to discuss opportunities and challenges regarding the implementation of sustainability in a special and often neglected market: the butcher trade and meat market. Key challenges currently faced by the food trade and the meat industry include precarious employment and sustainable animal husbandry (Anthes 2019; Rehberg 2020). Meat processing companies such as butchers and slaughterhouses also need competencies that can counteract these existing challenges and at the same time address potential unforeseeable disruptive changes in the environment, economy, and society.

While butchery is one of the oldest traditional skilled professions in Germany and enjoys a high-standing reputation (Bahl 2017), in addition to slaughtering animals the work of a butcher today also includes tasks such as meat refinement (Bahl 2017) and developing innovative new products to meet the high expectations of customers (German Butchers' Association 2021; Anthes 2019; Ingenbleek and Zhao 2019). In Germany a decrease can be observed in the overall number of butcheries, which fell from 20,359 in 2005 to just 12,898 in 2018. In addition, the butchery trade is facing the growing challenges of talent acquisition and retention. Over the last decade, the number of employees has fallen by almost 13,000, which corresponds to the loss of about one in ten jobs or training places. According to the 2019 annual report of the German Butchers' Association (2021), over the last 19 years the number of apprenticeship contracts has decreased from almost 10,000 in 2000 to around just 1,195 in 2019 (German Butchers' Association 2021), as the number of apprentices learning this trade is declining. Therefore, the small and medium-sized butcher shops which still exist need to renew or adapt their business model (Bildungszentrum Fleischerhandwerk 2020) in order to assert themselves against discounters and large (organic and non-organic) supermarket chains in the long term and also to increase their attractiveness as a place of work for the younger generation. Consequently, education programs for butchers, and especially vocational training, also need to adapt to new requirements. In view of the public debates about sustainability, climate change (IATP 2020), animal welfare and meat consumption, these issues need to be taken into consideration when opting to modernize and/or adapt vocational training for butchers.

Furthermore, trends in meat consumption (Umweltbundesamt 2019) and dietary trends (Ingenbleek and Zhao 2019) are also putting pressure on traditional butchers, for example due to customers switching from traditional butchers to discount store due to cheap prices or vegetarianism and veganism trends. On the other hand, several innovative business models geared towards sustainability (Schulze Steinmann 2019; have recently proven that they are economically feasible, while addressing the pressing sustainability issues of the meat industry, for example alternative butchery communities like crowdbutching ("http://www.buyacow.uk") or butchers with modern marketing concepts for traditional products (e.g. http://www.kumpelundkeule.de in Berlin, Germany). The Concept of crowdbutching is to share a cow with about eight to ten other consumers. Animals are only butchered from small farming businesses that are raised and fed in a sustainable way that respects animal welfare (Schulze Steinmann 2019).

Addressing sustainability issues to enable new visions for the butchery profession is relevant not only in the butchery trade but also in the training and apprenticeships of future butchers. Vocational education must therefore enable these future butchers to incorporate new mindsets, skills, and knowledge, for example with regard to rearing, stable hygiene, animal welfare, and resource conservation, also in terms of sustainability.

8.2 Theoretical Background

The starting point for our project is the development of specific competencies for sustainable action in today's organizations (Teece et al. 2016; Prahalad and Hamel 1990). It is a generally accepted scientific view (Teece et al. 2016; Erpenbeck and Sauter 2017) that in a rapidly changing organizational environment, conventional approaches to skills development are only capable to a limited extent of meeting the challenges of future work and life reality as well as the interconnectedness of organizations with their environment (Auer 2003). Recent research shows (Gomes and Wojahn 2017) that strategic competency management is particularly successful if it is geared towards permeability and de-institutionalization. In this development a so-called "transversal" exchange of competency takes place, an exchange across all organizational silos (Dahlmeier et al. 2017). The concept of "transversal competency management" aims to build bridges across systems and between different contexts of action as well as within different economic and educational institutions (Dahlmeier et al. 2017). The core of such a system is a distributed, connectable, and dynamic competency model. Within our model project, we attempt to create in-house tools for the vocational training of butchers to implement sustainable thinking and acting with a view to transversal competency enhancement, starting at the apprenticeship stage while at the same time addressing and raising awareness within the entire organization.

To explore the integration of sustainability-related competencies in the vocational training of future butchers, we started out with two assumptions: There is a high degree of uncertainty in the sustainable strategies of organizations, especially SMEs such as butcher shops, and at the same time these businesses lack or have limited possibilities to integrate sustainability because an institutional development towards sustainability of associations, guild or trade is missing. This reflects the highly complex challenges companies are facing currently and in the future in dealing with new and disruptive requirements and developments in all areas surrounding an organization when dealing with sustainability (Müller and Siakala 2020). Furthermore, the instruments and educational formats are often lacking at an individual level to build up the necessary knowledge and competency to achieve these goals, particularly in organizations with a small or medium-sized structure (Cordova and Celone 2019).

It is generally assumed that skills can only be understood as formally conveyed qualifications to a limited extent (Erpenbeck and Rosenstiel 2007). Instead, competencies should be understood as abilities and skills tied to individuals that enable people to "do something right" in a situation characterized by uncertainty (Teece et al. 2016). The right skills enable individuals to act independently and make autonomous decisions to properly assess uncertain situations and make decisions to cope with them (Wals and Corcoran 2012). North and Reinhardt (2005) describe competency as a relationship between the demands placed on a person or group and their abilities to cope with them. More precisely, competencies create the potential to meet these demands (de Haan 2008). In this perspective, isolated competency development within a single organization or task no longer provides the necessary context (North and Reinhardt 2005). Current application-oriented research shows that efforts to establish competency management as a formalized management approach in organizations are stagnating (North et al. 2018) and that efforts are limited to isolated implementations of individual organizations without achieving synergy effects among each other or creating a broad impact. Transversal competency management proposes a view that extends competency management to a transversal and holistic view (Dahlmeier et al. 2017). It is an individual competency development that takes place in practical everyday work inside organizations, in all relevant operational situations, without this being limited to organizational boundaries or being linearly predictable and is furthermore not limited to pre-structured learning situations (Dahlmeier et al. 2017).

8.2.1 Current Research Gap: Transversal Competency Development Across Organizational Borders

A future-oriented concept for developing sustainability-related competencies in organizations must therefore be able to provide alternatives to an isolated perspective that is reduced to the individual level. From a theoretical point of view, combining the discussion on the development of organizational competencies with a stronger focus on the individual stakeholders to promote learning environment innovations in the area of sustainability offers fresh new impetus. Especially in the meat industry there are a number of urgent issues (e.g. climate change, loss of biodiversity etc.) that have a disruptive effect on sustainability. However, conventional systems for learning in this profession exhibit weaknesses with regard to developing specific sustainability skills and the lack of systematic learning, particularly in terms of developing sustainability-oriented action competencies. This leads to the research question of how transversal competency management needs to be designed in the context of vocational education and training so that the relevant actors can act more responsibly and in line with the Sustainable Development Goals of the United Nations (United Nations 2019).

The primary aim of this pilot project is to design systems, roles, and instruments that link the strategic sustainability goals with actors' competencies in order to minimize qualification risks and within that make competency development actor-oriented. In-company training represents a central hinge point where junior experts are introduced to the issues of sustainability in their occupational profiles at an early stage in their careers. At the same time, training personnel already anchored in the sector and in professional life can be addressed within the framework of their training tasks and integrated into the process of competency development to foster sustainability within collaborative learning scenarios (Dillenbourg 1999).

8.2.2 Competencies and Learning Approaches to Promote Sustainability

The project "Trans-Sustain" was set up for the purposes of the model-based research and development of a holistic and transversal competency framework for vocational education. It was designed to support the associated competency-promoting environments and instruments in the field of vocational training in small and medium-sized butcher's shops operating in slaughtering or meat processing as well as the sale of meat and sausage products. In learning situations, competency frameworks can provide an overview of which competencies exist or are expected for a task (Erpenbeck and Rosenstiel 2007). The structure of competency frameworks is determined by the choice of categorization, with the contents indicating a clear task or profession. Furthermore, a degree of differentiation should be determined by which the skills are characterized. The form and degree of differentiation determine the content of a skills profile (Erpenbeck and Sauter 2017). In this research project, apprentices form the focus of our interest. They are subject to sustainability issues in their vocational training environment. Learning approaches that ensure sustainability are also defined within Education for Sustainable Development (ESD) as an overall objective rather than a defined body of information and knowledge (Hopkins 2009). UNESCO outlines this as follows:

> ESD empowers learners to take informed decisions and responsible actions for environmental integrity, economic viability and a just society for present and future generations, while respecting cultural diversity. [...] ESD is holistic and transformational education which addresses learning content and outcomes, pedagogy and the learning environment. It achieves its purpose by transforming society. (UNESCO 2020)

The Trans-Sustain pilot project locates itself as an active and self-reflective training program and focuses on the development of sustainability-oriented skills. Sustainability topics for this specific occupational field and concrete points of reference for training in the development of sustainability-oriented competencies thus need to be considered when addressing current challenges for the profession.

The goal of the project is to enable butchery companies to develop employee competencies in a transverse, self-directed, and future-oriented way. As part of this process, the potential for sustainable action for their own operational practice will be identified and implemented in independent development projects.

8.3 Research Design

The aim of the research design (Fig. 8.1) is to gain insights into the very specific training practices, already established sustainable processes, and also opportunities and challenges for the butchery profession. Methodologically, the focus is primarily on explorative methods, qualitative interviews, and model developments that will allow us to identify concrete potential for optimization at the interface between the learning system and the application of sustainability and future-oriented competencies in this specific field of practice and to initiate interventions.

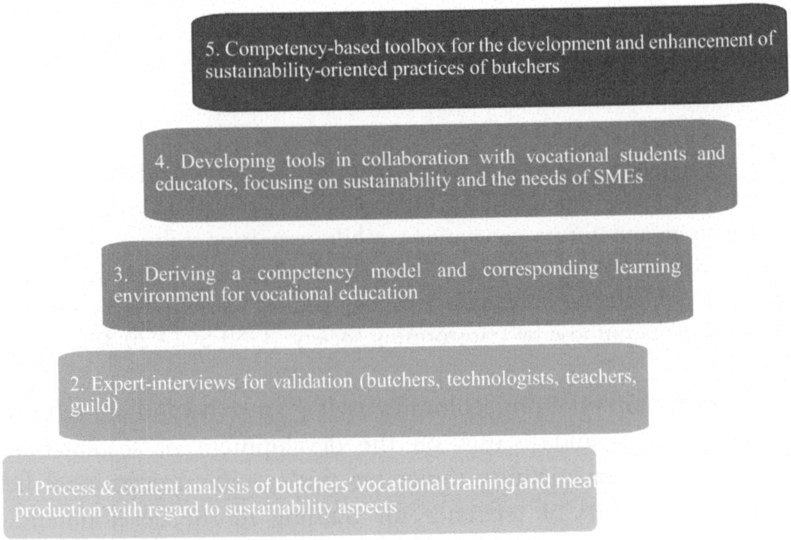

Fig. 8.1 Research design (*Source* Author's own work)

8.3.1 The Interviews

Initial access to the status quo of the butchery trade and an assessment of the need for future butchers was achieved through eight qualitative expert interviews in Germany. An interview guideline was therefore developed in German. The interview partners were selected based on their extensive personal experience in the meat industry. The aim was to acquire interview partners which mirror the whole field of expertise that is needed for a change towards sustainability in vocational training and transversal competencies in the area of meat production. Access to interview partners was gained via a previous bachelor's thesis in the field and through personal contacts and active networking at relevant events and conferences.

We started the interviews with two experts (interviews A and B) who both have over three decades of experience in various fields of meat production. Subsequent interviews were conducted with experts in specific areas of meat production, for example a sustainable butcher and a teacher for vocational training. Nine in-depth interviews were carried out in total to provide sufficient comprehension of the topic and its different perspectives (Table 8.1). The expert interviews were conducted within small and medium-sized businesses, industrial and family-owned businesses, sustainable and non-sustainable businesses, within the butcher's guild, with a supervisor and an engineer for meat production, a vocational teacher and a trainer for the butchery trade in Thuringia, Brandenburg, Bavaria, and Berlin (Table 8.1).

The interview partners are structured into two categories: One group is closely involved in the dual education system for butchers; the other group is active within the applied and practical field of the profession. The qualitative guideline-based interviews lasted for about an hour and were conducted between December 2018 and May 2019. The time period was comparably long because finding interview partners in this area of expertise took longer than expected. The interviews were analyzed according to the simplified transcription rules established by Kuckartz (2016, pp. 166–169). The interviews were evaluated based on Mayring's (2013, p. 3f) qualitative content analysis using pre-defined categories supplemented by new categories during the evaluation.

Table 8.1 Overview of interview partners

Expert	Profession/business	State
A	Expert in food safety, meat industry, and butcher's craft with over 30 years of experience	Northrhine Westphalia
B	Master butcher with 40 years of experience, family-owned business	Brandenburg
C	Vocational schoolteacher for butchers trade	Berlin
D	Sustainable butcher and wife, family-owned business	Berlin
E	Medium-sized conventional butcher	Bavaria
F	Chairman of butchers guild	Berlin
G	Small-sized conventional butcher, family-owned business	Baden-Wurttemberg
H	Medium-sized meat producer	Thuringia
I	Vocational in house—trainer meat industry	Thuringia

Source Author's own work

8.4 Preliminary Results

8.4.1 Opportunities and Challenges for Butchers

Initial findings from our theoretical literature research and from the expert interviews were compiled in an overview of key sustainable development fields (Fig. 8.2) for presentation to educational personnel and businesses in the butchery trade. The findings also provide a basis for discussing the implementation of sustainability in vocational education. These key fields are not only relevant for businesses with regard to their sustainability strategy but also for the future orientation of the trade.

We identified the six main subject fields for sustainability and future orientation of businesses and trade in which knowledge, skills, and competencies need to be achieved as followed:

8.4.1.1 Livestock Farming

Sustainable animal husbandry entails the concepts of "animal welfare" and "animal justice". This includes the handling of animals, the type of husbandry, animal health, as well as animal transport and the method of slaughter.

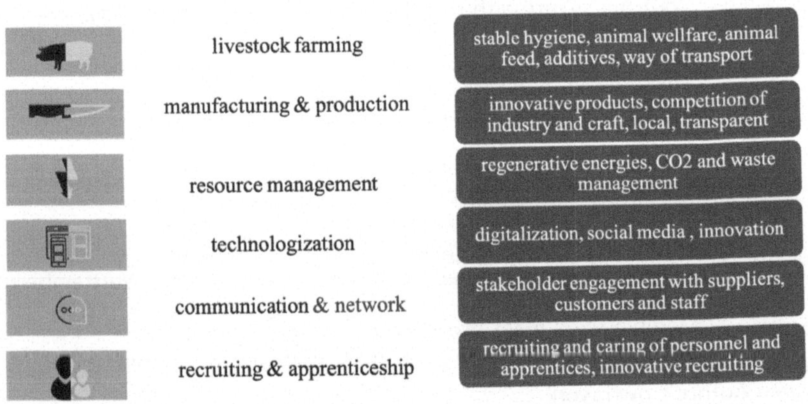

Fig. 8.2 Six fields of sustainable and future-oriented development for butchers' education (*Source* Author's own work)

> So that perhaps more and more farmers can be supported, that there is more sustainable agriculture in the future and if possible, people eat more consciously, convince people that this is our vision. (Meat producer, interview G)

8.4.1.2 Manufacturing and Production

Transparency in all stages of production, no waste ("from nose to tail"), no additives, colorings, or preservatives, local or organic ingredients such as herbs or spices, economical and sustainable packaging.

> So, inventing and making new things again and again in order to be able to sell really everything, not to throw anything away, not to throw away any, yes what can I say, yes really the animals [...]. From nose to tail completely. (Sustainable master butcher and wife, interview D)

In addition to sustainability and food trends, various other competencies are also essential for the success of butchery businesses.

8.4.1.3 Resource Management

Resource management ranges from energy management to sustainable packaging and films, and as much recycling as possible with correspondingly minimal residual waste.

> (I recycle) 95%. I try to recycle relatively much of the animals. Because I also always tell my customers that the animal lived, it died for us [...]. (Master butcher, interview B)

8.4.1.4 Technologization

Technologization and digitalization also include new distribution and communication channels, new materials, machines, and new programs. One sustainable and prosperous butchery business actively uses new media and tools. Especially when looking for new trainees and employees, media competency is therefore a prerequisite. The butcher's wife, for example, also publishes job advertisements on Facebook, Google Plus, and on her own website to find reinforcements for the team. New media are also used in the butcher's salesroom. In the butcher's shop windows there is an electronic picture frame on which numerous photos of local farmers and businesses can be seen (interview D).

> "For example, we are currently working on packaging. That we are reducing the proportion of film in packaging, replacing it with recycled materials, whatever. This topic, we have set up a special counter in the factory outlet for customers who come in with cans. (Meat producer, interview H)

8.4.1.5 Communication and Network

Sustainable action must be communicated (as stated in interview A, B, D, E, and I). This includes all stakeholders in the production chain, from suppliers and employees to customers, local authorities and schools. Regional partner networks facilitate sustainable action at the local and national level, strengthen business, and promote positive communication of the companies to the outside world.

> We are also doing a great deal to ensure that we visit schools, that we pay attention to classes in which vocational training or later working life is the main focus, and that we give lectures together with other companies [...]. (Vocational in-house trainer, interview I)

8.4.1.6 Recruiting and Apprenticeship

Not only the master butcher but also the entire staff of the butcher's shop must be convinced of the concept of sustainability (interview B and C). System competency is important here because the employees should be able to advise customers at all times and provide information on the subject of sustainability (interview A). The employees receive this knowledge within the scope of daily operating procedures; separate training is not necessary for knowledge acquisition. Securing the next generation and a lack of personnel can be existential issues for butchery businesses in Germany.

> You will need more social skills, such as communication skills for good customer orientation, but also reliability [...]. (Master butcher, interview B)

Sustainable action enhances companies' credibility and strengthens their image. Competencies for sustainable action will become increasingly important for future generations and learning a sustainable business can make the profession of the butcher more attractive for the next generation. For vocational education in organizations, this means achieving a new set of competencies (Hahne 2009) which can help to cope with the so-called "wicked problems" (Tulder 2003) of "unsustainability", while at the same time preparing apprentices for future-oriented challenges of the profession.

8.4.2 Emerging Competency Areas in the Butchery Profession

First findings in the literature research and the outcome of the expert interviews confirm that competency development in SMEs is no longer limited to the isolated context of an institution or a single professional situation but takes place across all situations, developmental stages, and organizational cultures. The competency bearer thus becomes the center of competency development (e.g. Wals and Corcoran 2012; Bormann and de Haan 2008; Rieckmann 2018) as a self-directed thinking and acting subject within his or her life context and environment. The tasks, roles, and decisions mastered become temporary and deformable. In this way, the discussion about the training and development of skills has moved from a more structural–functional perspective of human resource management to the actual competency owner. This is also seen by the educational staff and the butchers' guild, by the vocational trainer and vocational schoolteacher (in interviews C, F, and I). Based on these first indications, it is possible to define specific areas in which a profound development of competencies within the framework

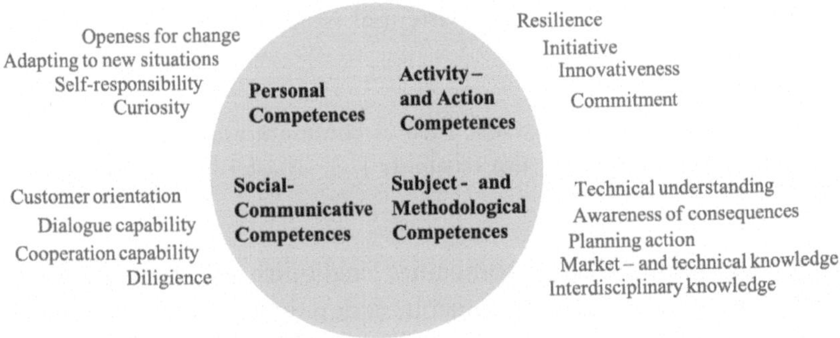

Fig. 8.3 Key competencies for the "Sustainable Butcher" (*Source* Author's own figure, referring to Heise and Erpenbeck [2007])

of vocational training can lead to improved sustainability competencies in organizations.

With regard to the further development of the identified areas for a sustainability and future- oriented competency framework, we can address these as a construct for key competency areas and corresponding sub-competencies for vocational education in the pilot project geared towards "The Sustainable Butcher" of the future (Fig. 8.3).

The outcome of the discussions with the experts already indicates a need for further qualification of trainees and apprentices which can be integrated into competency orientation to promote sustainable thinking and acting (see Fig. 8.4).

The examples in Fig. 8.4 show the link between profession-related competencies and approaches to sustainability and the corresponding sub-competencies. The initial findings within this competency model for sustainable butchers can serve as the basis for designing learning tools and learning environments that can be applied to vocational education and training.

8.5 Conclusion and Next Steps

The results that have been found so far through the interviews and literature research will be examined in close collaboration with model

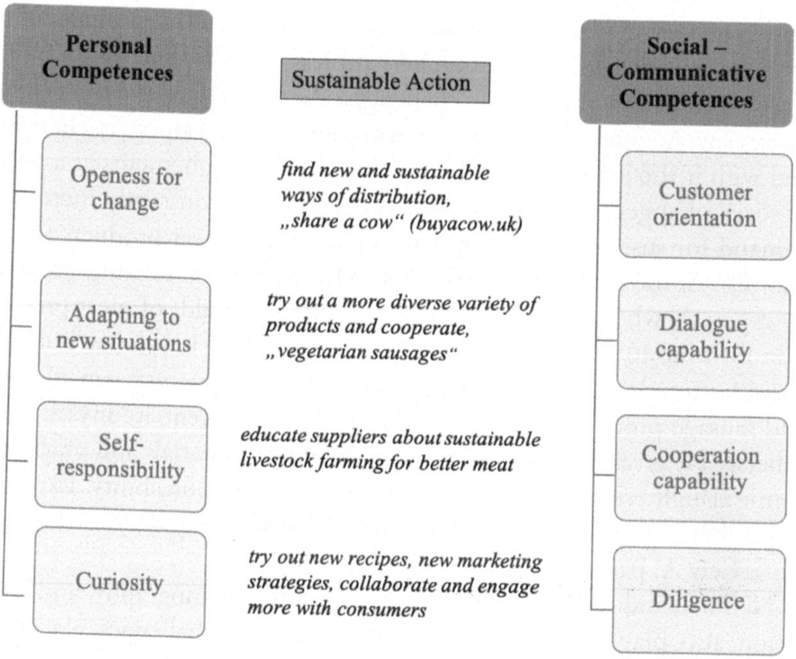

Fig. 8.4 Example for competency-related action towards sustainability (*Source* Author's own work)

enterprises and vocational trainers and will also be discussed with apprentices and trainers in upcoming workshops. In addition to the discussion on ways to implement sustainability in organizations such as small and medium-sized butcheries, the individual and specific needs of the profession also need to be integrated into new learning approaches in order to engage in a future-oriented perspective. In line with that orientation, not only professional competencies need to be addressed, but within that also a holistic perspective to create a different kind of mindset for sustainable thinking and acting. This was also stated as important future goals for the apprenticeship in butchery trade by the sustainable butcher and his wife (interview D).

Overall, this holistic view should be integrated within the competency framework and the targeted "toolbox", that needs to be developed for educational purposes within the organization. Furthermore, a broader view is needed to place the butchery profession in the wider context of its local and global aspects. The butchery profession today and in the future faces a multitude of different challenges. As highlighted by the experts (interview A, interview B), the market for meat products is changing and with it the job profile of the butcher and its requirements as a result of social changes, for example the trend towards a constantly increasing demand for sustainably and organically produced meat products (interview D). At the same time, a so-called "differentiator" is missing, as stated by expert A, who has been in business in different fields of meat production for over 40 years (interview A, paragraph 7f.). He believes butchers should strongly differentiate themselves from the mainstream of meat and sausage production by asking "How can I differentiate myself from others?" He gives the example of using other raw materials and practicing gentle slaughtering to show that a butcher takes responsibility. Expert A states that this even has a very positive effect on the quality of the meat (interview A, paragraph 7 f.).

National and international changes in politics, demography, and legislation also play a major role in influencing the challenges placed on the occupational profile (European Union 2013). In the medium-sized butchery trade, competitive pressure continues to increase due to large industrial corporations, which was also stated by several experts (interview A, B and F). We are aware of sustainability-related advantages and discussions about vegetarian and vegan diets. Since this research is a model-based attempt to implement sustainability in meat production, we will not engage with the discussion about dietary aspects at this point.

In the future, it will therefore be increasingly important for butchers to sustain demand in conventional butcher's shops by maintaining intensive customer contact and meeting special interpersonal needs (interview A, B, and E). The challenge for the butcher's job profile in concrete terms is therefore to fulfil these demands. Social and interpersonal skills are also gaining in importance (Bahl 2017) and present butchers with the challenge of acquiring and applying such skills (interview C and F). In the field of sustainable meat production, a significant trend has also been discernible together with other organic products for some years. The popularity of sustainably produced meat products or those with an organic seal has been rising steadily for years and no change in this trend is expected in the future. Today's challenges for butchers also result from the fact that the skills which are needed to meet this demand must be an essential part of the updated job profile (as stated by expert A, B, and F). This means that butchers today and also in the future need to be knowledgeable about sustainable and organic value chains and be able to apply this knowledge in a targeted and holistic manner.

The initial findings lead to the next step of competency-based learning approaches for these requirements which will be designed and tested and discussed in prototyping workshops with apprentices as well as with other different stakeholders within the companies. Concerning the group of apprentices, the butchery education experts pointed out that this interest group is very heterogenic with ambitious learners who will take over their parents' butcher shops in the future and also educationally disadvantaged learners (interview A, B, and C). What they do have in common is that they are digital natives and communicate naturally in various possibilities and situations (expert B, paragraph 15).

At the same time, learning new content in the applied business context of butchery is not easy to achieve because the daily work of butchers is tightly timed and there is no time for extra learning input (as stated in interview A and B). Learning tools should therefore focus foremost on digital and game-based formats, for example an app—concept.

Further interviews with trainers and apprentices will take place within in-house visits in businesses in Thuringia to verify our initial findings and to discuss new initiatives concerning teaching and learning approaches for the integration of sustainability not only with professional experts, but also with our main target group, the apprentices. As part of this objective, our research links the topic of transversal competency management with concrete applications in the meat industry and the craft of butchery. The ultimate aim is to provide an integrated and applied approach in the form of a "competence-based toolbox" for (re-)skilling these organizations in the context of sustainability and the future orientation of the respective businesses—starting with the apprentices first.

Acknowledgements The Project Trans-Sustain ("Transversal Competency Management for the enhancement of Sustainability in the butchers trade and in the meat processing industry") is funded by the German Federal Institute for Vocational Education and Training (BIBB) and the German Ministry of Education and Research (BMBF): HTW/21BBNE2701.

References

Anthes, Daniel. "Weniger is(s)t mehr, 'Flexitarier' wirbeln Fleisch-Industrie auf." *Forum Nachhaltig Wirtschaften* 4 (2019). Accessed February 3, 2020. https://www.forumcsr.net/News/9688/Wenigerisstmehr.html.

Auer, Thomas. *Sustainability in context of knowledge society and demography.* Zürich: Schweizer Arbeitsgeber, 2003.

Bahl, Anke. *Die professionelle Praxis der Ausbilder. Eine kulturanthropolgische Analyse.* Frankfurt: Campus Verlag, 2017.

BNE—Bildung für Nachhaltige Entwicklung. "Wie kann Bildung für nachhaltige Entwicklung in der beruflichen Bildung angewendet werden?" Accessed January 22, 2020. https://www.bne-portal.de/de/einstieg/bildungsbereiche/berufliche-bildung.

Bormann, Inka, and Gerhard de Haan (Eds.). *Kompetenzen der Bildung für nachhaltige Entwicklung*, Wiesbaden: Springer, 2008.

Bundeszentrum für Ernährung. "Fleischersatzprodukte, Seitan, Tofu, Lupine, Quorn - Das 'who is who' der Fleisch-Alternativen." Accessed January 24, 2020. https://www.bzfe.de/inhalt/fleischersatzprodukte-33298.html.

Cordova, Maria Federica, and Andrea Celone. "SDGs and innovation in the business context literature review." *Sustainability* 11(7043) (2019): 1–14. Accessed February 3, 2020. https://doi.org/10.3390/su11247043.

Dahlmeier, Matthias Patrick, Reinhardt, Kai, and Georg Schnauffer. "Die Zukunft des Kompetenzmanagements: Vorschlag für ein transversales „System-Modell" zur Kompetenzvernetzung zwischen Wissenschaft und Industrie als Voraussetzung für effektive Wissensarbeit." *GfWM Themen-Spezial* (2017): 3–28.

Deutsche UNESCO-Kommission e.V. "Nationaler Aktionsplan." Accessed August 25, 2020. https://www.bne-portal.de/de/nationaler-aktionsplan.

de Haan, Gerhard. *Gestaltungskompetenz als Kompetenzkonzept für Bildung für Nachhaltige Entwicklung*. Wiesbaden: Springer, 2008.

Dillenbourg, Pierre (Ed.). *Collaborative learning. Cognitive and computational approaches.* Oxford: Emerald, 1999.

Erpenbeck, John, and Werner Sauter. *Wertungen, Werte. Das Fieldbook für erfolgreiches Wertemanagement*. Wiesbaden: Springer, 2017.

Erpenbeck, John, and Lutz von Rosenstiel (Eds.). *Handbuch Kompetenzmessung – erkennen, verstehen und bewerten von Kompetenzen in der betrieblichen, pädagogischen uns psychologischen Praxis.* Stuttgart: Schäfer-Poeschel, 2007.

European Union. *European classification of skills/competences, qualifications and occupations. The first public release.* Publications Office of the European Union Luxembourg: European Union, 2013.

Fleischerschule - Bildungszentrum Fleischerhandwerk. "Metzgermeister". Accessed February 14, 2020. https://www.fleischerschule.de.

German Butchers' Association. Zahlen und Fakten. https://www.fleischerhandwerk.de/presse/jahrbuchzahlen-und-fakten.html. Accessed August 05, 2021.

Gomes, Giancarlo, and Rafaele Matte Wojahn. "Organizational learning capability, innovation and performance: Study in small and medium-sized enterprises (SMES)." *Revista de Administraçao* 52 (2017): 163–175. Accessed September 14, 2020. https://doi.org/10.1016/j.rausp.2016.12.003.

Hahne, Klaus. "Benötigt Berufsbildung für nachhaltige Entwicklung ein erweitertes Verständnis von Kompetenzentwicklung?" *Berufsbildung in Wissenschaft und Praxis - Nachhaltigkeit in der beruflichen Bildung* (2009): 13–17.

Heise, Volker, and John Erpenbeck. *Kompetenzmanagement: Methoden, Vorgehen, KODE(R) und KODE(R)X im Praxistest (Kompetenzmanagement in der Praxis).* Münster: Waxmann, 2007.

Hopkins, Charles. "Reflections on 20+ years of ESD." *Journal of Education for Sustainable Development* 6(1) (2009): 21–35.

IATP—Institute for Agriculture and Trade Policy. "How big meat and dairy are heating up the planet." Accessed February 2, 2020. https://www.iatp.org/emissions-impossible.

Ingenbleek, Paul T.M., and Yhuang Zhao. "The Vegetarian Butcher: on its way to becoming the world's biggest 'meat' producer?". *International Food and Agribusiness Management Review* 22(2) (2019): 295–307. Accessed February 11, 2020. https://doi.org/10.22434/IFAMR2018.005.

Kuckartz, Ulf. *Qualitative Inhaltsanalyse: Methoden, Praxis, Computerunterstützung* (3rd edition). Weinheim und Basel: Beltz Juventa, 2016.

Mayring, Phillip. Qualitative Inhaltsanalyse. In *Dorsch Lexikon der Psychologie*. Edited by Markus Antonius Wirtz: 1278. (16 edition). Bern: Huber Hogrefe, 2013.

Müller, Martin, and Sara Siakala. *Nachhaltigkeitslieferkettenmanagement. Von der Strategie zur Umsetzung*. Berlin: de Gruyter, 2020.

North, Klaus, and Kai Reinhardt. *Kompetenzmanagement in der Praxis: Mitarbeiterkompetenzen systematisch identifizieren, nutzen und entwickeln*. Wiesbaden: Gabler, 2005.

North, Klaus, Reinhardt, Kai, and Barbara Sieber-Suter. *Kompetenzmanagement in der Praxis: Mitarbeiterkompetenzen systematisch identifizieren, nutzen und entwickeln* (3rd edition). Wiesbaden: Springer, 2018.

Prahalad, C.K., and Gary Hamel. "The core competence of the corporation." *Harvard Business Review* 68(3) (1990): 79–91. Accessed February 2, 2020. https://ssrn.com/abstract=1505251.

Rehberg, Carina. "Die Clean Eating Methode." Accessed February 10, 2020. https://www.zentrum-der-gesundheit.de/clean-eating-ia.html.

Rieckmann, Marko. "Learning to transform the world: Key competencies in ESD." In *Issued and trends in education for sustainable development*, edited by Alexander Leicht et al., 39–59. Paris: United Nations Educational, Scientific and Cultural Organization, 2018.

Schulze Steinmann, Matthias. "Big brother is watching Kuh." *F3-farm, food, future*. Summer issue 2019, 55.

Teece, David, Peteraf, Margaret A., and Sovieh Leih. "Dynamic capabilities and organizational agility: Risk, uncertainty and strategy in the innovation economy." *California Management Review* 58(4) (2016): 13–35. Accessed February 13, 2020.

Tulder, Rob V. (Ed.). *Business & the sustainable development goals: A framework for effective corporate involvement*. Rotterdam School of Management. Rotterdam: Erasmus University Press, 2003.

UN—United Nations. "Decade of action." 2019. Accessed 14 February 2020. https://www.un.org/sustainabledevelopment/decade-of-action/.

UNESCO "What is ESD". https://en.unesco.org/themes/education-sustainable-development/what-is-esd. Accessed February 3, 2020.

Umweltbundesamt. *Die Zukunft im Blick: Fleisch der Zukunft*. Dessau-Roßlau: Umweltbundesamt, 2019.

Wals, Arjen E.J., and Peter B. Corcoran. *Learning for sustainability in times of accelerating change*. Wageningen: Wageningen Academic Publishers, 2012.

9

In Search of Morphogenetic Mechanisms to Transform Marketing Systems from Linear to Circular Structural Arrangements

Nicola J. R. Thomas

9.1 Introduction

The need for sustainability challenges established production and consumption processes that shape global marketing systems. The traditional linear take-make-dispose model generates significant economic opportunities. However, these gains generate significant social and environmental costs, including unsustainable natural resource use, ecosystem degradation and social injustices (Murray et al. 2017). Proposed as a sustainable alternative, the Circular Economy (hereafter CE) seeks to transform market structures, resources and material flows from linear to circular arrangements. While CE draws on theoretical approaches largely developed by environmental economists (e.g. Andersen 2007) and industrial ecologists (Saavedra et al. 2018), scant theoretical attention has been paid to how marketing systems transition and transform from a

N. J. R. Thomas (✉)
De Montfort University, Leicester, UK
e-mail: nicola@dissertology.com

C. Simões et al. (eds.), *Corporate Responsibility, Sustainability and Markets*, Palgrave Studies in Governance, Leadership and Responsibility,
https://doi.org/10.1007/978-3-030-79660-0_9

socio-cultural perspective (Hobson 2016). As humans, not structures, act (Akram 2013), this lack of theorizing restrains society's ability to shift towards a circular economy. To this end, this book chapter explores the application of Archer's social realist theory, The Morphogenetic Approach (Archer 1982), to better understand how these systemic shifts could be better realized in the global fashion system.

This chapter's core contribution to the book's theme, namely Corporate Responsibility, Sustainability and Markets, lies in its systemic identification of how human agency and structures interact to reproduce linearity, that is, it reveals what is holding back the sustainable transition to a circular business model. It also identifies those interactions that are, or could be, responsible for transitioning the system towards circularity. Simply put, its research sheds light on why CE's uptake currently remains low, despite its broad market appeal.

The need to transition to a circular economy is now widely accepted among firms, institutions and academics (Ghisellini et al. 2016). While CE is prevalent in today's business discourse, its need was recognized five decades ago by Kenneth Boulding. From an environmental economics perspective, Boulding (1966) proposed a 'spaceman economy' where society is focused on 'stock maintenance, and any technological change which results in the maintenance of a given total stock with a lessened throughput (that is, less production and consumption) [as] clearly a gain'. Two decades later Pearce and Turner (1990) coined the term circular economy where underpriced or unpriced externalities are internalized within the economy to sustain human, economic and environmental processes and activities.

While CE's roots originate in environmental economics, and many schools of thought now tackle CE issues (Zink and Geyer 2017), the field is dominated by industrial ecology. Here, the material and metabolic pathways of industrial processes are decoupled from environmental systems, by closing the material and energy loops inherent to industry systems and processes. More recently, CE has expanded by drawing on related concepts. These include: 'cradle to cradle' (McDonough and Braungart 2009), regenerative design (Cole et al. 2013), biomimicry (Benyus 1997), the sharing economy (Benkler 2004), product-service systems (Tukker 2015) and the performance economy (Stahel 2016). As

CE has morphed into an umbrella conceptualization, this chapter adopts the widely cited definition by Ellen Macarthur Foundation (2013):

> an industrial system that is restorative or regenerative by intention and design. It replaces the 'end-of-life' concept with restoration, shifts towards the use of renewable energy, eliminates the use of toxic chemicals, which impair reuse, and aims for the elimination of waste through the superior design of materials, products, systems, and, within this, business models.

As CE commits to innovating business models, this demands radical systemic change. However, while research must give due attention to system structures and their arrangements, such as technological processes, there is a need to move beyond the tendency to view the world as an engineered system (Zink and Geyer 2017). Instead, attention is equally warranted towards understanding human agency and social interactions with market structures (Murray et al. 2017).

9.2 Research Background

Extant research focused on transitioning to a circular economy is largely focused at the macro level. These studies tend to focus on national initiatives, across economic blocks, in particular the European Union (McDowall et al. 2017), or on regional developments, such as eco parks and 'industrial symbiosis' clusters (Mathews and Tan 2011). An emerging macro trend considers social structures. Prominent among these are institutional factors, where several studies (e.g. Dubey et al. 2016) find that external pressures, such as coercive pressures (e.g. derived from government policies, market demand and competitors), normative pressures (e.g. perceived industry norms) and mimetic pressures, where entities mimic system actor behaviors, collectively place macro, top-down pressures on downstream 'actors', such as firms, to adopt circular practices. These institutional pressures can act as a barrier, for instance, by stifling innovation (Walker et al. 2008), by lacking enforcement or by constituting highly complex, overlapping or fragmented regulations (Tura et al. 2019). However, an apparent commonality at the macro level is the adherence to the social fact paradigm, where 'a social fact is any way of acting, whether fixed or not, capable of exerting over the individual an external constraint' (Durkheim 1982, p. 59). From this perspective, the role of human agency is either rejected, or neglected, or at least remains unclear how system actors—from manufacturers, recyclers, managers to citizen-consumers—reproduce or transform these institutional and macroeconomic structures.

At the firm level, both macro 'top-down' factors and those 'bottom-up' needs of its customers need to be considered alongside its organizational environment and employee needs. For instance, a company's culture pertains to a firm's ethos, values and habits towards CE (Liu and Bai 2014). While mostly cited as a barrier, it may, with experience, become a CE enabler (Rizos et al. 2016). Furthermore, firms committed to sustainability are more likely to adopt CE activities (Guldmann and Huulgaard 2020). However, for some firms, structural restraints are more problematic, irrespective of company culture or experience. Barriers include a lack of capital and information, technological know-how, as well as bureaucratic burdens (Rizos et al. 2016). Studies also focus on employee agency. For instance, employees can struggle to navigate firmly embedded linear processes if 'business as usual' remains the implicit company norm (Guldmann and Huulgaard 2020). Furthermore, while top-management support for CE is identified as a key enabler of employee CE efforts, so too is building effective teamwork strategies and the provision of cross-level employee training to provide the necessary skills to fully support CE initiatives (Kurilova-Palisaitiene et al. 2018). However, a dearth of research theorizes how company culture-employee interactions shape emergent outcomes. Moreover, cross-level research tends to undertheorize agency-structural interactions.

Several CE studies also focus on the consumer. Those CE specific behaviors empirically studied include consumer willingness to pay for products made from recycled content (Magnier et al. 2019), leasing and renting products (Raihanian Mashhadi et al. 2019), engaging in waste related practices (Hebrok and Heidenstrøm 2019), purchasing remanufactured products (Singhal et al. 2019), sharing and collaborative consumption practices (Khan and Rundle-Thiele 2019), repair and maintenance strategies (Ackermann 2018) and participating in product take-back schemes (Kant Hvass and Pedersen 2019). Furthermore, due to CE's unique particularities in terms of challenging the dominant ownership norm (e.g. sharing, renting, leasing), several novel psycho-sociological constructs have emerged. For instance, lack of service familiarity, customer confusion and an apparent reluctance to sacrifice the benefits of ownership (Poppelaars et al. 2018). Nonetheless, at the micro level, despite a few notable exceptions (e.g. Hebrok and Heidenstrøm 2019; Hazen et al. 2017; Mylan et al. 2016), the majority of consumer-centric CE studies adhere to the agency paradigm, which overlooks consumer interdependencies with other systemic levels, for example, firms and macro forces (Thomas 2018). While these differences may be in part due to paradigm incommensurability, and/or a pragmatic division of labor between micro, meso and macro perspectives, transitioning from linear to circular arrangements demands a whole systems perspective.

9.2.1 Meta-Theoretical Approach

To resolve this apparent incommensurability between agency and structure, this study adopted the Morphogenetic Approach (Archer 1982). Its core premise is that any agent, individual or corporate, enters an existing situation (T^1), where existing structures and culture will condition social interactions. However, while human agency is constrained and/or enabled by situational constraints during social interactions (T^2–T^3), humans can reproduce or transform structures (T^4), due to their inherent agency. As morphogenesis is informed by critical realism, it adheres to the stance that agency-structural interactions and systemic outcomes are context and activity dependent. This study is contextualized to the global fashion industry, as fashion circularity is now recognized as a strategic imperative (McKinsey & Company 2019). Its activity focuses on shifting from an ownership to a rental business model. This attention is warranted given that CE activities need to maximize the value of product use before remanufacturing is considered (Korhonen et al. 2018). For instance, the UK Government's Audit Committee (2019) reports that more than $500 billion of value is lost every year due to clothing underutilization and lack of recycling. Renting, rather than owning clothes, therefore provides an opportunity to maximize value while reducing environmental impact.

Using the Scopus database, initial broad searches were made to identify key search terms to maximize relevant inclusivity. The final Boolean search consisted of: 'fashion' OR 'apparel' AND 'product service system' OR 'collaborative consumption' OR 'rent*', OR 'subscri*' to identify articles published in English between 2004 and 2019. This 15 year time frame was considered substantial, given that circular fashion is a relatively new term in the fashion industry (Green Strategy, n.d.). All abstracts of identified papers were manually inspected for relevance, by checking whether the paper addressed at least one barrier and/or incentive to participate in a fashion rental business model. The final consideration set consisted of 28 academic papers. Given the study's purpose, each paper was thoroughly examined within NVivo 12, where focused coding was employed to identify units of information belonging to two parent codes, namely enabling or constraining factors, and their nested three sub-codes, namely agency, structure and culture. As guided by the Morphogenetic Approach, causation coding was then undertaken to identify and understand interactions between agency, structure and culture (T^2–T^3), and to understand why particular outcomes (T^4) came about. Causal coding examined content for antecedent (e.g. motives) and mediating variables, as well as consequences and context. Where explicit causation information was missing or unclear, retroductive reasoning was undertaken. For example, could X occur without Y happening first? Causation pathways were iteratively visualized using causal loop diagramming (CLD) with Kumu.io mapping software. Conventional CLD notation guidelines were adhered to (e.g. Sedlacko et al. 2012), where coded variables are connected by arrows denoting the causal influences between them. Each causal link was assigned polarity, either positive (+) or negative (−) to indicate how each variable changes when the preceding variable changes. A positive link is assigned, for instance, where trust increases (or decreases) lead to increases (or decreases) in loyalty. In contrast, negative links are assigned where a variable increase (or decreases), and leads to decreases (or increases). As such, link polarities do not describe variable behavior, they instead describe what would happen *if* there were a change. Moreover, important loops were highlighted by a loop identifier, either positive (amplifying) or negative (balancing). It is important to note that positive loop identifiers do not necessarily consist of only positive links as they can contain an *even* number of negative links. Furthermore, positive loop identifiers should not necessarily be confused with positive effects; a positive loop can denote the amplification of negative impacts. Lastly, due to the unwieldy size of the emergent CLD, the final task involved splitting the overall diagram into four contextually relevant CLDs, or mechanisms, that work interdependently to reproduce or transform the system under study.

9.3 Results and Discussion

Emergent findings identified four mechanisms, deliberated below, that synergistically interact to reproduce the linear fashion system, as well as explain the emergence of circular fashion activities that are currently constrained to a small scale.

9.3.1 Egocentric Motivational Push and Pull

Consumers experience a motivational 'push and pull' when considering their intentions to rent fashion (Fig. 9.1). Extant research implicates a mix of utilitarian motivations when consumers consider product-service characteristics such as cost, convenience, selection choices, information availability, lack of sociality and product customization (Ramkumar and Woo 2018). Furthermore, rental intentions can also be amplified by hedonistic motivations. These include keeping up with trends, stimulation, value, authority and status. Collectively, these motivations positively impact rental attitudes, and in turn, influence rental intentions (Ramkumar and Woo 2018). However, while these motivations implicate felt gratifications, people also integrate risks, and other factors, into their decision-making processes.

As Fig. 9.1 conveys, perceived risks can override intentional agency by dampening motivations. Three key types of risks are evidenced, namely

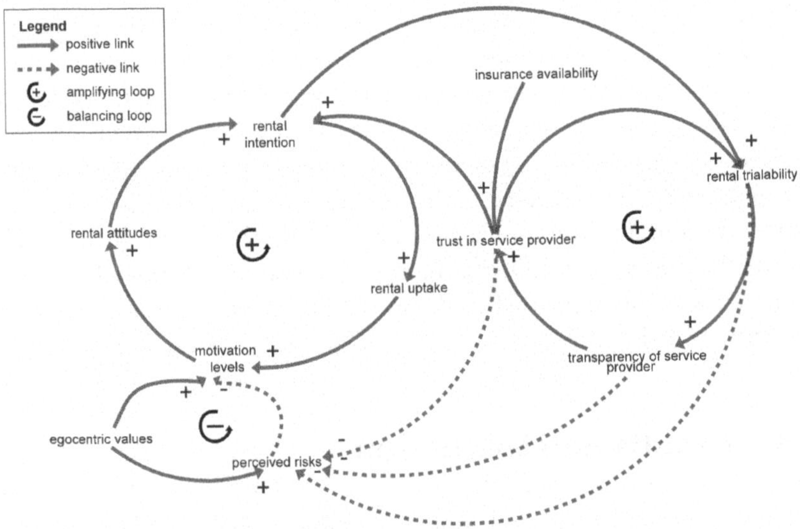

Fig. 9.1 Egocentric motivational push and pull mechanism

financial, hygiene and performance (Lang 2018; Becker-Leifhold and Iran 2018). Perceived financial risks occur when consumers fear a financial loss. While renting does appeal due to lower upfront investments (Schaefers et al. 2016), some consumers fear renting is a waste of money, for example, due a lack of ownership, short usage periods, unmet expectations as well as perceived liabilities for damaged rented items (Lang 2018). Likewise, hygiene risks (e.g. mites, disease, odors) can also override any potential rental advantages (Becker-Leifhold and Iran 2018). Hygiene risks, among others, also contribute to perceived performance risks, where rental products may not live up to expectations.

To avoid egocentric motivations and risk perceptions 'cancelling each other out', transparency of, and trust in service providers needs to be strengthened to reduce the causal power of risk perceptions (Armstrong et al. 2015). Insurance, too, could build trust, and override liability risks, if effectively communicated to end-users (Fernandes et al. 2019). Furthermore, Woo and Ramkumar (2017) propose as 'exploratory product acquisition', where consumers could sensitize themselves to risk. This could be achieved by hedonic eliciting surprises, for instance 'what's in the box?', or more likely, by offering trialability to reduce risk avoidance (Armstrong et al. 2016; Pedersen and Netter 2015).

9.3.2 Fluid Transformation of Self and Ownership

Operating in concert with egocentric motivations is the dynamic interplay between self and society's dominant ownership norm. Ownership's dominance arises, in part, from the emotional attachment consumers place on products (McNeill and Venter 2019), for instance by personifying the wearer or by embodying memories (Petersen and Riisberg 2017). While studies infer consumer 'need for uniqueness' can lead to emotional attachment to products and as such counter interest in renting due to materialism (Lang et al. 2016), fluidity of self-presentation, enabled by renting, could break this cycle (Fig. 9.2). This is where a rental user can differentially represent themselves for self and others, and therefore help rental users to both 'stand out' (self image) as well as 'fit in' due to the constant need to compare self with others and enhance social identity. In terms of social identity, renting can help the user to 'fit in' at a special event, being in a place with a distinct identity (work, play

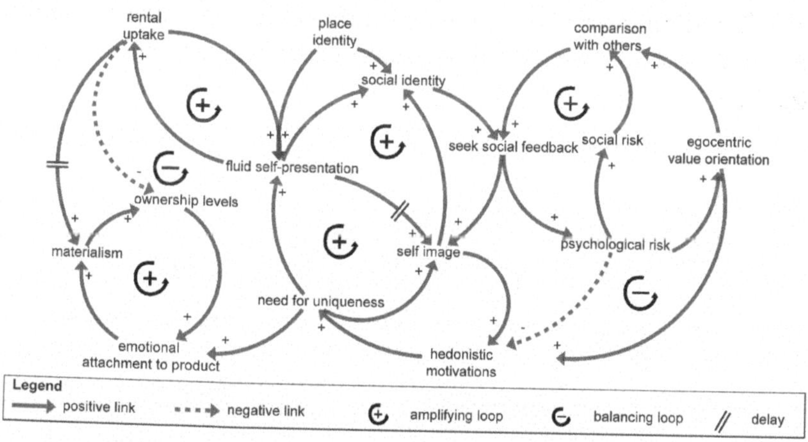

Fig. 9.2 Fluid transformation of self and ownership mechanism

or neighborhood) or entering a new life stage, such as teenager, pregnancy (Loussaïef et al. 2019). By fitting in, this also serves to reduce an individual's sense of risk, both psychologically and socially.

As shown in Fig. 9.2, renting can nurture a temporary extended self, and longer term, this fluidity could stabilize into preferences, and as such, transform both self image, and indirectly undermine the ownership norm. However, further research is needed to ensure that rental enabled fluidity of self does not increase materialism, for example, by renting far many more clothes than a person would normally own. If this causal link is substantiated this would call into question whether renting holds the causal power to act as a 'self-regulatory device' to curb excessive consumption (Petersen and Riisberg 2017).

Overall, this second mechanism indicates that increasing the contagion of rental use could be amplified by fluid self-presentation, by enhancing both self and social identity. However, to understand whether this amplification could occur, research must also consider the availability and quality of the rental service experience.

9.3.3 Experiential Rental Norm Amplification

Research indicates significant, but as yet unrealized potential to amplify the mass appeal and uptake of the fashion rental proposition. As Fig. 9.3

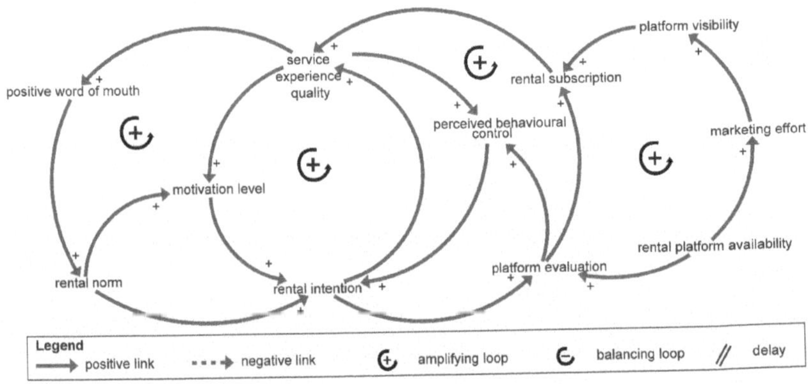

Fig. 9.3 Experiential rental norm amplification mechanism

demonstrates, rental intentions will remain unrealized if service platforms are unavailable, or if present, hindered by a lack of marketing efforts and platform visibility (Choi and He 2019). Therefore, while a few rental firms are attempting to disrupt the fashion industry (e.g. Rent-The-Runway, YCloset), their numbers are overshadowed by those reproducing the ownership model. Moreover, perceived behavioral control will fail to trigger rental intentions when rental models are non-existent or still in their infancy (Lang and Armstrong 2018). However, if available, particularly with evaluation options enabled by trialability (Tao and Xu 2018), this could amplify both perceived behavioral control and rental subscriptions. Moreover, positive WOM towards the relative advantages afforded by rental products and the subscription service itself, could reduce uncertainty in others (McKinney and Shin 2016). Therefore, positive word of mouth could amplify further consumer acceptance and erode the dominant ownership norm (Adam 2018).

Whether or not positive WOM is generated depends on the quality of the rental experience itself, particularly as customer satisfaction lies at the heart of the service economy (Hu et al. 2014). Rental service experiences will depend on the affordances of the technological platforms, as well as the overall service experience. In this regard, Tao and Xu (2018) find that complicated sign-up and cancellation processes, will deter from the experience. Furthermore, online reviews indicate the importance of service quality, including responsiveness, service reliability, timeliness, efficiency and the provision of information that is fit for task (McKinney and Shin 2016). Nonetheless, given the rental experience is dependent on a platform's existence, those factors that enable and/or constrain their availability in the marketplace, are considered more in depth next.

9.3.4 Constrained Firm Capabilities

Several interdependent factors currently constrain a firm's adaptive capabilities to meet current and potential rental market demands. The industry lacks the dynamic capabilities to respond effectively to rental demands, as its corporate agentic and structural dependencies are dominated by ownership, rather than rental norms (Fig. 9.4).

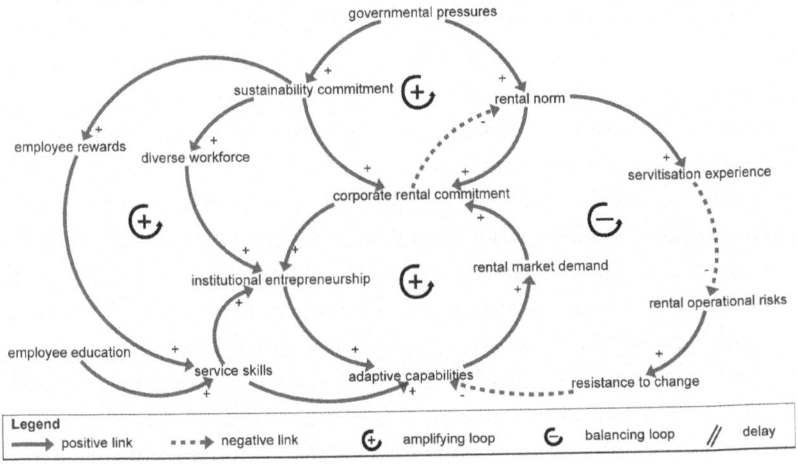

Fig. 9.4 Constrained firm capabilities mechanism

Research suggests a culture of institutional entrepreneurship is important to enable circular fashion (Cook and Hodges 2015). Yet despite the fashion industry's hypercompetitiveness, sustainable innovation rates remain slow (Global Fashion Agenda 2019). Moreover, its adaptive capacity is constrained by a lack of servitization skills and experience (Fig. 9.4), such as those involved in service transactions, laundry and maintenance and centralized disposal. The study by Adam (2018), for instance, strongly suggests that firms already successfully implementing rental service provision differ from ownership driven firms along several important dimensions. Firstly, rental providers enjoy more diverse, incentivized and well-educated workforces. Educated employees are more open to experiences, and a diverse, widely experienced workforce, particularly those recruited from service industries, are far more likely to adapt to and experiment with the rental model. Moreover, employees rewarded by profit-sharing, extensive training and employment security, are characteristic of those firms committed to the rental business model. Yet these 'ingredients for rental success' contrast starkly with current working conditions in the fashion industry; high employee turnover rates and a low wage culture are endemic (Lee and Ha-Brookshire 2017).

Dynamically coupled with employee commitment is an organization's corporate commitment to ownership and/or rental market demands. Unsurprisingly, those companies already committed to sustainability are more likely to commit to rental business models (Adam et al. 2017). However, this factor alone is insufficient to leverage robust commitments to rental. If a firm's strategic and operational focus remains implicitly wedded to the ownership model, and in the absence of governmental pressure, a lack of investment, perceived operational risks and resistance to change, the linear fashion business model will continue to prevail. Given this context, extant research strongly suggests many firms still lack the dynamic capabilities, internal and external pressures to enable a transition to circular business models. Nonetheless, with an increasing number of companies volunteering to experiment with rental (e.g. Business of Fashion, n.d.), and with more sustainable, rewarding recruitment and human resource strategies (Adam 2018), early adopter success could gradually break down the dominant ownership norm.

9.4 Conclusion and Recommendations

Emergent systemic findings, as guided by Archer's (1982) Morphogenetic Approach, strongly suggest why evidenced agentic commitments to a rental business model are not being realized. Despite fashion brands committing to CE oriented business models (Global Fashion Agenda, n.d.), several systemic constraints are holding back the transformational potential of circular economic principles in the global fashion industry.

Prominent among these systemic constraints is the friction caused by 'business as usual'. Exacerbated by a lack of external pressures, such as absent leadership from governmental actors, the fashion industry's traditional path dependency on product ownership means that transitioning to a rental proposition is unlikely to manifest without significant structural change. Yet structural changes are unlikely to materialize unless corporate agency is fully aligned with, and acts upon, CE principles. Nonetheless, with an increasing number of firms now bucking this 'business as usual' trend, mimetic and normative pressures could serve to undermine the dominant ownership norm, while increasing the likelihood of governmental and economic support if early adopter transitions prove successful. Several points of leverage emerged from this study, and together indicate the need to empower all system agents—consumers, employees, human resource managers, top management, rental marketers and policy makers—to realize this change.

Caution, however, is warranted in view of the paucity of research that considers the unintended consequences of CE initiatives (Zink and Geyer 2017). By way of example, while emergent findings suggest how the dominant ownership norm could be diminished, they also suggest that egocentric driven materialism could thrive in CE scenarios. As overly materialist values undermine human wellbeing (Dittmar et al. 2014), further research should explore whether the rental model exacerbates materialism, overconsumption and poor wellbeing outcomes. Moreover, while early research suggests that biocentric values hold little sway over consumer preferences for rental, biospheric values and concerns could help buffer the potential of materialistic driven rebound effects.

Collectively, this study contributes an interrelated series of evidence-based dynamic hypotheses, as depicted by causal loop diagrams, that require empirical testing to substantiate findings. Yet extant research is dominated by reductionist approaches, for example, by undertaking consumer or employee surveys to discover law-like, linear regularities in rental intentions. To move forward, a key recommendation for future research involves participatory modelling (e.g. Voinov and Bousquet 2010). Research demonstrates this approach can: (1) foster consensus and collaborative learning experiences between different stakeholders; (2) enhance strategic and citizen decision making, and (3) aid both theoretical development and system improvements. Moreover, by taking a hybrid modelling approach (Lättilä et al. 2010), research could explore how agent decision making gives rise to emergent structural-cultural changes, and if combined with system dynamic modelling, the opportunity to understand systemic changes at the industry level over different morphogenetic cycles. This type of approach is needed, as single studies focused on specific system levels, cannot foresee how changes in one part of the system, via interdependencies, cause knock-on effects, for better or worse, on other, sometimes distant parts of the system.

In conclusion, this chapter's value lies in its systemic exploration of how agency and systemic structures currently interact to reproduce the dominant linear system. Importantly, it also provides valuable insights into how systemic changes are beginning to, or could emerge. Extant research, systemically mined for insights, indicate several 'virtuous circles' could be leveraged and amplified, and therefore demonstrates how transformations from linear to circular economic arrangements could be achieved. Further research, investment, external and stakeholder pressure is required to not only aid better understanding, but to spread and accelerate these positive early transitions towards a circular economy.

References

Ackermann, Laura. 2018. "Design for Product Care: Enhancing Consumers' Repair and Maintenance Activities." *Design Journal* 21 (4): 543–51. https://doi.org/10.1080/14606925.2018.1469331.

Adam, Marcus. 2018. "The Role of Human Resource Management (HRM) for the Implementation of Sustainable Product-Service Systems (PSS)—An Analysis of Fashion Retailers." *Sustainability (Switzerland)* 10 (7): 2518. https://doi.org/10.3390/su10072518.

Adam, Marcus, Jochen Strähle, and Matthias Freise. 2017. "The Interaction of Product-Service Systems (PSS) and Corporate Environmental Management (CEM): Can PSS Drive Today's Fashion Industry toward More Environmental Sustainability?" *Service Science* 9 (3): 235–49. https://doi.org/10.1287/serv.2017.0182.

Akram, Sadiya. 2013. "Fully Unconscious and Prone to Habit: The Characteristics of Agency in the Structure and Agency Dialectic." *Journal for the Theory of Social Behaviour* 43 (1): 45–65. https://doi.org/10.1111/jtsb.12002.

Andersen, Mikael Skou. 2007. "An Introductory Note on the Environmental Economics of the Circular Economy." *Sustainability Science* 2 (1): 133–40. https://doi.org/10.1007/s11625-006-0013-6.

Antunes, Paula, Rui Santos, and Nuno Videira. 2006. "Participatory Decision Making for Sustainable Development—The Use of Mediated Modelling

Techniques." *Land Use Policy* 23 (1): 44–52. https://doi.org/10.1016/j.landusepol.2004.08.014.

Archer, Margaret S. 1982. "Morphogenesis Versus Structuration: On Combining Structure and Action." *The British Journal of Sociology* 33 (4): 455. https://doi.org/10.2307/589357.

Armstrong, Cosette M., Kirsi Niinimäki, Sari Kujala, Essi Karell, and Chunmin Lang. 2015. "Sustainable Product-Service Systems for Clothing: Exploring Consumer Perceptions of Consumption Alternatives in Finland." *Journal of Cleaner Production* 97 (June): 30–39. https://doi.org/10.1016/j.jclepro.2014.01.046.

Armstrong, Cosette M., Kirsi Niinimäki, Chunmin Lang, and Sari Kujala. 2016. "A Use-Oriented Clothing Economy? Preliminary Affirmation for Sustainable Clothing Consumption Alternatives." *Sustainable Development* 24 (1): 18–31. https://doi.org/10.1002/sd.1602.

Audit Committee, Environmental. 2019. "Fixing Fashion: Clothing Consumption and Sustainability Sixteenth Report of Session 2017–19 FIXING FASHION: Clothing Consumption and Sustainability." https://publications.parliament.uk/pa/cm201719/cmselect/cmenvaud/1952/1952.pdf.

Becker-Leifhold, Carolin, and Samira Iran. 2018. "Collaborative Fashion Consumption—Drivers, Barriers and Future Pathways." *Journal of Fashion Marketing and Management* 22 (2): 189–208. https://doi.org/10.1108/JFMM-10-2017-0109.

Becker-Leifhold, Carolin Viktoria. 2018. "The Role of Values in Collaborative Fashion Consumption—A Critical Investigation Through the Lenses of the Theory of Planned Behavior." *Journal of Cleaner Production* 199 (October): 781–91. https://doi.org/10.1016/j.jclepro.2018.06.296.

Benkler, Yochai. 2004. "Sharing Nicely: On Shareable Goods and the Emergence of Sharing as a Modality of Economic Production." *Yale Law Journal* 114. https://heinonline.org/HOL/Page?handle=hein.journals/ylr114&id=291&div=18&collection=journals.

Benyus, Janine M. 1997. *Biomimicry: Innovation Inspired by Nature*. Morrow.

Boulding, Kenneth E. 1966. "The Economics of the Coming Spaceship Earth." In *Environmental Quality in a Growing Economy*, 3–14. Resources for the Future/Johns Hopkins University Press.

Business of Fashion. n.d. "Rental." Accessed November 30, 2019. https://www.businessoffashion.com/articles/tags/topics/rental.

Choi, Tsan Ming, and Yanyan He. 2019. "Peer-to-Peer Collaborative Consumption for Fashion Products in the Sharing Economy: Platform

Operations." *Transportation Research Part E: Logistics and Transportation Review* 126 (June): 49–65. https://doi.org/10.1016/j.tre.2019.03.016.

Cole, Raymond J., Amy Oliver, and John Robinson. 2013. "Regenerative Design, Socio-Ecological Systems and Co-Evolution." *Building Research & Information* 41 (2): 237–47. https://doi.org/10.1080/09613218.2013.747130.

Cook, Sasikarn C, and Nancy Hodges. 2015. "Exploring Non-Ownership Apparel Consumption Through Online Fashion Product Rental Services: An Application of Institutional Theory." Vol. 12. https://lib.dr.iastate.edu/itaa_proceedings/2015/posters/20.

Dittmar, Helga, Rod Bond, Megan Hurst, and Tim Kasser. 2014. "The Relationship Between Materialism and Personal Well-Being: A Meta-Analysis." *Journal of Personality and Social Psychology* 107 (5): 879–924. https://doi.org/10.1037/a0037409.

Dubey, Rameshwar, Angappa Gunasekaran, Stephen J. Childe, Thanos Papadopoulos, Samuel Fosso Wamba, and Malin Song. 2016. "Towards a Theory of Sustainable Consumption and Production: Constructs and Measurement." *Resources, Conservation and Recycling* 106 (January): 78–89. https://doi.org/10.1016/j.resconrec.2015.11.008.

Durkheim, Emile. 1982. *The Rules of Sociological Method*. The Free Press.

Fernandes, Solange, José Lucas, Maria José Madeira, Alexandra Cruchinho, and Isabela Dias Honório. 2019. "Circular and Collaborative Economies as a Propulsion of Environmental Sustainability in the New Fashion Business Models." In *Lecture Notes in Electrical Engineering*, Vol. 505, 925–32. Springer Verlag. https://doi.org/10.1007/978-3-319-91334-6_127.

Foundation, Ellen Macarthur. 2013. "Towards the Circular Economy". https://www.ellenmacarthurfoundation.org/assets/downloads/publications/Ellen-MacArthur-Foundation-Towards-the-Circular-Economy-vol.1.pdf.

Ghisellini, Patrizia, Catia Cialani, and Sergio Ulgiati. 2016. "A Review on Circular Economy: The Expected Transition to a Balanced Interplay of Environmental and Economic Systems." *Journal of Cleaner Production* 114 (February): 11–32. https://doi.org/10.1016/j.jclepro.2015.09.007.

"Global Fashion Agenda—2020 Commitment." n.d. Accessed December 1, 2019. https://www.globalfashionagenda.com/commitment/.

"Global Fashion Agenda—Pulse 2019." n.d. Accessed November 30, 2019. https://www.globalfashionagenda.com/pulse-2019-update/#.

Guldmann, Eva, and Rikke Dorothea Huulgaard. 2020. "Barriers to Circular Business Model Innovation: A Multiple-Case Study." *Journal of Cleaner*

Production 243 (January): 118–160. https://doi.org/10.1016/j.jclepro.2019.118160.

Hazen, Benjamin T., Diane A. Mollenkopf, and Yacan Wang. 2017. "Remanufacturing for the Circular Economy: An Examination of Consumer Switching Behavior." *Business Strategy and the Environment* 26 (4): 451–64. https://doi.org/10.1002/bse.1929.

Hebrok, Marie, and Nina Heidenstrøm. 2019. "Contextualising Food Waste Prevention—Decisive Moments within Everyday Practices." *Journal of Cleaner Production* 210 (February): 1435–48. https://doi.org/10.1016/j.jclepro.2018.11.141.

Hobson, Kersty. 2016. "Closing the Loop or Squaring the Circle? Locating Generative Spaces for the Circular Economy." *Progress in Human Geography* 40 (1): 88–104. https://doi.org/10.1177/0309132514566342.

Hu, Zhi-Hua, Qing Li, Xian-Juan Chen, and Yan-Feng Wang. 2014. "Sustainable Rent-Based Closed-Loop Supply Chain for Fashion Products." *Sustainability* 6 (10): 7063–88. https://doi.org/10.3390/su6107063.

Kant Hvass, Kerli, and Esben Rahbek Gjerdrum Pedersen. 2019. "Toward Circular Economy of Fashion: Experiences from a Brand's Product Take-Back Initiative." *Journal of Fashion Marketing and Management* 23 (3): 345–65. https://doi.org/10.1108/JFMM-04-2018-0059.

Khan, Jashim, and Sharyn Rundle-Thiele. 2019. "Factors Explaining Shared Clothes Consumption in China: Individual Benefit or Planet Concern?" *International Journal of Nonprofit and Voluntary Sector Marketing* 24 (4): 1465–4520. https://doi.org/10.1002/nvsm.1652.

Korhonen, Jouni, Antero Honkasalo, and Jyri Seppälä. 2018. "Circular Economy: The Concept and Its Limitations." *Ecological Economics* 143 (January): 37–46. https://doi.org/10.1016/j.ecolecon.2017.06.041.

Kurilova-Palisaitiene, Jelena, Erik Sundin, and Bonnie Poksinska. 2018. "Remanufacturing Challenges and Possible Lean Improvements." *Journal of Cleaner Production* 172 (January): 3225–36. https://doi.org/10.1016/j.jclepro.2017.11.023.

Lang, Chunmin. 2018. "Perceived Risks and Enjoyment of Access-Based Consumption: Identifying Barriers and Motivations to Fashion Renting." *Fashion and Textiles* 5 (1). https://doi.org/10.1186/s40691-018-0139-z.

Lang, Chunmin, Cosette M. Armstrong, and Chuanlan Liu. 2016. "Creativity and Sustainable Apparel Retail Models: Does Consumers' Tendency for Creative Choice Counter-Conformity Matter in Sustainability?" *Fashion and Textiles* 3 (1). https://doi.org/10.1186/s40691-016-0076-7.

Lang, Chunmin, and Cosette M. Joyner Armstrong. 2018. "Fashion Leadership and Intention Toward Clothing Product-Service Retail Models." *Journal of Fashion Marketing and Management* 22 (4): 571–87. https://doi.org/10.1108/JFMM-12-2017-0142.

Lättilä, Lauri, Per Hilletofth, and Bishan Lin. 2010. "Hybrid Simulation Models—When, Why, How?" *Expert Systems with Applications* 37 (12): 7969–75. https://doi.org/10.1016/j.eswa.2010.04.039.

Lee, Stacy, and Jung Ha-Brookshire. 2017. "Ethical Climate and Job Attitude in Fashion Retail Employees' Turnover Intention, and Perceived Organizational Sustainability Performance: A Cross-Sectional Study." *Sustainability* 9 (3): 465. https://doi.org/10.3390/su9030465.

Liu, Yong, and Yin Bai. 2014. "An Exploration of Firms' Awareness and Behavior of Developing Circular Economy: An Empirical Research in China." *Resources, Conservation and Recycling* 87: 145–52. https://doi.org/10.1016/j.resconrec.2014.04.002.

Loussaïef, Leïla, Isabelle Ulrich, and Coralie Damay. 2019. "How Does Access to Luxury Fashion Challenge Self-Identity? Exploring Women's Practices of Joint and Non-Ownership." *Journal of Business Research* 102 (September): 263–72. https://doi.org/10.1016/j.jbusres.2019.02.020.

Magnier, Lise, Ruth Mugge, and Jan Schoormans. 2019. "Turning Ocean Garbage into Products—Consumers' Evaluations of Products Made of Recycled Ocean Plastic." *Journal of Cleaner Production* 215 (April): 84–98. https://doi.org/10.1016/j.jclepro.2018.12.246.

Mathews, John A., and Hao Tan. 2011. "Progress Toward a Circular Economy in China." *Journal of Industrial Ecology* 15 (3): 435–57. https://doi.org/10.1111/j.1530-9290.2011.00332.x.

McDonough, William, and Michael Braungart. 2009. *Cradle to Cradle : Remaking the Way We Make Things*. Vintage.

McDowall, Will, Yong Geng, Beijia Huang, Eva Barteková, Raimund Bleischwitz, Serdar Türkeli, René Kemp, and Teresa Doménech. 2017. "Circular Economy Policies in China and Europe." *Journal of Industrial Ecology* 21 (3): 651–61. https://doi.org/10.1111/jiec.12597.

McKinney, Ellen, and Eonyou Shin. 2016. "Exploring Criteria Consumers Use in Evaluating Their Online Formal Wear Rental Experience." *Clothing and Textiles Research Journal* 34 (4): 272–86. https://doi.org/10.1177/0887302X16654269.

McKinsey & Company. 2019. "The State of Fashion 2019." https://www.mckinsey.com/~/media/McKinsey/Industries/Retail/OurInsights/TheStateofFashion2019Ayearofawakening/The-State-of-Fashion-2019-final.ashx.

McNeill, Lisa, and Brittany Venter. 2019. "Identity, Self-Concept and Young Women's Engagement with Collaborative, Sustainable Fashion Consumption Models." *International Journal of Consumer Studies* 43 (4): 368–78. https://doi.org/10.1111/ijcs.12516.

Murray, Alan, Keith Skene, and Kathryn Haynes. 2017. "The Circular Economy: An Interdisciplinary Exploration of the Concept and Application in a Global Context." *Journal of Business Ethics* 140 (3): 369–80. https://doi.org/10.1007/s10551-015-2693-2.

Mylan, Josephine, Helen Holmes, and Jessica Paddock. 2016. "Re-Introducing Consumption to the 'Circular Economy': A Sociotechnical Analysis of Domestic Food Provisioning." *Sustainability (Switzerland)* 8 (8). https://doi.org/10.3390/su8080794.

Pearce, David W., and R. Kerry Turner. *Economics of natural resources and the environment*. JHU Press, 1990.

Pedersen, Esben Rahbek Gjerdrum, and Sarah Netter. 2015. "Collaborative Consumption: Business Model Opportunities and Barriers for Fashion Libraries." *Journal of Fashion Marketing and Management* 19 (3): 258–73. https://doi.org/10.1108/JFMM-05-2013-0073.

Petersen, Trine Brun, and Vibeke Riisberg. 2017. "Cultivating User-Ship? Developing a Circular System for the Acquisition and Use of Baby Clothing." *Fashion Practice* 9 (2): 214–34. https://doi.org/10.1080/17569370.2017.1313600.

Poppelaars, Flora, Conny Bakker, and Jo van Engelen. 2018. "Does Access Trump Ownership? Exploring Consumer Acceptance of Access-Based Consumption in the Case of Smartphones." *Sustainability (Switzerland)* 10 (7). https://doi.org/10.3390/su10072133.

Raihanian Mashhadi, Ardeshir, Aditya Vedantam, and Sara Behdad. 2019. "Investigation of Consumer's Acceptance of Product-Service-Systems: A Case Study of Cell Phone Leasing." *Resources, Conservation and Recycling* 143 (April): 36–44. https://doi.org/10.1016/j.resconrec.2018.12.006.

Ramkumar, Bharath, and Hongjoo Woo. 2018. "Modeling Consumers' Intention to Use Fashion and Beauty Subscription-Based Online Services (SOS)." *Fashion and Textiles* 5 (1). https://doi.org/10.1186/s40691-018-0137-1.

Rizos, Vasileios, Arno Behrens, Wytze van der Gaast, Erwin Hofman, Anastasia Ioannou, Terri Kafyeke, Alexandros Flamos, et al. 2016. "Implementation of Circular Economy Business Models by Small and Medium-Sized Enterprises (SMEs): Barriers and Enablers." *Sustainability (Switzerland)* 8 (11). https://doi.org/10.3390/su8111212.

Saavedra, Yovana M.B., Diego R. Iritani, Ana L.R. Pavan, and Aldo R. Ometto. 2018. "Theoretical Contribution of Industrial Ecology to Circular Economy." *Journal of Cleaner Production* 170 (January): 1514–22. https://doi.org/10.1016/j.jclepro.2017.09.260.

Schaefers, Tobias, Stephanie J. Lawson, and Monika Kukar-Kinney. 2016. "How the Burdens of Ownership Promote Consumer Usage of Access-Based Services." *Marketing Letters* 27 (3): 569–77. https://doi.org/10.1007/s11002-015-9366-x.

Sedlacko, M, A Martinuzzi, I Røpke, N Videira, P Antunes, and F Schneider. 2012. "Aalborg Universitet Utilising Systems Thinking for Sustainable Consumption How Participatory Systems Mapping Achieves Four Types of Insight Utilising Systems Thinking for Sustainable Consumption: How Participatory Systems Mapping Achieves Four Types of In." In *SEE 2012 Conference—Ecological Economics and Rio+20: Challenges and Contributions for a Green Economy*. Rio de Janeiro, Brazil.

Singhal, Deepak, Sarat Kumar Jena, and Sushanta Tripathy. 2019. "Factors Influencing the Purchase Intention of Consumers towards Remanufactured Products: A Systematic Review and Meta-Analysis." *International Journal of Production Research* 57 (23): 7289–99. https://doi.org/10.1080/00207543.2019.1598590.

Stahel, Walter R. 2016. "The Circular Economy." *Nature* 531 (7595): 435–38. https://doi.org/10.1038/531435a.

Strategy, Green. n.d. "Origin and Definition of Circular Fashion—Green Strategy | Sustainable and Circular Fashion Consulting." Accessed September 25, 2020. https://www.greenstrategy.se/circular-fashion-definition/.

Tao, Qiong, and Yingjiao Xu. 2018. "Fashion Subscription Retailing: An Exploratory Study of Consumer Perceptions." *Journal of Fashion Marketing and Management* 22 (4): 494–508. https://doi.org/10.1108/JFMM-11-2017-0123.

Thomas, Nicola J. R. 2018. "Sustainability Marketing. The Need for a Realistic Whole Systems Approach." *Journal of Marketing Management* 34 (17–18): 1530–56. https://doi.org/10.1080/0267257X.2018.1547782.

Tukker, Arnold. 2015. "Product Services for a Resource-Efficient and Circular Economy—A Review." *Journal of Cleaner Production* 97 (June): 76–91. https://doi.org/10.1016/j.jclepro.2013.11.049.

Tura, Nina, Jyri Hanski, Tuomas Ahola, Matias Ståhle, Sini Piiparinen, and Pasi Valkokari. 2019. "Unlocking Circular Business: A Framework of Barriers and Drivers." *Journal of Cleaner Production* 212 (March): 90–98. https://doi.org/10.1016/j.jclepro.2018.11.202.

Voinov, Alexey, and Francois Bousquet. 2010. "Modelling with Stakeholders." *Environmental Modelling and Software* 25 (11): 1268–81. https://doi.org/10.1016/j.envsoft.2010.03.007.

Walker, Helen, Lucio Di Sisto, and Darian McBain. 2008. "Drivers and Barriers to Environmental Supply Chain Management Practices: Lessons from the Public and Private Sectors." *Journal of Purchasing and Supply Management* 14 (1): 69–85. https://doi.org/10.1016/j.pursup.2008.01.007.

Woo, Hongjoo, and Bharath Ramkumar. 2017. "Who Seeks a Surprise Box? Predictors of Consumers' Use of Fashion and Beauty Subscription-Based Online Services (SOS)." *Journal of Retailing and Consumer Services* 41 (March): 121–30. https://doi.org/10.1016/j.jretconser.2017.11.011.

Zeng, Huixiang, Xiaohong Chen, Xu Xiao, and Zhifang Zhou. 2016. "Institutional Pressures, Sustainable Supply Chain Management, and Circular Economy Capability: Empirical Evidence from Chinese Eco-Industrial Park Firms." *Journal of Cleaner Production* 155 (2): 54–65. https://doi.org/10.1016/j.jclepro.2016.10.093.

Zink, Trevor, and Roland Geyer. 2017. "Circular Economy Rebound." *Journal of Industrial Ecology* 21 (3): 593–602. https://doi.org/10.1111/jiec.12545.

10

'Fruits of the Same Tree'? A Systematic Review of Corporate Social Responsibility and Social Enterprise Comparative Literature

Sadaf Shariat and Zahra Khamseh

10.1 Introduction

Social Enterprise (SE) and Corporate Social Responsibility (CSR) movements both aim to bring social change, yet they follow different approaches in making this change. Social enterprise is a growing sector globally, a modern construct viewed as catalyst of social change by providing innovative solutions for social needs (Mair and Marti 2006). Corporate Social Responsibility strategy promotes the idea that corporations ought to move beyond merely satisfying their direct financial interest. Carroll proposed that 'companies have not only economic and

S. Shariat (✉)
University of South Wales Business School, Cardiff, UK
e-mail: sadaf.shariat@southwales.ac.uk

Z. Khamseh
University of Minho, Braga, Portugal

C. Simões et al. (eds.), *Corporate Responsibility, Sustainability and Markets*, Palgrave Studies in Governance, Leadership and Responsibility, https://doi.org/10.1007/978-3-030-79660-0_10

legal obligations, but ethical and discretionary (philanthropic) responsibilities as well' (Carroll 1979, 499; Carroll 1991, 40). Reviewing the literature related to the two schemes, it is arguable that SE and the CSR have much in common, for instance achieving the ultimate aim of building a 'better' world (Page and Katz 2010, 1353) by encouraging more businesses to take the interests of non-shareholder stakeholders more seriously and to participate meaningfully in addressing emerging social and environmental problems. Although social enterprise is 'connected to CSR in profound and interesting ways' (Page and Katz 2010, 1353), it is questionable 'how, where and why SE and CSR might overlap' (Grant and Palakshappa 2018, 1).

Reviewing the relevant literature, different views regarding the overlap between SE and CSR will be discussed. SE may be viewed as a CSR model (Permana and Mursitama 2018), and one may argue that SE and CSR seem like 'fruits of the same tree' (Page and Katz 2010, 1376), or that they are 'both socially constructed societal processes' (Grant and Palakshappa 2018, 6). Nevertheless, some critics find the differences between CSR and SE more striking than similarities, with some CSR proponents finding such differences 'lamentable' (Page and Katz 2010, 1384). It is argued that CSR and SE receive support from different sources, adopt different approaches to social change and embrace different social missions and intended beneficiaries (Page and Katz 2010). This chapter investigates previous studies which compared these two concepts in order to shed light on the ambiguity in current SE and CSR comparative literature.

Under the same line of analysis that this book follows, that evolving marketing purposes in organizations link to the purpose of CSR, sustainability practices or societal values, this chapter aims to highlight the importance of differentiating SE and CSR platforms by reviewing the past comparative studies of SE and CSR. Given that social marketing practices are relevant to both SE and CSR (Grant and Palakshappa 2018), the review of past comparative literature with the purpose of shedding light on the conceptualization of SE and CSR as value-driven societal processes will be helpful to clarify the links to marketing theory and practice, as 'capturing' and 'conveying the value' is considered the key purpose of 'marketing in the context of needing to "do good"'

(McWilliams and Siegel 2011; Grant and Palakshappa 2018, 2). Furthermore, increasing interest in SE and CSR calls for a deeper understanding of existing literature at this juncture, particularly a solid knowledge of differences, similarities, links and overlaps which, among all various other benefits, will assist to leverage effectively the corporation's marketing and communication approach.

This chapter proceeds in four parts. Part I and II provide a brief introduction to the topic, an overview of SE and CSR and the methods employed in this research to review the relevant literature. Part III explains the themes emerging from the review, analysing the comparative studies of the overlaps, differences and conflicts between two concepts. In light of the themes identified and discussed, part IV highlights potential gaps in the selected literature and ways to address the less attended aspects.

Social Enterprise (SE) is an umbrella term which contains many forms of organization with a vast array of activities and typologies based on their diverse legal forms, mechanisms of governance, organizational designs and management models (Nicholls 2009; Kickul and Lyons 2012; Ridley-Duff and Bull 2014). There is no single, clear-cut definition of 'social enterprise' or 'social entrepreneurship', therefore it is especially important that authors apply the terms to achieve a better understanding of the concepts (Peredo and McLean 2006). Yet there is no scholarly consensus on what SEs precisely imply (OECD 1999; Dacin et al. 2010) and most of the time social entrepreneurship and social enterprise are used interchangeably. On a global scale, SEs are known as important means of development both economically and socially. Their approach and organizational objective are different from previous conventional business as social value creation is prioritized in their mission and financial benefit is often used to maintain the durability of value created for beneficiaries (Mair and Marti 2006).

In addition to innovative not-for-profit ventures, social entrepreneurship can include social purpose business ventures, such as for-profit community development banks and hybrid organizations mixing not-for-profit and for-profit elements, such as homeless shelters that start businesses to train and employ their residents. SEs should be viewed primarily as businesses which target both financial and social sustainability (Wang et al. 2015), the intersection of social purpose and commercial activity (Grant and Palakshappa 2018). SEs' main mission is to serve community interests by helping to eliminate unemployment, poverty and other unmet social needs. It is generally recognized that SEs are active in several social areas, offering value in female emancipation, the empowerment of women (Haugh and Talwas 2016) and minorities, international development, environment protection, introduction of renewable sources of energy, local community development (Clark and Ucak 2006), social sustainability (DiVito and Bohnsack 2017), natural disasters (Lewis 2013), solutions to homelessness and, more generally, improving quality of life.

In this vein, SEs include a range of activities such as not-for-profits engaging in market activity, co-operatives, social service organizations contracting with governments to provide services to the community and social businesses (Grant 2008; Teasdale 2010; Thompson and Doherty 2006). Curtis (2008) suggests that no single theory can fully explain SE. Furthermore, there is no agreed definition for SE (Dart 2004; Haugh 2005; Jones and Keogh 2006), which could be partly connected to its diverse forms and processes. SE can be considered both a noun and a verb, an 'entity' and an 'action' (Borzaga et al. 2012; Shaw and Carter 2007). It is argued that SE should borrow existing theory from conventional business (Haugh 2012). Consequently, Nicholls (2010, 612), suggests it as 'pre-paradigmatic' as a lack of established epistemology and proposes 'fluid institutional space for dominant actors to shape and exploit'. The idea of SE as a 'singular construct' is challenged (Grant and Palakshappa 2018) and a range of models are developed in relation to SE where each model is influenced by slightly different motives and ideologies.

Similar to what is discussed in relation to SEs as an 'umbrella term' (Peredo and McLean 2006), Matten and Moon (2008) liken CSR to an 'umbrella concept'. The difficulty of providing a definitive definition of CSR is also highlighted in relevant literature (Benn and Bolton 2011). The notion of integrating social aspects of business into the core business strategies of corporations in a move to go beyond what is required by law is what Sethi (1975) developed as the foundations of CSR. Carroll

(1979, 499) emphasized the responsibility of businesses beyond their direct economic and legal obligations and their working towards 'ethical and discretionary (philanthropic) responsibilities' (Carroll 1991, 40).

The continued development and transformation of CSR into an alternative thematic framework was highlighted by Carroll (1999) where he referred to the evolution of CSR definitions, the conceptualization of which can be traced back several decades. Given the alleged role of CSR as a base point for related themes and concepts, like corporate social performance, business ethics and corporate citizenship, CSR is more than a stand-alone definition and relates to a broad context (Carroll 1999). Although CSR has its fundamental idea practices related to philanthropy, social responsibility and working conditions, the publication of Howard Bowns's 1953 book, known as the first book on CSR (Lockett et al. 2006; Carroll 1991), triggered the continuous challenge and development of the concept by academics and practitioners. A diverse range of sub-strands and transmutations have been developed, dependent on or related to CSR (Lockett et al. 2006): 'Corporate Social Performance' (Clarkson 1995), 'Corporate Citizenship' (Waddock 2004), 'Corporate Social Responsiveness', 'Corporate Responsibility' and 'Corporate Environmentalism' (Menon and Menon 1997), to name a few. Waddock (2004) calls these concepts the branches from the tree trunk of CSR, coexisting side by side rather than having developed one after another. Carroll (1999) asserts that CSR is the source and common denominator that these branches share.

This brief review of CSR demonstrates that implementation of CSR initiatives and integration of social and business dimensions may occur in many forms and across various levels of organizations. This broad contextualization may lead to overlaps with SE. The present research therefore focuses primarily on these core literature streams to conduct a search for literature accordingly. Our identified areas of interest, the SE and CSR Literature, fit well within these boundaries.

10.2 Methods

10.2.1 Search Strategy and Databases Used

In order to identify the strengths and weaknesses of existing literature and any potential gaps, a systematic literature review of SE and CSR was conducted. The present review includes the SE and CSR literature published in studies up to 1st January 2020. We used the search terms 'Corporate Social Responsibility' AND 'Social Enterprise' in Google Scholar, JSTOR, Web of Science and Scopus. To ensure a wider range of information in different databases was covered, we extended the search to what could effectively be Corporate Social Responsibility or Social Enterprise, i.e. synonyms and abbreviated forms of the two terms i.e. SE and CSR, 'social responsibility', 'social entrepreneurship', and 'social venture'. Furthermore, a backward search was conducted from the reference list of the sample identified in Step 1, in order to identify additional relevant materials.

10.2.2 Selection Procedure

After collecting relevant materials, the sample was screened according to the inclusion criteria of the review. For the purposes of final selection, the research should contain both keywords (CSR and SE) in the title in a way that suggests it is a comparative study of the two concepts. The sample was as such screened first for relevance on the basis of title and abstract. The inclusion criteria were as follows: (1) the title of the research should contain both CSR and SE; (2) it should discuss and compare CSR and SE; (3) it should be a journal article, conference paper, book chapter, or thesis published between 1 January 2000 and 1 January 2020; (4) it should be written in English, and the text should be available in full.

From the 250 results identified by the search process, 50 pieces of research were selected for the screening of titles and abstracts. Among these, only 25 reviewed studies met the inclusion criteria. The selected sample provided a comparative analysis of CSR and SE published during the period 1 January 2000 to 1 January 2020.

10.2.3 Data Analysis

A thematic approach was employed for identification and analysis of the existing themes. The main aim of the review was to provide a thematic analysis of the issues identified previously in the selected comparative studies of CSR and SE concerning the relationship between these two subjects. To address the above objective, there has to be a systematic approach in data analysis so that the results can be communicated to others transparently (Malterud 2001; Sandelowski 1995). The thematic analysis method was employed to analyse the final sample due to the effectiveness of the approach in identifying, analysing, organizing, describing and reporting themes found within a data set (Braun and Clarke 2006). We specifically investigated the research objectives of the selected research works, their study approach, the key findings of the sample with reference to relationship between SE and CSR and the data analysis methods and, finally, the validity and reliability of the selected research. The final selected sample was screened by the authors who then coded the text of research works according to meaning and content. To ensure the integrity of coding, authors assessed and analysed each individually before comparing results and reaching a consensus. Subsequently, all selected research was allocated to a specific theme and some articles more than one theme. The contents of all the research were summarized and described for future discussion and as a guide for categorization under each stream, as well as for possible identification of any special pattern in the data e.g. on the birth and evolution of themes according to the bibliographic date of the sample. On the basis of our coding procedure, we distinguish five research streams emerging from the final selected sample. The next section will discuss the findings of our research based on the themes identified in the selected literature. The emergent streams are discussed in hierarchical order according to the frequency of the identified theme under each stream within the selected final sample.

10.3 Research Streams

10.3.1 Introduction

This section aims to provide a brief overview of the selected comparative literature regarding the nature of arguments, possible patterns and changes in the manner in which literature on SE and CSR have been compared and discussed, taking into account the date of the bibliographic references as the concepts under review and its relations have evolved during the 20-year period. The earliest published work identified in the sample that deals with SE and CSR literature was written in 2007 by Baron, well-articulated research with the aim of defining CSR and SE by applying CSR theories. No research work (compatible with the adopted inclusion criteria) was found in the first half of the first decade in current research (2000–2005). In the second half of the first decade in the current study, the number of comparative reviews on the topic remains very limited, although a number of rigorous works such as Baron (2007) and Cornelius et al. (2008) contributed significantly to the body of knowledge and paved the path for the future comparative studies of SE and CSR.

The second decade studied in the selected sample (2010–2020) commenced with the call in literature for SE scholars to engage further with and move towards using established theories, (e.g. Zeyen et al. 2013) including CSR theories for the SE, and to bridge these two bodies of literature that 'potentially have much to say to one another' as Littlewood and Holt (2018) put it. The move first led to studies aiming to clarify the scope of SE and to discuss whether the Social Enterprise is the new Corporate Social Responsibility (Page and Katz 2010), followed by more comparative studies trying to identify the differences between the two concepts (e.g. Page and Katz 2010; Crisan and Borza 2012; Saatci and Upper 2013; Priede et al. 2014; Nino 2015).

There also exists a significant number of publications in the selected sample in the second decade, the majority related to post-2016, highlighting the nature of CSR and SE as value-driven societal processes (e.g. Szeged et al. 2016; Uddin et al. 2016; Amelio 2017; Tiba et al. 2019; Grant and Palakshappa 2018; Palakshappa and Grant 2018). Although some studies discussed the role of CSR and SE quite early in the second decade of the reviewed literature (Page and Katz 2010; Mitra and Borza, 2011, 2012; Hiller 2013), the majority of work regarding the importance of CSR to support SE (or vice versa) relates to recent years, particularly between 2016 and 2018 (e.g. Uddin et al. 2016; Singh et al. 2017; Sinha et al. 2017; Littlewood and Holt 2018; Natsvlishvili 2018; Pasricha et al. 2018; Amelio 2017). The positive contribution of such literature has resulted in a recent pattern of proposals for innovative models dealing with both concepts (e.g. Szegedi et al. 2016; Bredhammar and Slesinski 2019; Littlewood and Holt 2018).

Even now there are only limited studies that have analysed the intersection of and relationships between social entrepreneurship and CSR (identified and discussed also by Littlewood and Holt 2018).

10.3.2 Research Stream 1: The Importance of CSR to Support SE (or Vice Versa)

The first stream of Social Enterprise and Corporate Social Responsibility literature focuses on the impact of CSR on SE and vice versa. This stream particularly emphasizes the importance of CSR in supporting Social Entrepreneurship and the role of SE in promoting CSR and bridging the gap between business and society (e.g. Uddin et al. 2016; Sinha et al. 2017; Pasricha et al. 2018; Igwe et al. 2018; Littlewood and Holt 2018). In this stream, we identified studies which applied a number of CSR theories in a social enterprise context (e.g. Littlewood and Holt 2018). Other research in this stream describes CSR as a crucial consideration for Social Enterprises. For instance, in a study of CSR and SE in Romania Crisan and Borza (2012) highlight the literature concerning the CSR as an important lever to support Social Enterprises.

Furthermore, the importance of SE in supporting CSR and bridging the gap between business and society is discussed extensively in the literature. It is argued that the innovative models of CSR identified in the cases studied in India indicate the efficiency of models to benefit both business and society in an effective and sustainable way (e.g. Singh et al. 2017 in a study of CSR and SE in an Indian context). Other research in this stream examines the positive impact of ethical leadership on CSR practices and the significant insight it provides for SEs in their endeavours to become socially responsive, leading to stronger potential for creating a positive social impact (e.g. Pasricha et al. 2018). Natsvlishvili (2018) shows the importance of strengthening CSR to create steps towards development of social entrepreneurship. The study focuses on social entrepreneurship in Georgia and suggests that SEs should balance efficiency and equity to achieve company success and serving social interests. In that particular context, CSR in selected companies is not well-aligned with their business plan. The article also discusses factors such as lack of legal definition for SE (i.e. acting as a nongovernmental organization), the limited nature of their organizational capacity and low organization maturity to reason why the existing efforts in terms of balancing and implementing CSR are insufficient.

Some literature in this stream focuses on how linking CSR and SE can help corporations to benefit from a wider range of opportunities. In a study conducted in the context of Bangladesh, Uddin et al. (2016) completed 62 interviews with SEs and stakeholders and concluded that linking CSR practices with SEs helps companies to view and benefit from opportunities more effectively. The article asserts that, in the process of exploring and understanding opportunities, CSR practices, as a potential source of opportunities, help to generate and confer unique benefits to a firm from their engagement of activities and in this way a unique interface can benefit both business and society.

Lastly, the role of CSR in supporting SE is widely recognized in the sample directly studied for the purpose of current research or important studies which were referred to in research works from our sample. For instance, Amelio (2017) highlights the role of CSR as an important lever in supporting Social Entrepreneurship (referring to Austin 2001, 2006; Austin and Reavis 2002) and the impact CSR has in the social value creation process for both businesses and social purpose organizations, citing Crisan and Borza (2012).

It was also suggested that developing applicable forms of SE in pursuit of CSR policies can be beneficial for corporations as it is equally for SEs to 'incorporate corporate involvement in their funding and operational mechanisms' (Nicolopoulou and Karatas-Ozkan 2009). The mutual benefit which corporations and SEs have in deploying applicable features of their strategies and structure can be utilized effectively in 'pursuit of generating social capital'. (Nicolopoulou and Karatas-Ozkan 2009).

10.3.3 Research Stream 2: CSR and SE as Value-Driven Societal Processes

The second stream addresses the commonality between CSR and SE as socially constructed processes (e.g. Grant and Palakshappa 2018; Palakshappa and Grant 2018; Mitra and Borza 2010; Uddin et al. 2016; Szegedi et al. 2016; Sinha et al. 2017; Singh et al. 2017; Amelio 2017; Asensio et al. 2019; Tiba et al. 2019). Academic comments such as those of McWilliams and Siegel (2011) are cited to explain the benefit of conceptualizing SE and CSR as value-driven social processes. The benefit appears to be the fact that, because a primary purpose of marketing in the context of needing to 'do good' is to capture and convey value, conceptualizing SE and CSR clarifies the links to marketing theory and practice (McWilliams and Siegel 2011).

Grant and Palakshappa (2018) highlight the overlap bewteen CSR and SE, refering to related literature (e.g. the works of Grant and Dart 2008; Kurucz et al. 2008; Teasdale 2010) concerning CSR and SE as value-driven societal processes. The article states that 'value is a common theme in both concepts, albeit in different forms' (Grant and Palakshappa 2018, 3). Furthermore, some important arguments were referred to in this stream, such as social value as a creation of SEs (Di Domenico et al. 2010) and economic value as an outcome of CSR strategies (Husted, Allen, and Kock 2015). It was also argued that value could be generated through social alliances between a not for profit organization and a business (Grant and Palakshappa 2013, 11). They defined SE push strategy that is undertaken from an organizational perspective and interpret push and pull influences of SE and CSR that may generate concrete forms of value, concluding that SEs impacts may 'push' change at micro levels of activity, whereas CSR 'pull' may have impact at meso or macro levels of activity (Grant and Palakshappa 2018, 4).

In this stream, the important interaction between an individual's personal values and consumption behaviour was also discussed, citing scholars such as Doran (2009) and concluding that the contribution of values to our belief system (influencing our actions accordingly), contributes in turn to our epistemological understanding of concepts such as SE and CSR (Grant and Palakshappa 2018, 2). In a later study, the same authors (Palakshappa and Grant 2018) focus on SEs and CSR to demonstrate in more depth their similarities and differences from an epistemological perspective, confirming that although both concepts are different, they overlap in generating 'value' and 'sustainabilities'. The emphasis is placed on the commonalities that SEs and CSR share through their sustainability which leads to 'humanism', indicating that 'humanism' in business generates social value (Nicolopoulou 2014). Similarly, the generation of value in social, collaborative and strategic forms through the Triple Bottom Line was highlighted as the central theme of both concepts (Palakshappa and Grant 2018). Blaga and Gica's research (2019) also aimed to deepen awareness and understanding of 'social value creation' by what authors explain as analysis and comparison of the 'extent of "social value creation" by organizations that dedicate themselves to CSR principles' and also 'the "social value creation" by social enterprises' in an attempt to explore the links and relationship between the two concepts.

10.3.4 Research Stream 3: Receiving Support from Different Sources, Having Different Social Missions and Different Intended Beneficiaries

A third stream of SE and CSR literature focuses on the differences between SE and CSR, mostly differences in their social missions and intended beneficiaries and the issues surrounding SE and CSR receiving support from different sources (e.g. Baron 2007; Page and Katz 2010; Crisan and Borza 2012; Saatci and Upper 2013; Priede et al. 2014; Nino 2015; Igwe et al. 2018). In terms of receiving support from different sources, it is argued that the SE movement operates in a setting different from the CSR movement (e.g. see Page and Katz 2010). CSR and SE draw support from different sources. The vision of SE, 'realized and embodied in new organizational forms rather than existing corporations' (Page and Katz 2010, 1353) with an emphasis on the individual social entrepreneur, is an indication of 'a more libertarian orientation, unlike more robust iterations of CSR that strike some as socialistic' (Page and Katz 2010, 1384). As discussed in the previous stream CSR and SE can benefit society through value creation with their CSR activities, though it is also important to emphasize how contribution to sustainable development can benefit a firm (Tiba et al. 2019). In fact, CSR is able to support the startup of SEs, since SEs come as a response to the needs and expectations of society and, in this way, CSR practices ensure the accessibility of value for people to live a quality life (Nino 2015).

Priede et al. (2014) identify and discuss CSR and SE as two related concepts but with different underlying natures, reasons to exist and measurements of success. Both social and commercial businesses adopt CSR initiatives and practices as business strategy although with differences in the stage at which it is implemented. Social enterprises tend to develop it at the early stage of the company's formation as opposed to commercial organizations which implement it at the later stage of the company's operations. Furthermore, it is discussed that both business types pursue economic sustainability. SEs aim to make profit to solve social problems, maximizing community benefits and eco-friendly products and minimizing exploitation of natural resources, whereas commercial businesses attempt to maintain competitive advantage as well as maximize profit for the shareholder's sake (Igwe et al. , 43). Therefore, CSR is viewed by some scholars as an important tool for maintaining 'profitability, stakeholder relationships and business reputation' (Igwe et al. 2018, 42).

CSR is sometimes defined as 'application of new considerations (responsibilities) to existing business models within an existing profit-making paradigm', whereas social enterprise is seen as an entity that 'takes those business models and applies them to unresolved social problems, partly by redefining that same paradigm from shareholder wealth creation to social wealth creation' (Page and Katz 2010, 3). In this stream, academic comments have been made to prove that social enterprise involves 'a broader array of social missions' and 'intended beneficiaries than those encouraged by CSR'. CSR initiatives target 'general society' or 'satisfaction of stakeholder expectations' while SEs aim at 'the poorest of the poor' or those in most urgent need (e.g. Sattci and Urper 2013, 3).

10.3.5 Research Stream 4: Social Enterprise as a CSR Model

The fourth stream examines the CSR in SEs, and most importantly how CSR initiatives may fit into an SE model and whether the choice of SE affects customers' perceptions regarding the CSR value the firm is involved in. The aim of these research works appears to be the assessment of SE as a model for implementation of CSR initiatives. Chew et al. (2016) provide a comparative analysis of the estimate of the CSR in an SE (a macro-focused labour union) and non-SE commercial firm. The study concluded that the customers value the CSR of the SE more highly than the commercial firm studied in the article. Furthermore, SE was found to be more successful in achieving private benefit while implementing CSR initiatives compared to the traditional firm engaged in CSR activities at the same level.

Other research in this stream provides a critical evaluation of the level of acceptance of social responsibility practices in the EU, particularly the EU's role in promoting SE as a business model. The article emphasizes the importance of CSR as it is practiced in SEs to redistribute a part of a corporation's profits to social causes (Amelio 2017, 345) and the role of the 2014 EU directive in forcing some private entrepreneurs (PEs) to become social entrepreneurs (Amelio 2017, 349). Using the Aristotelian-informed capabilities approach (Nussbaum 1999; Cornelius 2002), Cornelius et al. (2008) focus on CSR in SEs in general and internal dimensions of CSR in SEs in particular, in that SEs have a strong orientation towards their external stakeholders. The study proposes CSR frameworks to test both internal and external stakeholders. In a later study, Spence (2016) explores CSR theories in the context of SEs, small enterprises underrepresented in CSR and social responsibility research.

In recent research, Littlewood and Holt (2018, 10) identified still inadequate attention to the application of a CSR lens to social enterprises and provided robust discussion of the insights, application and value of CSR theory for social entrepreneurship research and in the study of social entrepreneurship.

10.3.6 Research Stream 5: Proposal for Innovative Approaches Combining CSR and SE

This research stream focuses on studies proposing innovative approaches in addressing SE and CSR. One approach identified in the literature suggests combining CSR research and social entrepreneurship theory (Bredhammar and Slesinski 2019; Singh et al. 2017). Bredhammar and Slesinski (2019) in their research identified a gap which allegedly hinders the practical success of CSR. The gap is claimed to be the current trade-off that CSR decreases the economic profits of the firms. The study further analysed the existing CSR theories, focusing on the Carroll's pyramid (Carroll 1991) and the strategic CSR model (Burke and Logsdon 1996), and concluded that although both models are valid, they fail to effectively solve the issues of the trades-off. To link strategic CSR dimensions and social entrepreneurship components, it is important to create both economic and social value (Bredhammar and Slesinski 2019). Therefore, the study proposed a conceptual model of economic and social value creation which adds the social entrepreneurship components to the strategic CSR conceptual model (Bredhammar and Slesinski 2019, 48).

Other research in this stream proposed the integrated model of Corporate Social Responsibility, Social Innovation and Social Entrepreneurship (Szegedi et al. 2016). Szegedi et al. (2016, 5) argue that 'Social Enterprises, which go a step beyond accepting Corporate Social Responsibility, may become an important driver of social development'. The analysis of CSR and SE and Social Innovation literature confirms that CSR that is integrated into corporate strategy can itself be considered a social innovation. The studies in this stream often differentiate between SE and CSR initiatives based on the priority of either social or economic standpoints.

In their study Mitra and Borza (2011) highlighted different types of collaboration between social organizations and companies that led to more social impact. Through empirical research they identify the position of social enterprise and commercial enterprise, such as a common trend of social involvement. In some cases, if the social involvement does not have a positive contribution to a company's development, CSR implementation is minimized or even eliminated. The article proposed a social entrepreneurship model which can manifest as collaborations or partnerships with social enterprises to help and sustain CSR implementation (Mitra and Borza 2011, 252).

Nicolopoulou and Karatas-Ozkan (2009) proposed a convergent model to link CSR with SEs. The article defined that both concepts interrelated through the framework of the triple bottom line. The proposed model suggests the study of two social phenomena in a way that the external activity of firms is the outcome of an interplay between micro, meso and macro levels of activities initiated by internal strategic vision and actions. In this way, SEs and corporations can benefit from adapting CSR structure and strategies in pursuit of their social interest and social capital. Further proposed models have been developed with both CSR and SE in mind including the Littlewood and Holt's (2018) application of CSR theories—stakeholder theory and the pyramid of CSR—in a social enterprise context to develop a revised stakeholder theory of social enterprise and the social enterprise responsibility pyramid.

Having discussed the identified streams in SE and CSR literature, the next section will discuss briefly the strengths, weaknesses and challenges of the selected sample.

10.4 Discussion: Gaps and Challenges in the SE and CSR Comparative Studies

This section aims to identify challenges in the comparative studies of SE and CSR literature. As discussed earlier, the current qualitative literature review is designed to provide an overview of existing literature concerning the concepts of Social Enterprise and Corporate

Social Responsibility in comparative business and management studies. In management research, theory is understood as 'an account of constitutive, causal relationships between two or more concepts within a set of boundary conditions' (Gay and Weaver 2011, 26). In this section, we engage in a gap-finding mission in the SE and CSR comparative literature, based on this understanding of theory. We argue that filling the gaps identified will advance both CSR and social enterprise literature.

10.4.1 Strength of the Research Streams

CSR and SE literature has yielded several key insights in defining concepts and describing and integrating theoretical models to inspire initiative for social and sustainable development. A considerable proportion of previous research comparing these two concepts has focused on the common goal for both CSR and SE: allegedly, the creation of social value in line with financial sustainability. This generally considers SE and CSR as models to generate concrete form(s) of value. A significant focus of the selected literature is to identify the similarities, differences and overlap between two concepts (e.g. Saatci and Urper 2013; Nino 2015) in the absence of a clear, agreed upon definition for either concept. Despite some commonalities, research works often emphasize that CSR initiatives aim to reduce social and environmental negative impacts which result in profit-maximizing and that companies could only devote a small portion of their resources to social purposes. However, SEs' primary purpose is to provide solutions to unmet social problems and deliver social benefits in very large scale. Therefore, SEs attempt to pursue social changes by creation of social wealth.

A significant contribution to the body of knowledge is the development of new models in which, for instance, the combination of CSR and SE was proposed to enhance the corporate involvement in micro, meso and macro levels of institutional activities in the hope of sustainable creation of social value. As discussed in part III, there have been proposals to combine selected theories and concepts in order to maximize the effect and success of the proposed models (e.g. Szegedi et al. 2016; Bredhammar and Slesinski 2019; Littlewood and Holt 2018). Furthermore, the proposed models indicate that both concepts are complementary to build a healthy and dignified social system. Similarly, by combining CSR with SE components, one should only expect a more effective process to achieve economic and social value creation. The proposed models highlight the fact that, if SEs step beyond CSR components, this could drive social development. Finally, given that CSR theory is believed to have a significant contribution to make to the body of knowledge in social entrepreneurship, and that bridging CSR and social entrepreneurship literature is considered both possible and beneficial (as discussed in the identified research streams), critical examination of comparative literature of these two concepts, their links, overlaps and relationship, is important for policy and practice.

10.4.2 Lack of Clarity in Defining SE and CSR

As briefly discussed in part 1, one of the key challenges referred to in the individual studies of CSR and SE is the absence of a single, agreed upon definition for SE (Dart 2004; Haugh 2005; Jones and Keogh 2006) and CSR (Benn and Bolton 2011; Matten and Moon 2008). It is widely agreed that SE and CSR are ambiguous concepts (Grant and Dart 2008; Kurucz, et al. 2008; Teasdale 2010) for which there exists little consensus for a definition among scholars (Jones and Keogh 2006; Martin and Osberg 2007; Matten and Moon 2008; Sethi 1975). Both are known as socially constructed concepts and, as Grant and Palakshappa (2018, 2) put it, they 'have developed over time with advances in scholarship and practice to represent unique concepts and/or as all encompassing "umbrella" terms'.

The key question here is this: what should be the starting point in comparative studies of SE and CSR in the absence of an agreed definition? Additionally, could such absence affect the quality of comparative literature in SE and CSR? One may argue that the availability of an agreed upon definition for two concepts (that are the subjects of a review) is not a premise for producing effective comparative studies. The variation in definition/lack of an agreed upon definition for SE (and CSR) may be justified in relation to geographic, political, economic and cultural differences (Defourny and Kim 2011; Defourny and Nyssens 2006; Grant 2008; Kerlin 2006).

However, as is suggested in literature related to SE (e.g. Douglas and Grant, 2014), we argue that there should be a balance in the absence of any agreed definition. This is because, on the one hand, the application of a widely accepted definition may reduce the risk of a concept (including SE and CSR) 'becoming a meaningless, catch all expression' (Grant and Palakshappa 2018, 2) and, on the other hand, working within definitions that are too well defined, as Douglas and Grant (2014) mention, 'risks imposing normative or instrumental influences that may stifle the dynamic and fluid concept' (Grant and Palakshappa 2018, 2). If possible, it will be useful to develop and introduce an agreed upon conception of SE and CSR at an internal level. This will clearly delineate the nature of these constructs and their components in view of their complexity. This is expected to provide a clearer and easier start for a comparative literature of SE and CSR.

10.4.3 Approaches to Comparing SE and CSR (Impact/Success)

As the characterization of streams in part 3 shows, the SE and CSR comparative literature does not exhibit characteristics of a well-defined, comprehensive research stream. The majority of contributions is fundamentally descriptive rather than explanatory, and more importantly lack empirical evidence in support of arguments. For example, our review resulted in identification of only 7 pieces of research that used empirical methods and case study to measure and compare one or more aspects of the two concepts (Chew et al. [2016] in the context of Singapore; Mitra and Borza [2011, 2012] in the context of Romania; Uddin et al. [2016] in the context of Bangladesh; Pasricha et al. [2018] in the context of India, and Littlewood and Holt [2018] in the context of Sub-Saharan Africa with cases from Kenya, Zambia, Mozambique, South Africa).

A more balanced approach in using qualitative methods and collecting empirical data would have been constructive to analyse and compare how implementation of these concepts may help business success or how one may help implementation/success of the other. Further case studies could be considered in future empirical works which may provide a range of benefits, including developing a more accurate comparative analysis of a business CSR initiative and SE. More empirical research needs to be carried out to measure more accurately how these concepts may help each other, or how one can help the other to be implemented effectively and to quantify potential impact or success using quantitative/qualitative methods.

Admittedly, the gap identified regarding research methods used could be related to the limitations of our study. As discussed in the inclusion criteria, this study focuses on comparative SE and CSR literature where the title of research includes both SE and CSR. However, the comparison between the two concepts could occur in other studies focused specifically on CSR or SE but which at some point have compared the two concepts. It is possible that projects that do not aim specifically to compare both concepts (and are therefore excluded from our sample population) unintentionally have presented and evaluated some empirical data and therefore developed some useful results on our topic.

10.4.4 Analysis of the CSR and SE's Impact in Different Contexts

While some differences in theoretical and practical applications of SE and CSR are understandable, the literature review suggests insufficient analysis and comparison of SE and CSR in different contexts, for example economically or geographically. Grant and Palakshappa (2018) is a rigorous study to analyse the push and pull influences of SE and CSR in Fair Trade practices which may take place simultaneously, but on different levels. The article discusses how SE influences may push change at micro (individual) levels of activity, whereas CSR pull may be more apparent at meso (organization) and/or macro (national) levels of activity. It is important that future work includes more comparative discussion of this sort.

It is generally discussed that SE and CSR have presented differences in practice which could be explained using geographic, social, political and economic factors (see. Grant 2008; Kerlin 2006; Maignan and Ralston 2002; Matten and Moon 2008). Similarly, as discussed previously, definitional variation seems to be influenced by geographic, political, economic and cultural differences (Defourny and Kim 2011; Defourny and Nyssens 2006; Grant 2008; Kerlin 2006). It is however still questionable whether such differences justify the small number of comparative studies in the field of SE and CSR literature. There seem to exist benefits in conducting more research to compare and analyse the implementation of these concepts in different contexts e.g. geographical contexts or economic scales.

Although this review is not intended to provide a geographical or geopolitical view of the identified literature, through search and review it was found that geographic differences in interpretation and application are evident in CSR and SE comparative literature and scholarship. In this study, authors identified the opportunity to learn from analysis of samples of comparative review of SE and CSR from Asia (e.g. Uddin et al. 2016 Bangladesh; Pasricha et al. 2018; Singh et al. 2017 India; Chew et al. 2016 Singapore) to Africa (e.g. Littlewood & Holt 2018 within the context of Sub-Saharan Africa) and Europe (e.g. Cornelius et al., 2008 UK; Natsvlishvili 2018 Georgia; Mitra and Borza 2011, 2012 Romania; Szegedi et al. 2016 Hungary), where all presented very special experiences on their own merit. As a general observation, it was found that researchers in the context-specific studies mostly seek to identify and focus on peculiarities of CSR and SE in a given system, taking to account socio-economic, political, legal and cultural and market factors. This is reflected particularly in the context comparative reviews of CSR and SE in developing countries, for instance in the work of Natsvlishvili (2018) where the author refers to the limited organizational capacity and insufficient institutional maturity and absence of effective legislation and civil society development in Georgia in an effort to portray a realistic comparison of SE and CSR within the specific context of a post-soviet Georgia. Similarly, Littlewood and Holt (2018) provided a fruitful discussion of CSR and SE in Sub-Saharan Africa using cases from Kenya, Zambia, Mozambique and South Africa. Citing earlier research in the region such as Rivera-Santos et al. (2015) and Littlewood and Holt (2015), authors highlight the importance of African contextual factors, the choices of activities of social ventures, the relationship between Social Entrepreneurship and environmental characteristics and the relationship between Social Entrepreneurship, Broad-Based Black Economic Empowerment (BBBEE) and CSR (Littlewood and Holt 2018, 11).

There should be lessons to learn from such comparisons. Although concepts like SE are growing in different regions around the globe, 'developing their own flavour of SE' (Grant and Palakshappa 2018, 11), there should be more work to identify the differences in order to be able to compare the outcome of different systems, to explore the opportunities and 'to accommodate influences from diverse world views, as well as geographical, historical, political and social differences' (Grant and Palakshappa 2018, 16).

10.5 Conclusion

The current review examined the literature in analysis and comparison of Social Enterprise and Corporate Social Responsibility. Our search strategy and inclusion criteria yielded a sample of 25 studies comparing the concepts of SE and CSR. Using thematic analysis, five key research streams were identified in the selected literature. The research streams are: (a) the importance of CSR to support SE (or vice versa); (b) CSR and SE as value-driven societal processes; (c) receiving support from different sources, having different social missions and different intended beneficiaries; (d) SE as a CSR model; (e) a proposal for innovative approaches combining CSR and SE.

The review shows that there are challenges and weaknesses in the comparative SE and CSR literature and filling these gaps is an important task for future research. The findings of this review suggest that although the analysis of SE and CSR has received much attention recently, there are limited studies effectively comparing the two concepts in the form of an independent study. Furthermore the methodology still has a long way to go in order to embrace a more diverse range of methods, most importantly the qualitative data and empirical research. This will provide a better understanding of research trends and gaps in the above fields. Based on this review, we argued that both fields have long been troubled by a lack of consensus on definitions. This could affect the provision of effective comparative studies. Furthermore, many research works are of rather general character and treat the SE and CSR in a vacuum, within a limited and often theoretical context, not a critical comparative environment.

The findings of our review add to the growing body of SE and CSR research. The review offers a comprehensive analysis of comparative studies of SE and CSR to identify the common patterns, gaps and challenges in the selected literature. The findings gained from the review can inform researchers to fill the lacunae in the field, taking into account the weaknesses and challenges of existing literature discussed here. Similar to any other research, findings should be read in the lights of some limitations. The scope is limited to research works in English that compare SE and CSR (where the title of article implies such comparison and includes both SE and CSR in its wording). This approach might have resulted in the exclusion of literature that could offer additional insight into SE and CSR literature.

References

Amelio, Stefano. 2017. "CSR and Social Entrepreneurship: The Role of the European Union". *Management Dynamics in the Knowledge Economy.* 5 (3): 335–354.

Asensio, Eva, Jesús Perán, and Yolanda Rodríguez. 2019. "From Corporate Social Responsibility to Social Entrepreneurship: A New Methodology". In *Social Responsibility: Concepts, Methodologies, Tools, and Applications.* 534–548. IGI Global.

Austin, James E, and Cate Reavis. 2002. "*Starbucks and Conservation International.*" Harvard Business School Case 303–355. Cambridge, MA. (Revised May 2004).

Austin, James E. 2001. "Strategic Collaboration Between Nonprofits and Businesses". *Human Resources Abstracts.* 36 (1): 69–97.

Austin, James E. 2006. *Effective Management of Social Enterprises: Lessons from Businesses and Civil Society Organizations in Iberoamerica.* Cambridge, MA: Harvard University Press.

Baron, Robert A. 2007. "Behavioral and Cognitive Factors in Entrepreneurship: Entrepreneurs as the Active Element in New Venture Creation". *Strategic Entrepreneurship Journal.* 1: 167–182.

Benn, Suzanne, and Dianne Bolton. 2011. *Key Concepts in Corporate Social Responsibility.* London: Sage.

Blaga, Sorin, and Oana Gica. 2019. "Corporate Social Responsibility and Social Entrepreneurship". *Romanian Economic and Business Review.* 14 (4): 17–31.

Braun, Virginia, and Victoria Clarke. 2006. "Using Thematic Analysis in Psychology". *Qualitative Research in Psychology.* 3 (2): 77–101.

Bredhammar, Michelle, and Pia Slesinski. 2019. "Saving the World Cannot be a One-Man Show: Combining CSR Research and Social Entrepreneurship Theory for a Better Future". Master thesis, Linnaeus University.

Borzaga, Carlo, Sara Depedri, and Giulia Galera. 2012. "Interpreting Social Enterprises". *Revista de Administração.* 47 (3): 398–409.

Burke, Lee, and Jeanne M. Logsdon. 1996. "How Corporate Social Responsibility Pays Off". *Long Range Planning.* 29 (4): 495–502.

Carroll, Archie B. 1979. "A Three-Dimensional Conceptual Model of Corporate Performance". *The Academy of Management Review.* 4 (4): 497–505.

Carroll, Archie B. 1991. "The Pyramid of Corporate Social Responsibility: Toward the Moral Management of Organizational Stakeholders". *Business Horizons.* 34 (4): 39–48.

Carroll, Archie B. 1999. "Corporate Social Responsibility: Evolution of a Definitional Construct". *Business and Society.* 38 (3): 268–295.

Chew, Soon-Beng, Wei Quan Jeffrey Huang, Hui Ching Chia, and Huang Chi Soh. 2016. "Determinants of Corporate Social Responsibility of a Social Enterprise: An Empirical Analysis". *Review of Pacific Basin Financial Markets and Policies.* 19 (3): 1–20.

Clark, Catherine, and Selen Ucak. 2006. "Rise For-Profit Social Entrepreneur Report: Balancing Markets and Values". University of Illinois at Urbana-Champaign's Academy for Entrepreneurial Leadership Historical Research Reference in Entrepreneurship, Available at SSRN: https://ssrn.com/abstract=1509999.

Clarkson, Max B. E. 1995. *A Stakeholder Framework for Analyzing and Evaluating Corporate Social Performance.* Emmitsburg, MD: National Emergency Training Center.

Cornelius, Nelarine, Mathew Todres, Shaheena Janjuha-Jivraj, Adrian Woods, and James Wallace. 2008. "Corporate Social Responsibility and the Social Enterprise". *Journal of Business Ethics.* 81 (2): 355–370.

Cornelius, Nelarine. 2002. *Building Workplace Equality: Ethics, Diversity and Inclusion.* London: Thomson Learning.

Crisan (Mitra), Catalina, and Anca Borza. 2012. "Social Entrepreneurship and Corporate Social Responsibilities". *International Business Research.* 5 (2): 106–113.

Curtis, Tim. 2008. "Finding that Grit Makes a Pearl". *International Journal of Entrepreneurial Behavior & Research.* 14 (5): 276–290.

Dacin, Peter A., Tina M. Dacin, and Margaret Matear. 2010. "Social Entrepreneurship: Why We Don't Need a New Theory and How We Move Forward From Here". *Academy of Management Perspectives.* 24 (3): 37–57.

Dart, Raymond. 2004. "The Legitimacy of Social Enterprise". *Nonprofit Management & Leadership.* 14 (4): 411–424.

Defourny, Jacques, and Shin-Yang Kim. 2011. "Emerging Models of Social Enterprise in Eastern Asia: A Cross-country Analysis". *Social Enterprise Journal.* 7 (1): 86–111.

Defourney, Jaques, and Marthe Nyssens. 2006. Defining Social Enterprise, In *Social enterprise: at the crossroads of market, public policies and civil society.* Abingdon: Routledge.

Di Domenico, MariaLaura, Helen Haugh, and Paul Tracey. 2010. "Social Bricolage: Theorizing Social Value Creation in Social Enterprises". *Entrepreneurship Theory and Practice.* 34 (4): 681–703.

DiVito, Lori, and Rene Bohnsack. 2017. "Entrepreneurial Orientation and its Effect on Sustainability Decision Tradeoffs: The Case of Sustainable Fashion Firms". *Journal of Business Venturing.* 32 (5): 569–587.

Doran, Caroline J. 2009. "The Role of Personal Values in Fair Trade Consumption". *Journal of Business Ethics.* 84 (4): 549–563.

Douglas, H, and Grant, S. 2014. Social entrepreneurship and enterprise. Domain, dimensions and future directions. In H. Douglas, & S. Grant (Eds.), Social entrepreneurship and enterprise. Concepts in context (pp. 3–32). Melbourne: Tilde University Press.

Gay, Bruce, and Sue Weaver. 2011. "Theory Building and Paradigms: A Primer on the Nuances of Theory Construction". *American International Journal of Contemporary Research.* 1 (2): 24–32.

Grant, Suzanne. 2008. "Contextualising Social Enterprise in New Zealand". *Social Enterprise Journal.* 4 (1): 9–23.

Grant, Suzanne, and Raymond Dart. 2008. "The Social Construction of Social Enterprise". In *8th International Conference of the International Society for Third Sector Research, Universitat de Barcelona, Barcelona, Spain.*

Grant, Suzanne, and Nitha Palakshappa. 2013. "Social Enterprise and Corporate Social Responsibility: Towards a Deeper Understanding of the Links and Overlaps", 4th EMES International Research Conference on Social Enterprise. Liege, *EMES-SOCENT Conference Selected Papers, no. LG13–20.*

Grant, Suzanne, and Nitha Palakshappa. 2018. "Social Enterprise Push or Corporate Social Responsibility Pull? The Mainstreaming of Fair Trade". *International Journal of Nonprofit and Voluntary Sector Marketing.* 23 (4):16–25.

Haugh, Helen M. 2012. "The Importance of Theory in Social Enterprise Research". *Social Enterprise Journal*. 8 (1): 7–15.

Haugh, Helen M, and Alka Talwar. 2016. "Linking Social Entrepreneurship and Social Change: The Mediating Role of Empowerment". *Journal of Business Ethics.* 133 (4): 643–658.

Haugh, Helen M. 2005. "A Research Agenda for Social Entrepreneurship". *Social Enterprise Journal.* 1 (1): 1–12.

Hiller, Janine S. 2013. "The Benefit Corporation and Corporate Social Responsibility". *Journal of Business Ethics.* 118 (2): 287–301.

Husted, Bryan W, David Bruce Allen, and Ned Kock. 2015. "Value Creation Through Social Strategy". *Business & Society.* 54 (2): 147–186.

Igwe Paul A., Afam Icha-Ituma, and Nnamdi O. Madichie. 2018. "The Evaluation of CSR and Social Value Practices Among UK Commercial and Social Enterprises". *Entrepreneurial Business and Economics Review.* 6 (1): 37–52.

Jones, Declan, and William Keogh. 2006. "Social Enterprise: A Case of Terminological Ambiguity and Complexity". *Social Enterprise Journal.* 2 (1): 11–26.

Kerlin, Janelle A. 2006. "Social Enterprise in the United States and Europe: Understanding and Learning from the Differences". *International Journal of Voluntary and Nonprofit Organizations.* 17(3): 246–262.

Kickul, Jill, and Thomas S. Lyons. 2012. *Understanding Social Entrepreneurship: The Relentless Pursuit of Mission in an Ever Changing World*. New York: Routledge.

Kurucz, Elizabeth C, Barry A. Colbert, and David Wheeler. 2008. "The Business Case for Corporate Social Responsibility". *Oxford Handbook of Corporate Social Responsibility.* 83–112. Oxford Univerity Press: Oxford.

Lewis, Kate V. 2013. "The Power of Interaction Rituals: The Student Volunteer Army and the Christchurch Earthquakes". *International Small Business Journal*. 31 (7): 811–831.

Littlewood, David, and Diane Holt. 2015. "Social and Environmental Enterprises in Africa: Context, Convergence and Characteristics". *The Business of Social and Environmental Innovation: New Frontiers in Africa*. Springer International Publishing.

Littlewood, David, and Diane Holt. 2018. "Social Entrepreneurship in South Africa: Exploring the Influence of Environment". *Business & Society*. 57 (3): 525–561.

Lockett, Andy, Jeremy Moon, and Wayne Visser. 2006. "Corporate Social Responsibility in Management Research: Focus, Nature, Salience and Sources of Influence". *Journal of Management Studies*. 43 (1): 115–136.

Maignan, Isabelle, and David A. Ralston. 2002. "Corporate Social Responsibility in Europe and the US: Insights from Business Self-Presentations". *Journal of International Business Studies*. 33 (3): 497–515.

Mair, Johanna, and Ignasi Marti. 2006. "Social Entrepreneurship Research: A Source of Explanation, Prediction, and Delight". *Journal of World Business*. 41 (1): 36–44.

Malterud, Kirsti. 2001. *Qualitative Research: Standards, Challenges, and Guidelines*. The Lancet Publishing Group. 358 (9280): 483–488.

Martin, Roger L, and Sally Osberg. 2007. "Social Entrepreneurship: The Case for Definition". *Stanford Social Innovation Review*. Spring 2007: 28–39.

Matten, Dirk, and Jeremy Moon. 2008. ""Implicit" and "Explicit" CSR: A Conceptual Framework for a Comparative Understanding of Corporate Social Responsibility". *The Academy of Management Review*. 33 (2): 404–424.

McWilliams Abagail, and Siegel Donald. 2011. "Creating and Capturing Value: Strategic Corporate Social Responsibility, Resource-based theory, and Sustainable Competitive Advantage". *Journal of Management*. 37 (5): 1480–1495.

Menon, Ajay, and Anil Menon. 1997. "Enviropreneurial Marketing Strategy: The Emergence of Corporate Environmentalism as Market Strategy". *Journal of Marketing*. 61 (1): 51–67.

Mitra (Crisan), Catalina, and Anca Borza. 2010. "The role of corporate social responsibility in social entrepreneurship". *Management & Marketing Challenges for Knowledge Society*. 5 (2): 63–76.

Mitra (Crisan), Cătălina Silvia, and Anca Borza. 2011. "Social Entrepreneurship and Social Responsibility: Comparative Study". *Management & Marketing*. 6 (2): 1–12.

Natsvlishvili, Ia. 2018. "Social Entrepreneurship and Corporate Social Responsibility in the Context of a Moral Economy: Dilemma for Developing Countries (case of Georgia)". *Our Economy.* 64 (4): 49–59.

Nicholls, Alex. 2009. "'We Do Good Things, Don't We?': 'Blended Value Accounting' in social entrepreneurship". *Accounting Organizations and Society.* 34 (6–7): 755–769.

Nicholls, Alex. 2010. "The Legitimacy of Social Entrepreneurship: Reflexive Isomorphism in a Pre-Paradigmatic Field". *Entrepreneurship Theory and Practice.* 34 (4): 611–633.

Nicolopoulou, Katrina. 2014. "Social Entrepreneurship Between Cross-Currents: Toward a Framework for Theoretical Restructuring of the Field". *Journal of Small Business Management*. 52 (4): 678–702.

Nicolopoulou, Katrina, and Mine Karatas Ozkan. 2009. "CSR and Social Entrepreneurship: Future Global Opportunities and Challenges in Corporate Community Involvement Strategies". *International Journal of Business and Globalisation.* 3 (2): 173–187.

Niño, Andrea C. S. 2015. "Social Entrepreneurship and Corporate Social Responsibility: Differences and Points in Common". *Journal of Business & Economic Policy.* 2 (2): 85–93.

Nussbaum, Martha C. 1999. "Women and Equality: The Capabilities Approach". *International Labour Review.* 138 (3): 227–244.

OECD. (1999). *Social Enterprises*. Paris: OECD.

Page, Antony, and Robert A. Katz. 2010. "Is Social Enterprise the New Corporate Social Responsibility". *Seattle University Law Review.* 34: 1351–1384.

Palakshappa, Nitha, and Suzanne Grant. 2018. "Social Enterprise and Corporate Social Responsibility Toward a Deeper Understanding of the Links and Overlaps". *International Journal of Entrepreneurial Behavior & Research.* 24 (3): 606–625.

Pasricha, Palvi, Bindu Singh, and Pratibha Verma. 2018. "Ethical Leadership, Organic Organizational Cultures and Corporate Social Responsibility: An Empirical Study in Social Enterprises". *Journal of Business Ethics.* 151 (4): 941–958.

Peredo, Ana María, and Murdith McLean. 2006. "Social Entrepreneurship: A Critical Review of the Concept". *Journal of World Business.* 41 (1): 56–65.

Permana, Agus D, and Tirta N. Mursitama. 2018. "The Influence of Ideological Entrepreneurship to Social Enterprise's Success". *IOP Conference Series: Earth and Environmental Science.* 126 (1): 1–13.

Priede, Tiziana, Ivan Hilliard, and C. López-Cózar. 2014. "Parallel Paths—A Comparison of CSR Firms and Social Enterprises". *Journal of US-China Public Administration.* 11 (10): 852–861.

Ridley-Duff, Rory, and Mike Bull. 2014. "Entrepreneurship: Value-Added Ventures". In *Principles of responsible management: glocal sustainability, responsibility, and ethics.* Boston: South Western College Publishing.

Rivera-Santos, Miguel, Diane Holt, David Littlewood, and Ans Kolk. 2015. "Social Entrepreneurship in Sub-Saharan Africa". *Academy of Management Perspectives.* 29 (1): 72–91.

Saatci, Ezgi Yildirim, and Ceyda Urper. 2013. "Corporate Social Responsibility versus Social Business". *Journal of Economics, Business and Management.* 1 (1): 62–65.

Sandelowski, Margarete. 1995. "Triangles and Crystals: On the Geometry of Qualitative Research". *Research in Nursing & Health.* 18 (6): 569–574.

Sethi, Prakash S. 1975. "Dimensions of Corporate Social Performance: An Analytical Framework". *California Management Review.* 17 (3): 58–64.

Shaw, Eleanor, and Sara Carter. 2007. "Social Entrepreneurship: Theoretical Antecedents and Empirical Analysis of Entrepreneurial Processes and Outcomes". *Journal of Small Business and Enterprise Development.* 14 (3): 418–434.

Singh, Archana, Satyajit Majumdar, and Gordhan K. Saini. 2017. "Corporate Social Responsibility and Social Entrepreneurship: An Indian Context". *Journal of Entrepreneurship and Innovation in Emerging Economies.* 3 (1): 71–76.

Sinha, Deepti, Poonam Kain, and Sachin Sinha. 2017. "Corporate Social Responsibility and Social Entrepreneurship: A Symbiotic Association". *Apeejay Journal of Management Sciences and Technology.* 4 (3): 25–36.

Spence, Laura J. 2016. "Small Business Social Responsibility: Expanding Core CSR Theory". *Business and Society.* 55 (1): 23–55.

Szegedi, Krisztina, Gyula Fülöp, and Ádám Bereczk. 2016. "Relationships Between Social Entrepreneurship, CSR and Social Innovation: In Theory and Practice". *International Journal of Social, Behavioral, Educational, Economic, Business and Industrial Engineering.* 10 (5): 1402–1407.

Teasdale Simon. 2010. "How Can Social Enterprise Address Disadvantage? Evidence from an Inner City Community". *Journal of Nonprofit and Public Sector Marketing.* 22 (2): 89–107.

Thompson, John, and Bob Doherty. 2006. "The Diverse World of Social Enterprise". *International Journal of Social Economics.* 33 (5/6): 361–375.

Tiba, Sarah, Frank J. Rijnsoever, and Marko P. Hekkert. 2019. "Firms with Benefits: A Systematic Review of Responsible Entrepreneurship and Corporate Social Responsibility Literature". *Corporate Social Responsibility and Environmental Management.* 26 (2): 265–284.

Uddin, Md Mesbah, Matthew Hughes, and Paul Burrows. 2016. "Embedding corporate social responsibility (CSR) with entrepreneurship: a contested exploration to advance corporate social entrepreneurship". In Sustainability, Ethics, and Entrepreneurship (SEE) Conference. Denver, Colorado, USA, 16–18 May 2016.

Waddock, Sandra. 2004. "Parallel Universes: Companies, Academics, and the Progress of Corporate Citizenship". *Business and Society Review.* 109 (1): 5–42.

Wang, Hua, Ilan Alon, and Chris Kimble. 2015. "Dialogue in the Dark: Shedding Light on the Development of Social Enterprises in China". *Global Business and Organizational Excellence.* 34 (4): 60–69.

Zeyen, Anica, Markus Beckmann, Susan Mueller, Gregory J. Dees, Dmitry Khanin, Norris Krueger, Patrick J. Murphy. 2013. "Social Entrepreneurship and Broader Theories: Shedding New Light on the 'Bigger Picture'". *Journal of Social Entrepreneurship.* 4 (1): 88–107.

11

Ethics and Sustainability: The Role of Sustainable Policy Evaluation Tests

Inês Salgueiro

11.1 Introduction

Among ecological problems, what stands out is the lack of sustainability. The use our way of life makes of natural resources compromises not only "the ability of future generations to meet their own needs" (WCED 1987, 8) but also fails in doing environmental justice. Solving these problems requires a change in our way of life. This change must necessarily involve our economic, political, and social practices, but we must also become aware of the way our thinking is shaping our lives, namely in the field of ethical and moral foundations. Thus, the first step to be taken towards sustainability is to reflect on our ethical principles. It is necessary to examine the viability of traditional ethics to serve as the basis for a sustainable way of life.

I. Salgueiro (✉)
CECH, University of Coimbra, Coimbra, Portugal

IFILNOVA, Nova University of Lisbon, Lisbon, Portugal

C. Simões et al. (eds.), *Corporate Responsibility, Sustainability and Markets*, Palgrave Studies in Governance, Leadership and Responsibility, https://doi.org/10.1007/978-3-030-79660-0_11

This chapter aims to study the limitations and the possibilities in current ethical theories to solve environmental problems. It serves to connect issues in environmental ethics with the best work in classic deontological moral theory, understood here as shared duty. However, if the foundations of environmental ethics are difficult to develop, they are even more difficult to apply. This is due not only to the many faces of the problem and the number of agents involved but also, and mainly, to the interest-relative nature of our thought. By this I mean that our thinking has a characteristic that makes us judge according to our personal interest and not collectively. I intend to analyse this interest-relative nature and show that a solution to this problem must involve an interdisciplinary collaboration between philosophers, politicians, and economists to establish a link between politics, economics, and environmental ethics. Mark Sagoff (1988) was the first thinker to try to establish this link by making a distinction between consumer and citizen. I propose to discuss Sagoff's claims regarding the idea of cost–benefit and, from these remarks, expose the real evidences of the existence of self-interest in the preference for money. The analysis of this interest-relative nature allows us to understand how ethics are indispensable for solving the problem of sustainability, but it presents its weaknesses in both the theoretical and practical fields. Thus, due to an interest-relative constitution from our point of view as well as the practical problem of motivating collective responsibilities and our type of democracies, a solution to the problem seems very difficult to achieve. Given these reasons and owing to the great risk of serious damage to future generations and the natural environment, it can be concluded that the individual's autonomy, although necessary, is inadequate to solve problems that require collective action. To solve collective problems, it is essential to create political structures beneficial both to environmental justice and intergenerational justice. As an attempt to minimize the problem, this chapter presents a test, based on the general principles of classical deontology and utilitarian ethics, which allows the concrete intention of sustainability of certain policies in a political campaign to be verified.

The chapter is structured as follows. After the introduction, the second section provides an overview of traditional ethics and their limitations in addressing intergenerational and environmental justice. Next, the third section critically discusses Mark Sagoff's conflict between citizen and consumer. Finally, the fourth section presents the sustainable policy test. The conclusion summarizes the main insights.

11.2 An Overview of Traditional Ethics

Ethics refers to a system of moral principles that can be applied to our questions and our actions. Ethics conventions constitute the discourse of government leaders, business and economic programs, teachers, competitive sports and so on. Ethics is a concern with what is good for individuals, society and, recently, the planet. Ethics provides us with a map that guides us in our decision-making. So, for these reasons, we can define ethics as the most important code of the members of a society. Business ethics are linked to social responsibilities of business practices and, accordingly, they are strongly connected with environmental ethics. These include pollution control, preserving biodiversity, management of environmental resources, our obligation to future generations, and the natural environment.

Intuitively, we all recognize that we have obligations. The idea of sustainability corresponds to our obligation towards a responsible economic practice that bears in mind the limitations of ecosystems, their depletion and their weaknesses.

Sustainability is about the interdependency of the economic, political, and ecological spheres. It is the demand for environmental balance on the part of those who do not yet exist or who do not have a voice. Thus, this is an ethical issue. When we think about the suffering of future generations, individual specimens and species, the destruction and degradation of natural habitats and ocean pollution, for example, we do not consider this suffering to be the result of bad luck but rather we believe it is due to an immoral economic practice.

We all recognize that animals need a place to live. We all recognize plastics should not be in the sea. Such judgments involve the application of the categories of traditional ethical systems. It is our traditional ethical systems that allow us to make an ethical judgment about our obligations to future generations and to nature. I understand nature in the broad sense, that is, everything that is natural as opposed to artificial. Nature includes different individuals, populations, communities, and ecosystems, taking into account the five kingdoms[1] proposed by Whittaker (1969). It also includes the biotic balance of the experience shared between the different species, landscapes, oceans, rivers, lakes, and natural phenomena.

Pillars such as reversing global climate change, protecting biodiversity, developing sustainable food systems, creating renewable energies, and restoring the health of our oceans are strongly rooted in traditional ethics. However, these traditional ethical systems, although necessary to understand the problem, are insufficient to address the issues that arise. Our ethical categories are too anthropocentric. Environmental ethicists make a difference between strong/weak anthropocentric ethics. Here I am using the term in the strong sense, that is, ethics centred only on human privileges and that only intrinsically value human animals whereas non-human animals and the rest of biodiversity are considered to have a mere instrumental value.

Rachel Carson started this discussion in 1963 with "Silent Spring", which consists of a set of essays that document the harmful effects of pesticides on the environment, and the interest in the sustainability of ecosystems extended to Paul Ehrlich's work in "The Population Bomb" (1968) and Garrett Hardin's "The Tragedy of the Commons" (1968). Concerns in the 1960s arose from the observation that nature's resources and value were being lost. The following works sought to determine the central issues of environmental ethics, the way they are related to personal ethics and the need to review the paradigm of our relationship with nature. Among them are Næss' "The Shallow and the Deep, Long-Range Ecology Movement" (1973), Passmore's "Man's Responsibility for Nature" (1974), Singer's "Animal Liberation" (1975), "The Ethics of Environmental Concern" by Attfield (1983), "Philosophy Gone Wild" (1989) by Rolston, and "Feminism and the Mastery of Nature" (1993) by Val Plumwood.

---

[1] I am aware of the more recent organism classification systems but since this research is not about classifying organisms, I will adopt Whittaker's categorization.

Whether in the founding literature of environmental ethics or in more recent literature, it is possible to distinguish three dimensions of the relationship between the human and the natural world. The first is the consideration that we are dependent on natural resources. It is a utilitarian and consequentialist perspective, emphasizing the vulnerability of human beings and assigning an instrumental value to nature. In this dimension, the book "Morality's Progress" (2002) by Jamieson stands out. The second dimension of relationship is that which values nature in aesthetic terms, with the form of human accountability being the aesthetic appreciation of the environment. It is worth highlighting the views of eco-aesthetics, namely those of Berleant in "The Aesthetics of Environment" (1992) and Carlson and Lintott in "Nature, Aesthetics, and Environmentalism: From Beauty to Duty" (2008). Ecofeminism can also be included in this perspective, with Baier's research in "Moral Prejudices" (1994) and Gruen's research in "Entangled Empathy" (2015) being particularly important. A third dimension of relationship with the natural world emphasizes the subject's moral agency and gives intrinsic value to nature. In this perspective the concepts of duty, responsibility and respect are essential when applied to the environment. This is a dimension that includes "deep ecology" (Næss 1973), Regan's deontological foundations in "The Case for Animal Rights" (1983), Callicott's ecocentrism in "Thinking Like a Planet" (2013), and Korsgaard's argumentation in "Fellow Creatures" (2018). Indeed, the field of environmental ethics calls for new ethical ways of judging.

Nature is not only a mere instrument but has a value in itself, as Næss claims (1973), regardless of its usefulness to human beings. Nature already existed before the emergence of humans and will continue to be after humans disappear from the earth. An intrinsic value should be given to nature and to do that we must look beyond our immediate interests and include the interests of other living beings and future generations in our ethical deliberations. This is a metaphysical claim, but it provides the necessary background of all responsible actions. What is required is a change in the anthropomorphic way of considering nature as an instrument only useful to men and women and their economic practices. Moving towards Næss' demands will make it possible to restore nature's dignity and, at the same time, provide the ethical foundations for economic practices. Several thinkers defend this position. Bookchin (1980), for example, argues that the environmental problem must be seen as a social problem and, to that extent, the misuse of nature must be replaced by a form of nature conservation. O'Neill (1992, 1993) argues that human beings must have the necessary ethics to respect nature as an end in itself.

In the field of business ethics, environmental issues are connected to the moral obligations of the agents involved in the business activity. I agree with French (1979, 1984), Copp (2006), Hess (2014), and List and Pettit (2011) who consider that companies are "moral people" in the sense that they are morally responsible for their choices and actions. Corporate moral responsibility must integrate corporate sustainability[2] and to do that it must consider nature's intrinsic value. Environmental and intergenerational concerns are crucial for thinking about how individuals should make decisions in the context of business because it is about deciding what kind of world we want to live in.

These questions lead to a debate on whether environmental ethics should be constituted in a totally new way or whether they should be an extension of traditional ethics. I claim that it is not possible to constitute environmental ethics in a totally new way. Although there is an attempt in some environmental ethical theories to distance themselves from traditional ethics, this separation, although necessary in my view, cannot be total. Ethical tradition should be seen as the infrastructure on which new ethical systems depend. Some structures can and must be modified, but other structures do not have this capacity because they are, themselves, the foundations of ethical thinking on which new ethics are built, like new buildings in an ancient city. We cannot escape from the building models we construct to understand things.[3] We ought to recognize there is a common principle to all traditional ethics, which is "to want to make the world a better place". Consequentialism, social ecology, virtue ethics or Kantian deontological moral theory, for example, want the earth to be a better place to live. The wrong conditions in different historical periods lead us to think about new ethical systems. In our contemporaneity we

---

2 For further discussion see Crane et al. (2008).

3 For further discussion see Salgueiro (2020).

must accommodate the question of the natural environment and that is that.

I am now going to explain why I consider the deontological principles and the utilitarian principle of traditional ethics can be adapted to the requirements of the test that I propose to carry out. Let me start with Kant's deontological principles and then move on to the utilitarian principle.

Kant's categorical imperative is that the human will is an end in itself and because it is always an end and never a means to an end, it allows the application of moral law to the different circumstances of life. Its general formulation is as follows:

> Act as if the maxim of your action were to become by your will a universal law of nature. (Kant 1996a, 73)

Based on this general formulation, we can immediately conclude that environmental destruction cannot be considered a universal law of nature. Injustice to future generations can have no place in the moral law. Kant argues that men and women are responsible for giving themselves the law that they must obey. The human being is the author of the moral law and, therefore, obedience to that law is not given by any external coercion. The categorical imperative values human dignity insofar as it values the autonomy of rational will.

Korsgaard (1996) argues that Kant concludes that the will is autonomous because it is its own law or principle, but that argument leads to the problem of knowing the origin of this law. If the law is imposed outside the will, then the will cannot be considered free. In this sense, the will has to create the moral law. Thus, the problem is not the anthropomorphism of traditional ethics since the categorical imperative can be extended to nature, but the motivation of collective responsibilities.

It seems natural to apply the knowledge of what we consider to be a morally correct decision to a given situation. However, the question is not so simple because the will is not just determined by knowledge. In fact, mere knowledge is cold and external regarding the practical application of morality. We are not beings just endowed with reason; there are other factors that determine our will. Consequently, it is necessary for the agent to determine himself or herself as the cause of their actions. Determining ourselves as a cause is completely different from being moved by external causes; it is a movement of true autonomy.

The Kantian distinction between hypothetical and categorical imperative allows a better understanding of what is at stake. The categorical imperative establishes a law for each moral subject, but that law is not an indifferent and heteronomous law; it is a law that finds its strength in the rational will of each subject. Therefore, the subject is himself or herself the legislator and the executor of morality.

Potter (1997) argues that the categorical imperative is a synthetic a priori proposition because it postulates that rational beings can act for purely moral reasons, or, in other words, the categorical imperative expresses a principle of motivation of will. According to Potter, the categorical imperative must be linked to human motivation. Thus, the categorical imperative is a priori because it is not given to us by experience and is synthetic because it is a non-analytical imperative that, when confronted with a given situation, allows us to deduce moral injustice while requiring integrity on our part. Thus, moral concepts are exposed by the analytical method, but the categorical imperative is a synthetic because it adds to the moral law the motivation to want to act morally. To want to do good as the ultimate end, that good has a value in itself and that everyone has the will to achieve it in the world gives a non-analytical addition to morality, an effect visible in the world. This is the reason why Kant argues in "The Metaphysic of Morals" (1996b) that the supreme principle of the doctrine of law is analytical while the supreme principle of the doctrine of virtue is synthetic. The categorical imperative is based on the autonomy of the will, with a double aim, namely, to dignify men and women and cause good in the world, uniting it.

Given the formal characteristics of the categorical imperative, it is possible and easy to apply it in environmental ethics tests. But sometimes evidence suggests the categorical imperative is not enough to deal with specific situations that involve conflict. Sometimes there are struggles not resolvable by Kantian ethics. Sometimes we need to resort to the utilitarian principle. This principle considers that it is the consequences of the action that determine its morality. It is a calculation of possible damages and possible gains in relation to the consequences of the action. Sometimes principles are less important than the consequences of actions and, for this reason, I believe the utilitarian principle can be used in sustainable policy tests to complement deontology flaws in order to establish the course of some actions. It should be used because many environmental issues involve incompatible interests.

11.3 The Conflict Between Citizen and Consumer

In the previous section I showed the need to consider the intrinsic value of nature. We have seen that an extension of deontological Kantian moral theory to the environment is enough to restore nature's respect and dignity. But nature does not only have an intrinsic value. It also has an economic value. To conceal this is a naive utopia without practical effects. To that extent, a solution to the problem must involve the balance between considering the environment as having an intrinsic value and having an instrumental value.

Sagoff (1988, 2007) argues that one must seek to balance these two ways of valuing nature. He suggests it is possible to have "good economic performance" but at the same time "respect the sacredness of nature" (Sagoff 2007, 3). He claims that the theory of environmental policy fails because there are two contradictory ideas between groups of ecologists, on the one hand, and economists, on the other hand.

Sagoff's main objective is to reject cost–benefit analysis as a procedure for decision-making on public policies about the environment. The attempt to apply an economic assessment to environmental values is equivalent to treating the preferences an individual has as a citizen as being of the same type as those the same individual has as a consumer. Sagoff complains that the environment cannot be treated as a consumer good. His analyses lead us to reflect on the conflict of roles that we all experience in our daily lives. The behaviours expected of an individual or a certain group by society correspond to social models that condition the performance of that individual or group. People adjust their behaviours to the different contexts of their daily routine. Each person has several roles that can generate conflict. In certain situations, compatible behaviour between two or more roles may not be possible. In this case, an intraspecific conflict is created: the satisfaction of expectations regarding one role implies the inability to respond to the expectations of the other. In this sense, Sagoff argues that conflict arises not only between us, but also within us. This leads to a confrontation between what I want as an individual and what I believe as a citizen (Sagoff 1988, 60). The problem is therefore general and the conflict within individuals is large. The consumer is opposed to the moral agent and the concerned citizen (Sagoff 1988, 67).

Our way of judging is constituted in an identity. This identity requires self-care. But we have forgotten our identity. We have forgotten that we are individuals inserted in a society that interacts with nature and forms a system with it, that is to say, both its parts, whole and interactions, are one and need attention. This system must be recognized as our own identity and, in that sense, requires self-care. But most of the time we are not aware of this. Our identity, owing to many distractions such as consuming goods, is veiled to us. We forget that we have forgotten we are animals that are part of a rare biotic community needing certain conditions to survive and flourish. This forgetfulness is due to an interest-relative constitution that makes us believe that although other species and future generations have their importance, this is less important than our own personal interests because they are anonymous interests and not our own interests. This is the lie we live every day.

Given these circumstances, we can conclude that the value of nature cannot be based on a policy that considers nature to be a consumer good, but on a policy that values it as having an intrinsic value. Governments have a responsibility to help ensure the conditions in which the economy will function, defining and enforcing the rights of nature through legal reforms thus ensuring the sustainability of ecosystems. Citizens, for their part, "can support many social goals that are justified in themselves—as expressions of the intrinsic values of the community—and not simply or primarily because of their effects on the performance of the economy" (Sagoff 1988, 19).

The role played by consumers, citizens, companies, politicians, economists, and environmentalists is different and often incompatible.

Thus, following the idea of a social contract, citizens give up their individual freedom for a greater purpose—the collective interest. If that idea fails, states will collapse in the long run. It is in the need for survival of the concept of state and its functions that policies must have an environmental ethic as a guideline that considers economic development compatible with sustainability. Politics must seek the collective interest as an objective. The survival of our species and the survival of other species is in our collective interest. In this approach, the great majority of individuals represent the visibility of the policies followed.

11.4 Sustainable Policy Tests

The extension of Kantian ethics to the environment is sufficient to solve ecological problems, but since not all subjects are motivated to do so given the extreme complexity of following Kantian ethics, a solution grounded on the principles of law and not on the principles of virtue would be more efficient. Thus, in the presence of an unfair situation, the idea of justice, intuitively recognized by all of us, must be applied through coercive means based on policies that require strict legislation for economic practices that are not aimed either at our collective interest or at the collective interest of future generations and other species. Intergenerational issues and environmental justice must be present in the policies of the different states because there is a moral duty that underlies the political duty to ensure future generations and other species have an ecosystem favourable to life. Within this context, not attending to the rights of future generations and the natural environment should not be a political hypothesis.

The sustainable policy test appears as an attempt to solve this problem. It is easier for citizens to apply than to solve the conflict between citizen and consumer experienced in a supermarket (Sagoff 1988). This test must be a formal test that can be applied to any political program and is a viable way to verify such a program. It could be based on three deontological principles and on one utilitarian principle. The deontological principles are respect for the intrinsic value of ecosystems and biodiversity, intergenerational justice, and environmental non-maleficence.

The utilitarian principle is to maximize good and minimize harm for the survival of our species. These four principles should form part of common guidelines and serve as general guidelines for the actions of political parties.

Based on these principles, each political party must develop its policies in accordance with its ideologies if these allow them to pass the test of sustainable policy. In this way, the political ideals of each party are not at risk and are safeguarded. They must only adapt to respect the intrinsic value of ecosystems and biodiversity, intergenerational justice, and environmental non-maleficence. These indicators, although linked with an orientation towards sustainability, leave considerable space for the implementation of different political ideals in different economic and cultural situations and can therefore be applied in any country. This test will confer certainty on the goal of intergenerational justice and environmental justice. Accordingly, citizens will be freed from the burden of conflict between citizens and consumers. In other words, it will no longer be difficult for citizens to choose sustainability. Sustainability cannot be a personal decision. There is no point in imputing ecological responsibility to citizens because such accountability corresponds to a distortion of the idea of a social contract. Delegating ecological responsibility to a citizen's conscience without legal penalties is equivalent to delegating the responsibility of not killing another human being to a citizen's conscience without legal penalties.

The idea of a social contract arises from the need to alienate freedom in order to protect the common interest. In other words, the idea of a social contract also corresponds to a transfer of responsibility. Thus, it will only make sense to maintain the social contract if states fulfil their part of the agreement. In the case of a manifest breach of the state's responsibilities, a return to our natural state of freedom will be inevitable. The protection of citizens involves the protection of other species. The political organization of human beings only makes sense if it offers stability, security, and continuity of life. Thus, according to these principles, it is possible to analyse and assess the risk of political agreement according to the following indicators:

a. Promote renewable energies.

b. Ensure the sustainable use of resources.
c. Support intergenerational justice.
d. Respect human rights.
e. Respect nature's intrinsic value.

To apply the test, we must answer the following questions:

Question 1—Does this political party support non-renewable energies?
If the answer is yes, the political party passes the first question.
If the answer is no, ask:
Is this political party maximizing good and minimizing harm for the survival of our species by supporting non-renewable energies?

After this question, we should:

a. Identify alternative actions and those affected. The alternatives are to support renewable energies. Those affected include the non-renewable energy companies and their employees, stockholders, and suppliers as well as their customers and the society that uses non-renewable energies.
b. Determine benefits and costs for each alternative. Alternative 1—If politics does not support renewable energies, there is a high probability that the non-renewable energy companies will benefit in the short term from higher sales and profits and the marketing team will be rewarded. The employees, stockholders, suppliers, and customers will be happy. In the longer term, however, the resources will run out, biodiversity is compromised, pollution will increase, the air will be very polluted, diseases caused by pollution will increase, and the survival of our species will be compromised, and society will incur higher health care costs from the long-term effects of non-renewable energies. Alternative 2—If they do support renewable energies in the campaign, in the short term non-renewable companies will bear the costs of developing non-renewable energies and a new marketing approach and the marketers will be disappointed. The employees, stockholders, suppliers, and customers will be disappointed. However, in the long term, resources will not run out, biodiversity is less

compromised, pollution will decrease, the air will be less polluted, diseases caused by pollution will decrease, and the survival of our species will not be compromised, and society's costs will be lower.

Conclusion: To support renewable energies in the campaign corresponds to maximizing good and minimizing harm (Alternative 2). Not supporting them in the campaign corresponds to maximizing harm and minimizing good (Alternative 1).

Question 2—Does this political party ensure the sustainable use of resources?
If the answer is yes, the political party passes the second question.

If the answer is no, ask:
Is this political party defending the common good by not ensuring sustainable use of resources policies?

This question might help politicians understand that the common good may require that politicians give up some policies and that the common good of maximizing the beneficial effects of stability means that lobbying for an interest group needs to be restrained.
Conclusion: If a party-political action conflicts with the obligation to contribute to the common good, it is the wrong action.

Question 3—Does this political party ensure intergenerational justice?
If the answer is yes, the political party passes the third question.
If the answer is no, ask:
Is this political party defending the fair distribution of benefits and burdens by not ensuring intergenerational justice?

If everyone is equal, that is, has equal value as a human being, then everyone has an equal claim to a share. The default distribution is to give everyone an equal share since all are worth the same. This should be applied to future generations.
Conclusion: The present generations are getting all the benefits in this situation. The future generations are getting all the burdens. To be a fair distribution both generations would get benefits and burdens.

Question 4—Is this political party respecting human rights?

First, the right being upheld or violated should be identified. An extensive list of what many takes to be essential human rights is contained in the United Nations' Universal Declaration of Human Rights (1948) and in the resolution adopted by the Human Rights Council (2011).

If the political party respects all human rights, it passes the fourth question.

If this political party fails to respect the right to a decent environment, which is a human right, then this political party is not respecting human rights by not supporting eco-friendly policies.

Question 5—Is this political party respecting nature's intrinsic value?

First, what intrinsic value is should be identified. Intrinsic value is having value in itself and in that respect ecosystems and biodiversity must be maintained even if they are not useful to humankind.

If the political party respects ecosystems and biodiversity, it passes the fifth question.

If the political party does not protect ecosystems and biodiversity, that means it does not respect the intrinsic value of nature.

Although the questions are numbered, there is no specific order to apply the test because the idea is to focus on how different political programs are facing the points raised by the test's central questions in concrete terms. In this test I focus on intergenerational justice, sustainable use of resources, biodiversity, and some environmental issues. However, there are other environmental concerns that are not directly highlighted by the test, such as ecosystems, functional diversity, and population ethics, for example.

11.5 Conclusion

Applying tests to the policies defended in a political campaign can be quite beneficial to environmental sustainability because it allows the ecological risk in the choice of certain government leaders to be minimized and works as an anticipatory ethics in the field of government policies. The sustainable policy test would make it simpler to analyse the green policies, or the lack of them, behind the different political programs. Both consumers and companies will benefit from such clarity regarding political campaigns.

These tests can be applied by citizens, companies, the media, or social networks. Although at an early stage of development and still dealing with devising methods to improve them, these tests make a significant contribution to the questions raised about corporate responsibility, sustainability, and markets because they make it possible to gain a qualitative approximation of the importance of the policies concerning environmental ethics and intergenerational justice. Green economic policies would make it easier for companies to be socially responsible because it would benefit an economy based on long-term sustainability. A sustainable political strategy would also make it easier for consumers to be socially responsible citizens and to practise green behaviour.

Future research ought to develop more tests to verify how political programs are addressing the issues raised by both environmental and intergenerational justice concerns. It should also look at how these tests can be integrated into the programs of different political parties in different countries and languages. In general, empirical studies can help to reveal ecological intentions. Such work is essential to complement, inform and evaluate the efficacy of sustainable policy tests.

Acknowledgements This chapter was prepared with the support of the Portuguese Foundation for Science and Technology (FCT), grant number 2020.05875.BD.

References

Attfield, Robin. *The Ethics of Environmental Concern.* New York: Columbia University, Press, 1983.

Baier, Annette. *Moral Prejudices: Essays on Ethics*. Cambridge: Harvard University Press, 1994.

Berleant, Arnold. *The Aesthetics of Environment*. Philadelphia: Temple University Press, 1992.

Bookchin, Murray. *Toward an Ecological Society*. Montreal: Black Rose Books, 1980.

Callicott, Baird. *Thinking Like a Planet: The Land Ethic and Earth Ethic*. New York: Oxford University Press, 2013.

Carlson, Allen, and Sheila Lintott. *Nature, Aesthetics, and Environmentalism: From Beauty to Duty*. New York: Columbia University Press, 2008.

Carson, Rachel. *Silent Spring*. London: Hamish Hamilton, 1963.

Copp, David. "On the Agency of Certain Collective Entities: An Argument for "Normative Autonomy." *Midwest Studies in Philosophy* 30, no. 1 (2006): 194–221.

Crane, Andrew, Dirk Matten, and Jeremy Moon. *Corporations and Citizenship*. New York: Cambridge University Press, 2008.

Ehrlich, Paul. *The Population Bomb*. New York: Ballantine Books, 1968.

French, Peter. "The Corporation as a Moral Person." *American Philosophical Quarterly* 16, no. 3 (1979): 297–317.

French, Peter. *Collective and Corporate Responsibility*. New York: Columbia University Press, 1984.

Gruen, Lori. *Entangled Empathy: An Alternative Ethic for Our Relationships with Animals*. Brooklyn: Lantern Books, 2015.

Hardin, Garrett. "The Tragedy of the Commons." *Science* 162, no. 3859 (1968): 1243–1248.

Hess, Kendy. "The Free Will of Corporations (and Other Collectives)." *Philosophical Studies* 168, no. 1 (2014): 241–260.

Human Rights Council. (2011). Resolution 16/11. "Human Rights and the Environment" (UN HRC). Available at https://www2.ohchr.org/english/bodies/hrcouncil/docs/16session/A.HRC.RES.16.11_en.pdf (last accessed 11 August 2021).

Jamieson, Dale. *Morality's Progress*. Oxford: Clarendon Press, 2002.

Kant, Immanuel. *Groundwork of the Metaphysics of Morals*. Translated by Mary Gregor. Cambridge: Cambridge University Press, 1996a.

Kant, Immanuel. *The Metaphysics of Morals*. Translated by Mary Gregor. Cambridge: Cambridge University Press, 1996b.

Korsgaard, Christine. *The Sources of Normativity*. Cambridge: Cambridge University Press, 1996.

Korsgaard, Christine. *Fellow Creatures: Our Obligations to the Other Animals*. Oxford: Oxford University Press, 2018.
List, Christian, and Philip Pettit. *Group Agency: The Possibility, Design, and Status of Corporate Agents*. New York: Oxford University Press, 2011.
Næss, Arne. "The Shallow and the Deep, Long-Range Ecology Movement". *Inquiry* 16 (1973): 95–100.
O'Neill, John. "The Varieties of Intrinsic Value." *Monist* 75, no. 2 (1992):119–137.
O'Neill, John. *Ecology, Policy and Politics*. London: Routledge, 1993.
Passmore, John. *Man's Responsibility for Nature*. London: Duckworth & Co, 1974.
Plumwood, Val. *Feminism and the Mastery of Nature*. New York: Routledge, 1993.
Potter, Nelson. "The Synthetic a priori Proposition of Kant's Ethical Philosophy." *Jahrbuch für Recht und Ethik / Annual Review of Law and Ethics* 5, (1997): 437–459.
Regan, Tom. *The Case for Animal Rights*. London: Routledge and Kegan Paul, 1983.
Rolston, Holmes. *Philosophy Gone Wild*. Amherst: Prometheus Books, 1989.
Sagoff, Mark. *The Economy of the Earth*. Cambridge: Cambridge University Press, 1988.
Sagoff, Mark. *The Economy of the Earth: Philosophy, Law, and the Environment*, 2nd edn. Cambridge: Cambridge University Press, 2007.
Salgueiro, Inês. "Knowledge and Technology: Man as a Technological Animal." In *Knowledge, People and Digital Transformation: Approaches for a Sustainable Future*, edited by Florinda Matos, Valter Vairinhos, Isabel Salavisa, Leif Edvinsson and Maurizio Massaro, 25–36. Cham: Springer, 2020.
Singer, Peter. *Animal Liberation*. New York: Random House, 1975.
UN General Assembly. 1948. "Universal Declaration of Human Rights" (217 A [III]). Available at https://www.ohchr.org/EN/Issues/Education/Training/Compilation/Pages/UniversalDeclarationofHumanRights(1948).aspx (last accessed 11 August 2021).
WCED. 1987. *Our Common Future: The World Commission on Environment and Development*. Oxford: Oxford University Press.
Whittaker, Robert. "New Concepts of Kingdoms of Organisms." *Science* 163, no. 3863 (1969): 150–160.

12

Models of Capitalism, Institutions and Corporate Social Responsibility

Robert Kudłak

12.1 Introduction

To date, theoretical and empirical investigations on the causes of the involvement of enterprises in corporate social responsibility (CSR) have focused primarily on the ethical and strategic explanations of such activities. However, these studies have failed to take into account the institutional conditions in which economic entities operate. It was only the most recent decade of research on CSR that has brought a change in this regard. Of special importance were the studies by Campbell (2007) and Matten and Moon (2008) that have inspired many further theoretical and empirical studies analysing the impact of a broader institutional, cultural and political context on the behaviour of economic entities, including the level and form of their involvement in corporate social responsibility (Gjolberg 2009; Grosvold and Brammer 2011; Brammer et al. 2012; Campbell et al. 2012; Ioannou and Serafeim 2012). The

R. Kudłak (✉)
Adam Mickiewicz University, Poznań, Poland

C. Simões et al. (eds.), *Corporate Responsibility, Sustainability and Markets*, Palgrave Studies in Governance, Leadership and Responsibility,
https://doi.org/10.1007/978-3-030-79660-0_12

present work also refers to the institutional stream of CSR research and proposes an alternative explanation of the relationship between institutional environment and voluntary engagement in socially responsible activities. I argue that institutional conditions in a given country are a consequence of the adopted model of capitalism and, in particular, the model of the welfare state. In countries with a strong welfare state model (e.g. Western European countries), the state takes a large share of the responsibility for ensuring society's access to certain social services (e.g. universal, publicly-financed access to health care). To this end, it creates an institutional and legal system that ensures the creation and distribution of these services and obligates economic entities to be part of this process. This reduces the willingness of private actors to engage in voluntary activities in this area. In other words, strong institutional conditions "crowd out" CSR. On the other hand, in countries where the role of the state and the pressure of the institutional environment in this respect are smaller, the involvement of private entities in the provision of social services is greater. In short, the design of the institutional environment leads to a higher level ("crowds in") of engagement in corporate social responsibility.

12.2 The Rise of the European and American Models of the Welfare State

The term "welfare state" emerged after the Second World War, when a debate was launched in countries of Europe and North America over the responsibility of the state for the broadly construed social welfare and its redistribution between all the members of a society (Szarfenberg 2007). Undoubtedly, the process of expanding the state's involvement in social security has a longer tradition than the post-war period. It is worth mentioning here, for example, the compulsory health and unemployment insurance introduced by Bismarck (Suchiecka 2010) or the Beveridge Plan in the UK, which promoted social insurance and introduced public health services (Abel-Smith 1992). However, the post-war reconstruction of states and the growing level of industrialisation and urbanisation leading to the commoditisation of labour, intensified the efforts of successive governments to expand the scope of public intervention in order to ensure a more equitable access to welfare. These developments stimulated researchers to distinguish between different models of the welfare state (Esping-Andersen 1990; Castles and Mitchell 1993; Bonoli 1997). One of the most common typologies was proposed by Esping-Andersen (1990), who, on the basis of decommodification and stratification indices, singled out three models of the welfare state: liberal (residual), conservative and social democratic. The level and scope of state involvement in the broadly understood social policy are one of the basic elements that help to differentiate between these models.

The USA (but also Canada and Australia) is most often seen as an example of a liberal welfare state, regardless of the criteria adopted for delimiting the types of welfare state (e.g. Castles and Mitchell 1993; Bonoli 1997; Esping-Andersen 1999). This type is characterised by both the dominance of the market as a mechanism for redistributing wealth among the members of society and individualism. State intervention in the creation and redistribution of goods and services is very limited and concerns persons who are in fact unable to participate in the labour market (Arts and Gelissen 2002). These countries are characterised by a relatively low level of decommodification and a fairly pronounced degree of social economic disparity. In turn, in the social democratic model, the state is the most generous from the point of view of social policy (Esping-Andersen 1990). The state offers universal provision of social services and a high level of protection in case of unemployment (high decommodification). Therefore, the role of the state is strongly interventionist and manifests itself e.g. in a very extensive fiscal policy. In the conservative model, too, the level of social security and social services provided by the public sector is high (Esping-Andersen 1990). Differences in institutional conditions between the USA and European countries are the result of their specific, unique paths of historical development. At the end of the nineteenth century, both the United States and European countries were characterised by a similarly minimal range of the welfare state (Skocpol 1992). However, certain historical events contributed to the fact that the paths of these two regions of the world diverged in terms of creating and redistributing wealth.

The emergence of the USA as a federation of independent states restricted the possibility of establishing and conducting a central (nationwide) policy of wealth redistribution. According to Alesina et al. (2001), the political stability of the USA was the result of its eighteenth-century constitution, which guaranteed such a division of power between the federal government and the state authorities, protecting the latter from the influence and domination of the former. Researchers dealing with the American model of capitalism point out that elements of the welfare state in the USA began to emerge after the end of the Civil War in the form of pension schemes for war veterans (Skocpol 1992). Although this system was seen by some as the onset of a broader, universal system of social support, there were some factors that hindered its further development. These included social reluctance and mistrust of the central administration of the support system for veterans as well as the fact that the Civil War had deepened the internal divisions between the various states (Alesina et al. 2001). Court decisions, rejecting any legislative changes violating the rights of private entrepreneurs, also had a significant impact on limiting the development of the welfare state. Court jurisprudence in this area was a consequence of the American Constitution, whose primary objective was to protect private property rights (Alesina et al. 2001). The strength and independence of American courts were moreover important factors limiting the development of social legislation in the USA, which was not the case in the tradition and the legal systems of countries such as France or Germany (Alesina et al. 2001).

Given that a centrally managed, public system for redistributing wealth in the USA had not developed, the importance of private initiatives in this area began to grow, which is reflected in American culture to this day. Skocpol et al. (2000) have documented the role and importance of many NGOs (often nationwide), which since the beginning of American statehood have provided various social services benefiting their members and other target groups. These organisations have largely fulfilled the role played (to date) by European governments.

Alesina et al. (2001) moreover point to the fact that the USA has never developed an extensive and consistent movement safeguarding employees' rights, which could have contributed to the emergence and development of broadly construed social policy. While in nineteenth-century Europe, in the wake of the class struggle initiated by the communists, a workers' movement was created, American workers seemed to represent social Darwinism (Lipset and Marks 2000). In the USA, equality meant equality of opportunity, not equality of access to prosperity. The Great Depression of the 1930s was politically exploited by President Franklin Delano Roosevelt through the introduction of the New Deal programme of economic and social reforms, which made it possible to cater to the social demands of the traditional electorate of socialist parties, and which in effect prevented the emergence of such a political party in the USA (Alesina et al. 2001).

In turn, the European model of the welfare state was formed after the First World War, which completely reshaped the political order in Europe. The end of the war brought about the collapse of most of Europe's monarchies. This was accompanied by the development of workers' movements and parties whose pre-war activities (and those caused by social unrest) in countries such as Germany, Austria and Italy were limited by the presence of strong armies in those countries. States weakened by war could no longer significantly control and restrict the development of labour movements. All these processes made the newly adopted constitutions in European countries focus on the democratisation of state systems (e.g. by introducing proportional representation in parliament) and much less so than the American Constitution on protecting property rights (Alesina et al. 2001; Alesina and Glaeser 2006). Moreover, in his work Esping-Andersen (1990) draws attention to the birth of the middle class, whose support was greatly coveted by politicians, who extended the scope of the welfare state.

A more detailed and comprehensive analysis of the historical conditions that influenced the shape of contemporary welfare states and their institutional conditions is beyond the scope of this paper. However, the historical events mentioned above indicate the reasons for the entry of countries (i.e. the USA and Western European countries) onto the paths leading to the birth of different models of the welfare state and the corresponding institutional conditions determining the production and redistribution of welfare (and the role of the state and private entities in this respect).

12.3 Selected Differences Between the American and European Models of Welfare State

Institutional comparative analysis of welfare state models usually goes beyond the examination of individual institutional conditions. Rather, it aims at capturing certain common conditionalities in different countries. As Lange and Meadwell (1991) observe, the benefit of such an approach is that it characterises entire political and economic systems, bearing in mind, however, that certain features of these systems are similarly interlinked. The types of capitalist systems proposed by Esping-Andresen (1990, 1999) and by other authors differ from one another in terms of institutional conditions analysed, the level of public and private sector involvement in financing and providing social services, and the degree of distributing wealth among the members of society. Attempts to distinguish some ideal types of welfare state (Esping-Andersen 1990; Bradshaw et al. 1993; OECD 1997; De Beer et al. 2001) usually examine institutional determinants of the labour market (e.g. involvement of the state in the conduct and financing of active labour market policies, protection of workers in case of job loss, role and scope of tripartite agreements), health care, economic support for the unemployed (e.g. unemployment benefits and their determinants), maternity and parental leave, pension insurance and support for families. A detailed analysis of these conditions has been presented in many earlier works and goes beyond the scope of the present study. However, it is worth presenting, even in a simplified way, the differences between the USA and European countries in relation to one of the above spheres of social and economic life in order to highlight the differences between liberal (especially American) and European models of the welfare state.

One of the elementary differences between the countries representing liberal and European models of the welfare state (conservative and social democratic) concerns institutional conditions governing access to and the scope of health care. In European countries, the creation and redistribution of free and accessible health care, usually financed through compulsory taxes and contributions, is one of the fundamental tasks of the state (Moran 2000; Mossialos et al. 2002). Legislators in these countries form a set of institutions (legal and financial regulations) which involve all employees (and members of their families) as well as non-employed persons, in the medical care system. Therefore, in these countries, the responsibility for the establishment of the health care system lies with public entities and companies are obligatorily integrated into the system through a scheme of fiscal burdens. Health care systems cover not only those insured but also their family members and offer a very broad spectrum of entitlements in terms of financing medical appointments, hospitalisation or reimbursement of medicines. In the United States, on the other hand, institutionalised and publicly funded healthcare is in fact limited to two programmes, Medicare and Medicaid, which focus on the elderly and low-income individuals. These programmes are most often addressed exclusively at persons who meet certain age or income criteria, but not their family members. In 2010, a mere 14.5% of American population made use of Medicaid, while ca. 15.9% were covered by Medicare (DeNavas-Malt et al. 2010). In the USA, fees for medical appointments, hospitalisation and reimbursement of medicines are almost entirely covered the patients themselves. However, this lack of an institutionalised, centralised system of universal health care in the USA is compensated for by the insurance policies that employers offer to their employees. Over 60% of people of working age have health insurance financed by their employers (despite the absence of such a legal obligation) (DeNavas-Malt et al. 2010). In the USA, voluntary health insurance coverage by companies is seen as one of the most important obligations of businesses towards both employees and society in general. For example, Starbucks Coffee has since 2004 pursued a policy of providing healthcare to all employees working 20 hours or more a week (Starbucks 2004).

Another example demonstrating the important institutional differences between the USA and the countries of Western Europe in terms of social policy is that of the remuneration received by the worker during his or her illness. In most European countries, when sick, workers are guaranteed remuneration, typically around 70–80% of their regular pay. In the USA, however, only five states have introduced such an institutional and legal solution (Alesina et al. 2001). Moreover, even in these five states, the period of receiving such remuneration is much shorter (a maximum of 52 days) than in Western European countries, and its amount ranges from 18 to 63% of regular pay (Alesina et al. 2001). Similar institutional differences between the USA and European countries also apply to regulations concerning, among others, the labour market, social security as well as the support of families, the elderly and persons with disabilities.

Esping-Andresen's text referred to earlier (1990) triggered the emergence of many other empirical and theoretical works analysing different models of the welfare state in developed countries and promoting alternative typologies (e.g. Castles and Mitchell 1993; Ferrera 1996; Bonoli 1997). Without going into more detail on the differences between these proposals, it is reasonable to argue that research into welfare state models so far has led to some more general conclusions that are relevant to the issues addressed in this paper. First of all, it should be noted that the general dividing line runs between the USA and Western European countries (De Beer et al. 2001; Alesina and Glaeser 2004; Larsen 2008). Irrespective of some differences between them, European governments are much more inclined to centrally and institutionally redirect a significant part of the wealth generated in the country to the economically disadvantaged. In the USA, on the other hand, the government's share in this area is much smaller, which results from the conviction that people themselves are responsible for their own prosperity and that institutionalised assistance should be provided only to those who cannot be economically active (Bergqvist et al. 2013). Researchers point to a number of reasons for the above, including cultural and ethnic differences (Alesina et al. 2001; Larsen 2008; Jaeger 2009). Accordingly, the views and expectations of societies in these countries regarding the role of the public and private sectors in their involvement in the provision of certain social services are also different (Bielefeld et al. 2005; Jaeger 2009).

The above institutional differences between the USA and Western European countries are also reflected in the level of public and private social spending. According to Organisation for Economic Cooperation and Development (OECD 2019), the total European expenditure in this area, measured as a share of GDP, is in all cases higher than in the USA. The European countries presented here spend much more on social welfare goals than the average for OECD countries (21% of GDP), with France (31.7%), Finland (30.6%), Belgium (29.2%) and Italy (28.9%) spending the most, and Norway (23.9%) and the United Kingdom (21.5%) spending the least. The USA spends only 19% of its GDP on social purposes. On the other hand, an examination of private spending in this area shows that USA outlays (11.1%) are significantly higher than those in all European countries and more than 6 times the OECD average (1.8%). The level of spending on healthcare from public sources for all the countries discussed is quite similar and ranges from 5.5% (Norway) to 8.6% (France). However, a huge difference occurs again in the level of private expenditure, which in most European countries (except France and Germany) does not exceed 0.5% of GDP. In turn, in the USA it reaches 5.8% and is almost 10 times higher than the OECD average. A similar trend can be observed when comparing the level of public expenditure and private support for the elderly. The USA spends far less public money on this than European countries, while private money is spent many times higher. Finally, as regards to public expenditure on support and activation of the unemployed and support for families, this level is much higher in European countries than in the USA.

Hacker (2002) draws attention to another important difference between the two models under discussion (i.e. the American model and the European one): a dissimilar level of involvement of NGOs in the financing and delivery of social services. In more liberal systems, the importance and participation of these organisations are much greater. NGOs perform some quasi-public functions by providing social services to the general public (largely financed by the private sector). This was particularly visible in the USA in the 1980s, when the level of public goods and services provided to the society by the government dropped significantly. Salamon (1990) estimated that in this period NGOs provided about 50% of all social services and their activity was financed to a large extent from private funds. Therefore, the importance of these organisations in liberal models of capitalism is vital as they enable private entities to provide certain social services to society through the third sector, without the need to produce them themselves.

This does not mean, of course, that such organisations do not perform similar functions in European countries, but their importance in this respect is significantly lower (Hacker 2002).

The above body of literature and examples clearly show that the USA and Western European countries represent divergent models of the welfare state, which are in turn accompanied by different institutional conditions. In Western Europe, the role of the state in the creation and financing of social services is far greater. Therefore, the governments of these countries create institutional and legal environment guaranteeing universal and wide access to social services financed from public funds. This environment obligatorily involves private entities (first of all enterprises) in financing social welfare. In the United States, on the other hand, the share of the state in the creation and redistribution of social services is much smaller than in the countries of Western Europe, which also results in the fact that economic entities operating in the USA are subject to less institutional pressure to in this regard.

12.4 Institutional Crowding of the Private Provision of Social Services

The institutional differences in the provision of social services between the USA and Western European countries and the differences in the level of social spending clearly indicate that the production and redistribution of certain social services in European countries is mostly the domain of the state and is strongly codified and institutionalised. Business entities operating in these countries are subject to institutional conditions that determine the form, level and scope of mandatory involvement of the private sector in pro-social activities. These conditions reduce the willingness and actual involvement of enterprises in voluntarily, socially responsible activities, for example in the field of private provision of public collective goods. This results in a small participation of the private sector in the process of creation and redistribution of specific social services. On the other hand, in more liberal models of capitalism, such as the American one, the level of state involvement in this area is much lower, which is reflected in the fact that the pressure of institutional environment on enterprises as regards their obligatory participation in the provision of social services (e.g. through the tax system and the system of obligatory health insurance) is lower than in European countries. This means that private entities have far greater opportunities to voluntarily engage in socially responsible activities. Thus, when comparing institutional environments in these two regions of the world, one can see that these differences may serve to explain the relationship between institutional conditions and the level of CSR engagement. The stronger the institutional conditions determining universal access to publicly funded social services, the smaller the range of opportunities and the lower the willingness of enterprises to voluntarily engage in social activities such as health care, pension schemes, funding for education, research, higher education, social assistance, etc. In other words, strong institutional environment "crowd out" corporate social responsibility. Such a model of corporate behaviour is present in Western European countries, which engage in CSR much less frequently than American enterprises. On the other hand, in countries where the pressure of institutional environment in the area in question is lower (such as the USA), we are dealing with "crowding in" of CSR, i.e. a situation in which enterprises much more often engage in voluntary social activities.

There are a number of empirical studies confirming the above mechanism. Namely, high institutional pressure in the form of e.g. universal, institutionalised access to social services decreases the tendency of private entities, including enterprises, to voluntarily engage in this type of activity. Conversely, the reduction of this pressure leads to an increase in the involvement of private entities. The results of selected empirical studies documenting this phenomenon will be presented below with respect to health care, education and culture as well as social welfare. Indication will also be made of some phenomena accompanying "crowding out" and "crowding in", which may have an impact on the level and scope of the involvement of enterprises in corporate social responsibilities.

Numerous empirical studies analyse the phenomena of "crowding out" and "crowding in" in health care. For example, Cutler and Gruber

(1996) tried to estimate the extent to which the extension of Medicaid in the 1987–1992 period "crowded out" the involvement of private entrepreneurs in the provision of health insurance to the workforce. Medicaid was launched in the USA in 1965 and introduced health insurance to the indigent section of the population, especially to low-income women and children in single-parent families. In time, however, the eligibility criteria for the program got laxer and covered also pregnant women, children from more well-to-do families and those brought up by both parents (Cutler and Gruber 1996). Therefore, at the beginning of the 1990s, one third of all children in the USA and over 40% of women of childbearing age were entitled to Medicaid. Estimates made by Cutler and Gruber (1996) show that these changes had an impact on the percentage of the population that received private insurance. The results of their research may justify the conclusion that the expansion of the public health system has "crowded out" about 30–40% of the private insurance offered by companies to people for whom Medicaid has been extended. A similar survey was also conducted by Gruber and Simon (2008) who, using data from the Survey of Income and Program Participation 1996–2001, identified a 60% decline in the share of private insurance among those who were covered by public insurance. Hudson et al. (2005), in turn, studied the impact of the State Children's Health Insurance Program (SCHIP) on public and private insurance coverage of children and the proportion of children not covered by any insurance. They showed that the extension of eligibility to SCHIP increased the proportion of children insured under SCHIP, decreased the proportion of uninsured children, and significantly decreased the proportion of privately insured persons. The above and other studies (Aizer and Grogger 2003; LoSasso and Buchmueller 2004; Busch and Duchovny 2005) have shown that when the state institutionally changes its public health coverage, it can affect access to and coverage of private health insurance.

It can therefore be concluded that the strong institutional conditions prevailing in most European countries codifying in a formal and obligatory way the specific obligations of private entities with regard to, inter alia, healthcare and social security, significantly reduce the scope for voluntary involvement of economic entities in this respect. American companies, on the other hand, which are less exposed to this type of institutional environment, are more willing and have more flexibility to take voluntary actions towards workers and society in general. The above cited studies imply that the strong institutional conditions regarding health care "crowd out" voluntary action of companies which would go beyond the legal obligations of companies. Similar conclusions can be drawn from empirical studies concerning other spheres of social and economic life.

A review of studies carried out by de Witt and Bekkers (2016) demonstrates that ca. 2/3 of them confirm the negative relation between the strength of domestic institutional involvement and the level of provision of social services by the private sector. Scholars moreover indicate that residents of countries which represent dissimilar welfare state models demonstrate a different level of support for the state's extensive provision of social services (Svallfors 1997; Andress and Heien 2001). In countries where residents are accustomed to a high level of state involvement, their expectations concerning the role of private actors (individuals, businesses and NGOs) are relatively limited. In countries where the provision of social services is seen as a joint responsibility of public and private actors, the residents' expectations towards businesses in this regard are much higher (Svallfors 1997; Andress and Heien 2001).

There are also historical studies that explore the discussed mechanism over a longer period of time. For example, Gruber and Hungerman (2007) as well as Roberts (1984) analysed the impact of state intervention in the form of increased levels of goods and services provided to society during the Great Depression of the 1930s. Both studies confirmed the phenomenon of "crowding out" and Roberts (1984) pointed to the almost complete "crowding out" of private donations as a consequence of the overly excessive level of social protection financed and organised by the state. Similar conclusions were drawn by Abrams and Schmitz (1984).

Hiss (2009) uses the example of Germany to illustrate interesting institutional changes and their impact on corporate behaviour. In the 1950s and 1960s, Germany adopted a socio-economic development model that combined economic growth with relatively evenly distributed social welfare with a high level of corporate commitment. A significant range of economic activities was strictly regulated in order to promote social justice and a relatively equal participation by members of society in the welfare created. What has distinguished Germany from other countries is, among others, a significant share of the banking sector in financing the activities of enterprises (which gives preferences to long-term investments), the development of vocational education and a co-participation mechanism (with the participation of employees and their representatives) during the drafting and amending of the labour law (Hiss 2009).

The model based on institutionalised social solidarity (Kinderman 2012) described by Hiss (2009), as a result of increasing integration of the world economy, liberalisation of financial markets and growing deregulation of economies, began to erode slowly since ca. the mid-1980s. This led to the weakening of institutional conditions which guaranteed relatively universal access to social services for all members of the public and the role of the public sector in the provision of these services. This led to a weakening of the trade unions, which previously had safeguarded workers' rights, a weakening of collective labour agreements and an increase in dividends paid to shareholders at the expense of taxes paid to the state budget (Hiss 2009).

As a result, more and more German companies started to take voluntary measures that went beyond legal regulations (earlier attributed to the government and its agendas) in order to improve working conditions and establish work and environmental standards in the production chain. Summing up, the example described by Hiss (2009) implies that the weakening of institutional conditions and the role of the state in the creation and redistribution of social services triggers a heightened involvement of private enterprises in this respect, i.e. their involvement in corporate social responsibility.

12.5 Conclusions

In light of the arguments presented in this chapter, the involvement of enterprises in voluntary activities promoting social welfare is a function of the institutional environment which, in turn, is a consequence of the capitalism model adopted, in particular of the welfare state model. Specifically, the presented relationship implies that strong institutional pressure reflecting a high level of state involvement in the provision of social services reduces the level of voluntary engagement of economic entities in socially responsible activities ("crowds out" CSR), while low pressure increases this level ("crowds in" CSR). It seems that this relationship can effectively explain the level of CSR engagement of enterprises and the differences between developed countries, such as the USA and Western Europe, in this respect.

It seems that the explanation proposed in this chapter for the relationship between the institutional environment and the involvement of enterprises in CSR may be an interesting alternative to the theoretical considerations on the subject, dominant in the relevant literature, and may effectively explain the reasons for CSR implementation and the differences between countries and the world's regions in this regard. The phenomenon of institutional "crowding out" and "crowding in" of CSR described in this chapter is part of empirical research on corporate social responsibility and explains why in countries with a liberal welfare state model, such as the American one, the level of involvement of enterprises in CSR is much higher than, for example, in European countries.

The link between institutional determinants and CSR discussed in this chapter concerns only highly developed countries. Their capitalism models and existing institutional settings are stable and have developed as a result of a long process. The behaviour of enterprises is a consequence of these models and conditions. However, in countries other than highly developed ones (e.g. developing countries and countries undergoing a systemic transformation) it is difficult to clearly distinguish consistent models of capitalism which would be comparable with other models (e.g. Western European or American ones). It may be assumed that they are a combination of the existing institutional conditions and new institutions "imported" from highly developed economies, and therefore these countries cannot be the subject of comparative analysis in one group with highly developed countries (Ebbinghaus 2012). It is therefore necessary to explain in a different way how and under the influence of which conditions enterprises in developing countries and countries undergoing a systemic transformation undertake organisational practices in the field of CSR.

Interestingly, institutional changes leading to the state's withdrawal from the creation and distribution of certain social services (as presented for example by Hiss 2009) do not necessarily lead to automatic and unconditional filling of this gap by private sector entities. It should be borne in mind that institutional conditions are permanent, stable and less susceptible to change. Therefore, the current institutional landscape in market economy countries (regardless of the adopted capitalism model) is a consequence of a very long and slow process of institutional development, often unique and determined by the socially accepted development model and certain historical and political events. This does not mean that it is impossible to replace the role and position of the state by the private sector, but it is a rather slow process, determined by the current institutional conditions.

Acknowledgements The research underlying this chapter was funded by the Polish National Centre of Science (grant no. 2017/25/B/HS/00197 "Theoretical foundations of the relationship between institutional conditions and Corporate Social Responsibility").

References

Abel-Smith, Brian. "The Beveridge Report: Its origins and outcomes". *International Social Security Review* 45(1–2) (1992): 5–16.

Abrams, Burton A., and Mark D. Schmitz. "The crowding-out effect of governmental transfers on private charitable contributions: Cross-section evidence". *National Tax Journal* (1984): 563–568.

Aizer, Anna, and Jeffrey Grogger. "Parental Medicaid Expansions and Child Medicaid Coverage". NBER Working Paper #9907, August, 2003.

Alesina, Alberto, and Edward L. Glaeser. *Fighting poverty in the US and Europe: A world of difference*. Oxford: Oxford University Press, 2004.

Alesina, Alberto, and Edward L. Glaeser. "Why are welfare states in the US and Europe so different?". *Horizons Stratégiques* 2 (2006): 51–61.

Alesina, Alberto, Edward L. Glaeser, and Bruce Sacerdote. "Why doesn't the US have a European-style welfare system?" (No. w8524). National Bureau of Economic Research, 2001.

Andress, Hans-Jürgen, and Thorsten Heien. "Four worlds of welfare state attitudes? A comparison of Germany, Norway, and the United States". *European Sociological Review* 17(4) (2001): 337–356.

Arts, W., and John Gelissen. "Three worlds of welfare capitalism or more? A state-of-the-art report". *Journal of European Social Policy* 12(2) (2002): 137–158.

Bergqvist, Kersti, Monica A. Yngwe, M. Å., and Olle Lundberg. "Understanding the role of welfare state characteristics for health and inequalities—An analytical review". *BMC Public Health* 13(1) (2013): 1234.

Bielefeld, Wolfgang, Patrick Rooney, and Kathy Steinberg. "How do need, capacity, geography, and politics influence giving". In *Gifts of money in Americas communities*, ed. Arthur C. Brooks. Rowman & Littlefield Publishers, 2005, 127.

Bonoli, Giuliano. "Classifying welfare states: A two-dimension approach". *Journal of Social Policy* 26(3) (1997): 351–372.

Bradshaw, Jonathan, John Ditch, Hilary Holmes, and Peter Whiteford. "A comparative study of child support in fifteen countries". *Journal of European Social Policy* 3–4 (1993): 255–271.

Brammer, Stephen, Gregory Jackson, and Dirk Matten. "Corporate social responsibility and institutional theory: New perspectives on private governance". *Socio-economic Review* 10(1) (2012): 3–28.

Busch, Susan., and Noelia Duchovny. "Family coverage expansions: Impact on insurance coverage and health care utilization of parents". *Journal of Health Economics* 24(5) (2005): 876–890.

Campbell, John L. "Why would corporations behave in socially responsible ways? An institutional theory of corporate social responsibility". *Academy of Management Review* 32(3) (2007): 946–967.

Campbell, Joanna T., Lorraine Eden, and Stewart R. Miller. "Multinationals and corporate social responsibility in host countries: Does distance matter?" *Journal of International Business Studies* 43(1) (2012): 84–106.

Castles, F. G., Mitchell, D. "Worlds of welfare and families of nations". In *Families of nations: patterns of public policy in Western democracies*, ed. F.G. Castles. Aldreshot: Darthmouth Publishing Company, 1993, 94–112.

Cutler, D. M., and Gruber, J. "Does public insurance crowd out private insurance?" *Quarterly Journal of Economics* 111(2) (1996): 391–430.

De Beer, P., Vrooman, C., and Wildeboer Schut, J. M. "Measuring Welfare State Performance: Three or Two Worlds of Welfare Capitalism?" (No. 276). LIS Working Paper Series, 2001.

de Wit, A., and Bekkers, R. "Government support and charitable donations: A meta-analysis of the crowding-out hypothesis". *Journal of Public Administration Research and Theory* 27(2) (2016): 301–319.

DeNavas-Malt, C., Proctor, B.D., and Smith, "J.C. Income, poverty, and health insurance coverage in the United States: 2010". Current Population Reports, U.S. Census Bureau, Washington, DC, 2011.

Ebbinghaus, B. *Comparing welfare state regimes: Are typologies an ideal or realistic strategy*. Edinburg, UK: ESPAN, 2012, 1–20.

Esping-Andersen, G. *The three worlds of welfare capitalism*. Wiley, 1990.

Esping-Andersen, G. *Social foundations of postindustrial economies*. Oxford University Press, 1999.

Ferrera, M. "The Southern model of welfare in social Europe". *Journal of European Social Policy* 6(1) (1996): 17–37.

Gjolberg, M. "The origin of corporate social responsibility: Global forces of national legacies?" *Socio-Economic Review* 7 (2009): 605–637.

Grosvold, J., and Brammer, S. "National institutional systems as antecedents of female board representation: An empirical study". *Corporate Governance: An International Review* 19(2) (2011): 116–135.

Gruber, J., and Hungerman, D. M. "Faith-based charity and crowd-out during the great depression". *Journal of Public Economics* 91(5) (2007): 1043–1069.

Gruber, J. and Simon, K. "Crowd-out 10 years later: Have recent public insurance expansions crowded out private health insurance?" *Journal of Health Economics* 27 (2008): 201–217.

Hacker, J. S. *The divided welfare state: The battle over public and private social benefits in the United States*. Cambridge University Press, 2002.

Hiss, S. "From implicit to explicit corporate social responsibility: Institutional change as a fight for myths". *Business Ethics Quarterly* 19(3) (2009): 433–451.

Hudson, J. L., Selden, T. M., and Banthin, J. S. "The impact of SCHIP on insurance coverage of children". *INQUIRY: Journal of Health Care Organization, Provision, and Financing* 42(3) (2005): 232–254.

Ioannou, I., and Serafeim, G. "What drives corporate social performance? The role of nation-level institutions". *Journal of International Business Studies* 43(9) (2012): 834–864.

Jaeger, M. M. "United but divided: Welfare regimes and the level and variance in public support for redistribution". *European Sociological Review* 25(6) (2009): 723–737.

Kinderman, D. "'Free us up so we can be responsible!' The co-evolution of Corporate Social Responsibility and neo-liberalism in the UK, 1977–2010". *Socio-Economic Review* 10 (2012): 29–57.

Lange, P., and Meadwell, H. "Typologies of democratic systems: Form political inputs to political economy". In *New directions in comparative politics*, ed. H. J. Wiarda. Boulder, CO: Westview, 1991, 82–117.

Larsen, C. A. "The institutional logic of welfare attitudes: How welfare regimes influence public support". *Comparative Political Studies* 41(2) (2008): 145–168.

Lipset, S. M., and Marks, G. *It didn't happen here. Why Socialism Failed in the United States*. New York and London, 2000.

LoSasso, A. T., and Buchmueller, T. C. "The effect of the state children's health insurance program on health insurance coverage". *Journal of Health Economics* 23(5) (2004): 1059–1082.

Matten, D., and Moon, J. "'Implicit' and 'explicit' CSR: A conceptual framework for a comparative understanding of corporate social responsibility". *Academy of Management Review* 33(2): 404–424.

Moran, M. "Understanding the welfare state: The case of health care". *British Journal of Politics and International Relations* 2(2) (2000): 135–160.

Mossialos, E., Dixon, A., Figueras, J., and Kutzin, J., eds. *Funding health care: Options for Europe*, 2002.

OECD. *Making work pay: Taxation, benefits, employment and unemployment*. Paris: Organisation for Economic Co-operation and Development, 1997.

OECD. Database presenting governmental expenditures on social purposes, 2019. Derived from https://www.oecd.org/els/soc/statistics.htm on the 15 September 2019.

Roberts, R. D. "A positive model of private charity and public transfers". *Journal of Political Economy* 92(1) (1984): 136–148.

Salamon, L. M. "The nonprofit sector and government: The American experience in theory and practice". In *The third sector: Comparative studies of nonprofit organizations*, ed. H. Anheier & S. Wolfgang. Walter de Gruyter, 1990, 219–240.

Skocpol, T. *Protecting soldiers and mothers* (Vol. 992). Cambridge, MA: Harvard University Press, 1992.

Skocpol, T., Ganz, M., and Munson, Z. "A nation of organizers: The institutional origins of civic voluntarism in the United States". *American Political Science Review* 94(3) (2000): 527–546.

Starbucks, 2004. Focusing on healthcare and wellness. http://www.starbucks.com/aboutUSA/csr.asp.

Suchecka, J. (2010). *Ekonomia zdrowia i opieki zdrowotnej*. Warszawa: Wolters Kluwer.

Svallfors, S. "Worlds of welfare and attitudes to redistribution: A comparison of eight western nations". *European Sociological Review* 13(3) (1997): 283–304.

Szarfenberg, R. *Definicje, zakres i konteksty polityki społecznej. Polityka społeczna*. Warszawa: PWN, 2007.

Index

C. Simões et al. (eds.), *Corporate Responsibility, Sustainability and Markets*, Palgrave Studies in Governance, Leadership and Responsibility, https://doi.org/10.1007/978-3-030-79660-0

The manufacturer's authorised representative in the EU is Springer Nature Customer Service Centre GmbH, Europaplatz 3, 69115 Heidelberg, Germany. If you have any concerns regarding our products, please contact ProductSafety@springernature.com

Printed and bound by CPI Group (UK) Ltd, Croydon, CR0 4YY
22/09/2026
02221054-0007